Why I Believe What I Believe

The Foundations of Our Christian Faith

with

Study Group Questions and Discussion Points

Chris Laforêt

Why I Believe What I Believe
The Foundations of Our Christian Faith
First Edition

Copyright © 2013 by Chris Laforêt

All rights reserved. No portion of this book may be reproduced, stored in a retrieval system, or transmitted in any form or by any means—electronic, mechanical, photocopy, recording, scanning, or other—except for brief quotations in critical reviews, books, or articles, without the prior written permission of the publisher.

ISBN: 0989265307
ISBN-13: 978-0-9892653-0-0

Scriptures taken from the Holy Bible, New International Version®, NIV®. Copyright © 1973, 1978, 1984, 2011 by Biblica, Inc.™ Used by permission of Zondervan. All rights reserved worldwide. www.zondervan.com The "NIV" and "New International Version" are trademarks registered in the United States Patent and Trademark Office by Biblica, Inc.™

Cover Design and Photography: Chris Laforêt
Cover Fonts: Trajan Pro and Gautami
Text fonts: Trajan Pro and Calibri
Cover Photos from the Burlington Assembly of God, Burlington, North Carolina

 Like us on **Facebook**
www.facebook.com/WhyIBelieveWhatIBelieve

This book is dedicated to the people of God
who have formed a chain of faith through my life.

To sweet Miss Laird who taught me Bible stories and "Jesus loves me"
during my early years;
"Uncle" Clayton Guzman who introduced me to the faith of Abraham
and solid Christian writers in my early Christian walk;
my friend Dave Neathery who taught me I can completely trust the Word of God;
Pastor Howard Thompson who has been my shepherd for almost a decade and
under whose teaching I have gained a deeper respect of
God's character and nature;
and to the countless blessed brothers and sisters in the Lord
who have each sharpened me by their boundless faith.

Contents

Preface vii
1 Introducing This Book 1
2 Early Confessions, Hymns, and Creeds in Scripture 9
3 The Development of Creeds 15
4 Understanding Theological Tension 23
5 Authority 27
6 The Doctrine of God and His Revelation 35
7 "What is Truth?" 47
8 The Bible: The Written Word of God 55
9 God's Character and His Nature 69
10 The Doctrine of the Trinity 81
11 The Doctrine of Man 89
12 The Doctrine of Sin 105
13 The Person of Jesus 117
14 The Doctrine of the Atonement 131
15 The Holy Spirit 141
16 The Doctrine of the Church 151
17 The Eternal Realm 165
18 The Christian Walk 177
Epilogue: Called to Purity 189
Study Group Questions and Discussion Points 195
Appendix: Choosing and Using a Bible 205
Index 213
About the Author 222

Scan this to Like us and
follow the book on
Facebook

Preface

Beginning in the days of our childhood each of us forms our worldview by posing questions beginning with "why?" We humans are a curious creation living under God's sun, each seeking answers in the way of our inquiring and inquisitive natures. The word "why" epitomizes a quest for knowledge for we expect the answers to our "why" queries to widen the horizons of our minds. We petulantly question until an acceptable answer is forthcoming.

In these days, there has been a separation of belief and knowledge, of Church and of State. Instead of belief being considered, as it historically has been, a legitimate part of knowledge it has somehow become relegated to the backrooms of disrepute. This separation has cost Christians dearly. Instead of holding to a consistent worldview built upon their faith, they have become affected with a form of mental and spiritual multiple personality disorder caused by being one thing within the Church and completely another thing in the surrounding world. Many Christians do not *know* what they believe and thus live lives in which anything can usurp the Truth upon which they should be standing firmly.

This book attempts to hammer a stake into the hard ground of our intellectuality upon which the Truth of our Christian belief can be solidly attached. It declares definitively the "why" which resonates with some of our deepest questions and provides knowledge and understanding which will serve to undergird the beliefs of each and every Christian. "Why I believe what I believe" needs to become our creed. After all, we are not supposed to be "of the world" but rather "citizens of heaven." Therefore, we must not be ashamed to rest upon the Truth of the Gospel and must not be oblivious to the calling that we have each received.

While today we are dealing with the onslaught of post-modernism and relativistic truth, nothing is really new. The Church has always had to defend its position and the truths of its faith. In the early years, before the widespread dissemination of the Bible, it created memory-aids such as confessions and creeds to help each "rank-and-file" believer know the essential truths of the Christian theological position.

Throughout the centuries, the enemy may have changed from Gnostic to Docetist; Arianist to Monarchianist; from the Church of Rome selling indulgences to the modern day libertine Christianity; Mormonism to Scientology; but the one thing that has always allowed Christians to stand firm is a solid foundation on the Truth of their beliefs.

This book takes the Christian on an excursion of understanding the foundational principles of the faith. God's Word admonishes us to *"be still, and know that I am God."* (Psalm 46:10) Each of us needs to gain an understanding of the basic underpinnings of our beliefs. We must **know** God, the Person, and we must **know** about God through His revealed Word. It is my hope that this book will help each reader in building a stronger confession, a more faithful life, and a resistance to false teachings.

Throughout the chapters of this book you will notice that the Biblical text has been interspersed. Instead of merely pointing the reader to several different passages, it will hopefully make it more memorable by having the referenced Scriptural passages woven directly into the narrative. This is true in most cases when Scripture is referenced. I have also chosen to use the text of the New International Version because I feel that it treads the edge of being accurate to the underlying text, being readable, and its wording corresponds to our modern language patterns (see Chapter 8). The reader, however, is highly encouraged to look the Bible passages up in their favorite versions.

In closing, may this book help you and other Christians that you know to be better founded upon the principles of the Christian faith. May we all, as we voyage through the pages of this book, hearken closely to the words of the old hymn:

How firm a foundation, ye saints of the Lord,
Is laid for your faith in His excellent word!
What more can He say than to you He hath said—
To you who for refuge to Jesus have fled?

"Fear not, I am with thee, oh, be not dismayed,
For I am thy God, and will still give thee aid;

I'll strengthen thee, help thee, and cause thee to stand,
Upheld by My gracious, omnipotent hand.

"When through the deep waters I call thee to go,
The rivers of sorrow shall not overflow;
For I will be with thee thy trouble to bless,
And sanctify to thee thy deepest distress.

"When through fiery trials thy pathway shall lie,
My grace, all-sufficient, shall be thy supply;
The flame shall not harm thee; I only design
Thy dross to consume and thy gold to refine.

"The soul that on Jesus doth lean for repose,
I will not, I will not, desert to his foes;
That soul, though all hell should endeavor to shake,
I'll never, no never, no never forsake."[1]

- - - - -

I would like to take this opportunity to thank the many friends at Burlington Assembly and elsewhere who have encouraged me in the process of writing this book and who assisted by proof-reading and commenting on pre-release material. Thank you to my beloved wife, Sherry, for her encouragement, for patiently enduring hour after hour of my reading passages to her, and for spending countless additional hours reading sample chapter manuscripts.

A very special thank you to Dana Morris for agreeing to assume the role of editor and for her tireless work at proofing and fact checking my theology. Her suggestions made this book far more interesting and cohesive. Also, I would like to thank my co-worker and friend, Ed Crookshanks, who helped me through my learning the publishing process.

Burlington, NC
April, 2012

---

[1] Keith, John "How Firm a Foundation," first published in 1787

1 Introducing This Book

I came out of a confessional church background, having been born and raised as an Anglican until my mid-teens. I did the things "good Churchgoers" do—attending church for high feasts and even on occasional Sundays. I was christened as a baby and taught Catechism and Confirmed as I entered my second decade of life. I learned the creeds and the Lord's Prayer and many sayings and songs of the Liturgy still come to mind. However, I was not in any way a Christian...I may have known things about Christianity but did not know the Person of Christ.

That all changed when my mother moved us to Caracas, Venezuela during my teenage years. It was there that we were introduced to a nice English-speaking Southern Baptist congregation. It was at Bethel Baptist Church that I met the risen Lord and really learned the Bible. It was there that I heard His call and I yielded "my life and my all" to Him in April, 1980. What a lovely statement that makes, doesn't it. It is fair to say that I did yield my life in principle but the first years of my Christian walk was rocky. When the Savior touches our lives and heals us of our sin, the habits we formed and the pull of our old lives tend to yank us around. However, praise God for His goodness, He works on breaking those old chains that fetter us to our lives of sin.

I spent some of my formative years in a Southern Baptist college and followed by embarking on theological studies at Southeastern Baptist Seminary. In both places, I found myself wrestling with something that I saw. As shocking as it was, I wanted to deny it. Yet however much I tried, it kept coming back to haunt me. I believed then as I do now that the Lord was attempting to catch my attention.

What was so shocking to me? It was that the cults appeared to have been making major gains with Baptists, people who should have known the truth of the Word. After all, it was in such a church that I had heard the truth preached and had come to know Christ. Surely this could not be so! Yet, the statistics plainly demonstrated that heretical groups such as

Jehovah's Witnesses and Mormons seemed to "convert" a higher percentage of Southern Baptists than any other denomination. How could the they mislead such a large percentage of evangelical Christians who should know better? The answer turned out to be so simple that I was astounded.

Southern Baptists, like most Evangelical and Protestant denominations, adhere strictly to the philosophy of *Scriptural self-interpretation*. Now, don't get me wrong. There is nothing wrong with this; in fact, it is a major tenet in my very approach to Scripture! The problem comes out of the fact that too much of a good thing is not necessarily good. In many cases we who are in the Church tend to stand by and watch souls come to know Christ, be baptized, then learn some basics of scriptural interpretation from sermons and (maybe) Sunday School. We then cut them loose into a world where Satan and his heretical cults lurk like so many hungry wolves. We have forgotten the importance of discipleship in preparing strong believers. *Discipleship* is what increases the strength of believers and makes them resistant to false doctrine. While there are periods in which discipleship drives occur, not everyone has the opportunity or is able to schedule time to take these good courses.

Since those years many decades ago, the problem has been compounding. Not only do we have cults and other false teachings chewing away at mainstream believers, but we also have the believers themselves being taken captive by our post-modernistic mindset that claims that there is not a single objective truth. Thus, even as they come to Church and participate in the body of Christ, they hold fast to a belief that truth is relative! Anyone caught up in this mindset will live two distinct lives; the one of the pious churchgoer for an hour or two on a Sunday morning followed by the one in which an attitude of anything-goes rules his life for the remaining 166 hours of the week! If truth is relative and my truth and yours do not necessarily have to coincide, then what are we going to do with God's Truth? Once again, Satan will easily mislead the believer and manipulate him into anything but a life in which God is sovereign.

Our mainstream churches have also been suffering the ravages of a lack of solid doctrine. One popular pastor of a Megachurch has been known to remark in interviews that he believes he is offering one of the many ways to God (thus negating Jesus' words in John 14:6) and yet his flock are unable to decipher this as falsehood! Another well-known and respected pastor, and author of many books, has remarked that he does not believe in the Trinity. It appears that his followers do not demand that he explain the separate Persons of the Triune God Who are all co-existent and co-eternal!

Over the years, Megachurches have sprung up, many with large radio and television ministries, under the singular belief in a prosperity gospel. The prosperity gospel essentially states that "God wants you to be rich and will make you so" and flies in the face of Scriptural teaching such as James 2:5 and Matthew 19:23,24 in which poverty is not shunned by God, and is completely the opposite of the life modeled by Jesus Himself. Just as disturbing, statistics prove that those who occupy Church pews in America struggle with out-of-wedlock pregnancy, pornography, high divorce rates, gender confusion, substance abuse, not believing in absolute truth, and other ethical conflicts at rates that are close or even on par with that of non-believers.

All of this is shocking in light that Christians are called to serve God through Jesus, the Second Person of the Trinity. It is He who stated that *"I have come that they may have life, and have it to the full."* (John 10:10) Yet, the pew-bound who are called by His name are struggling with life as are the non believers in our society. What is wrong? Why are they foundering?

The Apostle Paul wrote in his final letter to Timothy that, *"the time will come when people will not put up with sound doctrine. Instead, to suit their own desires, they will gather around them a great number of teachers to say what their itching ears want to hear. They will turn their ears away from the truth and turn aside to myths."* (2 Timothy 4:3,4) We are certainly seeing a growing movement of this phenomenon both outside and within the Church. Paul's prescriptive formula to cure this is a truth which still stands today: *"Preach the word; be prepared in season and out of season; correct, rebuke and encourage—with great patience and careful instruction."* (2 Timothy 4:2) We must preach and teach, correcting and rebuking when appropriate, and encouraging one another in continuing to seek to understand both the Word and the will of God.

By God's grace, I have always known and remained firmly planted in the central truths of Christian belief. I have dealt on occasion with members of cults or members of misdirected Megachurches and they have not been able to interest me in what they have been selling. After years of careful thought and prayerful consideration, I have come to realize that this strength comes from a solid knowledge of the foundations of Christian faith.

As I mentioned before, my early life was spent in the Anglican Church. While I know that I was not saved during that time, I did however learn important doctrinal concepts which made perfect sense once I was exposed to the true grace of Christ in a Southern Baptist church. I realized then that over the years I had been repeating creeds by rote, words that made no difference to my life then, but which distilled the basic tenets of Christian belief into a few simple sentences! Many times it was the knowledge that I had gained there that helped me not to let go during the rocky times of temptation of my early Christian walk!

Over time, I have come to believe that each Christian must spend time developing a strong Theology. This, and only this, will provide the rigid framework upon which the defense of their faith will be built. We may live in relatively passive times but the moment for strong, reasoned defense of one's faith is fast approaching. In the days of the early Church, Christians had to be prepared to reason their faith and to die on its behalf. Wishy-washiness was not tolerated then, not by God (see Revelation 3:15,16) or by fellow Christians.

What the cults and false teachers are doing today is the work of culling out the wishy-washy Christians from within our midst. It is somewhat our fault for not doing the job for which we have been called, the making of "disciples of all nations" (Matthew 28:19) and our duty to "encourage one another and to build each other up" (1 Thessalonians 5:11a). It is indeed the responsibility of every Christian to build other Christians up, and those who are disciples to teach those who know less than them. We must be strong in theology and teach that strength to new Christians.

Now, understand that I am not espousing that non-liturgical and Evangelical denominations begin reciting creeds. After all, they are not creedal communities, and have not incorporated creeds into their worship rituals. Many Southern Baptists might be surprised to know that their denomination's belief system is outlined in a creedal confession called *The Baptist Faith and Message*. The Assemblies of God have their *Statement of Fundamental Truths*. Other church groups such as the Church of England (Anglican), Episcopalians, and Presbyterians are based on the

Westminster Confession of Faith. The Lutherans' articles of faith are encoded in the *Augsburg Confession* and the Methodists have their *Articles of Religion*. Check with your pastor and see what core doctrinal document forms the bedrock of your Church's beliefs. While all these Churches may not recite creeds, their basic theology is outlined in a core confessional document!

We have finally arrived at the focus for this book. The chapters in this book represent a small but palatable introduction of what is called *Systematic Theology*, the study of the major concepts of our wonderful faith. Instead of approaching these topics as academics (who begin with definitions of major theological concepts), we will outline the concepts as the early Christians did, through the simple creeds and confessions of the Church. These documents grew to encompass larger and larger territory as the Church faced increasing heretical beliefs. These statements were codified to be simple memory aids for the people who, unlike us, were not blessed with having a copy of the Bible readily available even if they could read.

Confessions, creeds and hymns thus form simplistic yet effective means of remembering key principles. They tend to contain condensed theology, small yet powerful expressions of faith. For example, consider the underlying theology to the following well-known hymn, one which we probably learned as children and may have taught our own children:

Jesus loves me! This I know,
for the Bible tells me so.
Little ones to Him belong,
they are weak but He is strong!

Jesus loves me! He who died.
Heaven's gate is open wide.
He will wash away my sin,
let His little child come in.

Jesus loves me! He will stay,
close beside me all the way.
He's prepared a home for me,
and some day His face I'll see.

Yes, Jesus loves me!
Yes, Jesus loves me!
Yes, Jesus loves me!
The Bible tells me so.[1]

These simple words, penned in the mid-19th century by Anna Bartlett Warner, touch on many major aspects of theology. First is the self-sacrificial love of God which led to the atonement by Jesus. There is the concept of complete salvation, the doctrine of the redeemable quality of man because God loves us even though we are fallen, the authority of Scripture, the fact that the Spirit of Christ lives in us, and an eschatological view of history (i.e. Christ will return). Wow! All of this in a simple song that we learned to sing as little children!

Quasi-creedal (quasi means "almost") confessions make it into modern Christian songs and hymns. Here is a sample of one popular Christian song "We Believe" written by Nathan DiGesare and Dan Scott and recorded by the contemporary Christian singer, Steve Green.

We believe in the Father, who created all that is,
and we believe the Universe and all therein is His.
As a loving heavenly Father, He yearned to save us all
to lift us from The Fall...
We believe.

We believe in Jesus, the Father's only Son.
Existing uncreated before time had begun.
A sacrifice for sin, He died then rose again,
to ransom sinful men...
We believe.

We believe in the Spirit who makes believers one.
Our hearts are filled with His presence, the Comforter has come.
The Kingdom unfolds in His plan unhindered by quarrels of man.
His Church upheld by His hand...
We believe.

Though the Earth be removed, and time be no more,
these truths are secure,
God's Word shall endure.

Whatever may change, these things are sure!
We believe.

So if the mountains are cast down into the plains,
when kingdoms all crumble, this One remains.

Our faith is not subject to seasons of men
with our fathers we Proclaim!
We believe our Lord will come as He said,
the land and the sea will give up their dead.
His children will reign with Him as their head.
We believe.
We believe.

This song contains many strong Christian affirmations. In it, among other subjects, we see shades of the doctrines of Creation, the Trinity, Atonement, Eschatology (the study of the End Times), the majesty of God, the sufficiency of Christ and many other concepts which we will touch upon later in this book.

This book will attempt to use the simple creedal confessions of the early Church as a framework to discuss the Scriptural truths which will strengthen us as believers. The creeds expose key concepts which we will then explore through the Word of God. Remember, as was stated earlier, many of these confessions were developed to counteract heresy which is what cults and other false teachers espouse today. It is my hope that this will become a handbook that will lead you to develop better understanding and stronger beliefs in God, Christ, the Trinity, atonement, salvation by faith, the return of Christ, and all the subjects which will help you to better combat doubts planted by Satan.

One final point which must be emphasized here is that creeds, confessions, and hymns (except for those revealed in Scripture) are man-made artifacts based upon Scriptural truths. It is necessary to test them in comparison with the Word of God. They have no binding authority whatsoever. However, if they do pass the scriptural litmus test, then they may be used as study guides to what God says in the Bible concerning specific subjects or as memory aids to remember difficult concepts. Most importantly, **creeds and confessions do not impart righteousness or have any special powers of their own**. They **cannot** impart saving grace. Their words are meaningless unless focused by the knowledge of the saved. They are *only* condensed, bite-sized chunks of theological truth.

---

[1] Warner, Anna "Jesus Loves Me," first published in 1860 as a poem. Set to music in 1862 by William Batchelder Bradbury who added the chorus with which we are familiar.

2 Early Confessions, Hymns, and Creeds in Scripture

Throughout the New Testament books it is not uncommon to uncover confessions and simple creeds that were in use in the first century Church. In many cases these confessional statements are simple and short. Among the simplest of these are the following:

That if you confess with your mouth, "<u>Jesus is Lord</u>," ... (Romans 10:9a)
Everyone who believes that <u>Jesus is the Christ</u> is born of God... (1 John 5:1a)

I have underlined the actual confessions within the Scriptural quotations. These simple statements actually meant the difference between life and death for early Christians facing Roman persecution. In many cases, merely confessing publicly that "Caesar is Lord" was all that was needed to preserve one's life. The confession that "Jesus is Lord" meant a prompt (and generally brutal) death sentence.

This underscores a point which must never be too far from our minds as we concentrate on this subject. Creeds and confessions always spring into existence in response to attacks on the Church, regardless of if the attacks are physical (as in persecution) or philosophical (as in heretical teachings).

Theological writer, Shirley Guthrie, in his book <u>Christian Doctrine</u> indicates that the "earliest Christian confession and the basic Christian affirmation repeated in different ways, in different times and places, in all creeds of the church is the simple New Testament confession 'Jesus is Lord' (Romans 10:9; Philippians 2:11)."[1] The previously-quoted simple confessions form the linchpin of our basic faith and hold it together. We all begin our Christian lives with the knowledge and affirmation that Jesus Christ is Lord of all and is the Messiah who came to redeem God's people!

The Apostle Paul seemed especially adept at weaving elements of commonly used confessions or confessional hymns into his writings, many times using them to punctuate some important concept which he was discussing. A good example of this is the confessional hymn which forms part of the majestic passage in Philippians 2:6-11:

Your attitude should be the same as that of Christ Jesus:

Who, being in very nature God,
did not consider equality with God something to be grasped,
but made himself nothing,
taking the very nature of a servant,
being made in human likeness.

And being found in appearance as a man,
he humbled himself
and became obedient to death—
even death on a cross!

Therefore God exalted him to the highest place
and gave him the name that is above every name,
that at the name of Jesus every knee should bow,
in heaven and on earth and under the earth,
and every tongue confess that Jesus Christ is Lord,
to the glory of God the Father. (Philippians 2:6-11)

This confession contains a rather involved discussion on the person of Christ and a very important *eschatological* view. Eschatological is the term used in theological circles to denote discussions and descriptions of the end times or the "last days." This confession indicates in a very real and powerful way that even though Christ *is* God, He abased Himself and became man. As the God-man, He subjugated His will to that of the Father and suffered death on the Cross. Because of His faithfulness, God made Him the One who shall receive the adoration of all Creation in the End Times. Every creature will have to pronounce the basic Christian confession that Jesus is indeed Lord. It is ironic that those very persons who have tortured and killed Christians through the ages for this affirmation of faith will in turn have to make the same statement when faced with the majesty of the Son of God!

In Galatians 1:3-5, Paul wrote a blessing to the readers which in itself is a *Christological* confession. Christological is another theological term which simply means something centering on, or referring to, Christ.

Grace and peace to you from God our Father
and the Lord Jesus Christ,
who gave himself for our sins to rescue us from the present evil age,
according to the will of our God and Father,
to whom be glory for ever and ever.
Amen. (Galatians 1:3-5)

Christ is viewed in this passage in terms of His work of Atonement, a theme which is recurrent in Christian creeds and confessions. In many discussions of the nature of the Trinity, the Godhead is portrayed as one being with three different parts or "Persons" who are defined in terms of each member's work. Even within this early confession we can see the beginning of this understanding of God's Triune nature which eventually flourished to become a major focal point of the early Church's creeds to preserve it against the attacks from the heretical teachings attacking the Godhead.

In Ephesians, Paul launched into another core confession:

There is one body and one Spirit—
just as you were called to one hope when you were called—
one Lord,
one faith,
one baptism;
one God and Father of all,
who is over all and through all and in all. (Ephesians 4:4-6)

Here we can see another primitive development of the doctrine of the Triune Godhead in balance with a strong monotheism. There is one God, the One Who created and rules over all. There is one Lord (Philippians 2:11) who we know as the Son or as Jesus Christ. There is one Spirit. There is one faith and one baptism which in this context demonstrates that all Christians are united through this common bond to form the one body. Thus, we should clearly discern that within this confession there is a developing sense of the oneness of the Church which is based on the oneness of the Godhead. Anyone who believes the central truths and who is truly saved through faith is a member of the one body.

Another early Christian confession or hymn is quoted by Paul in his first epistle to Timothy:

Beyond all question, the mystery of godliness is great:
He appeared in a body,
was vindicated by the Spirit,
was seen by angels,
was preached among the nations,
was believed on in the world,
was taken up in glory. (1 Timothy 3:16)

This is a Christological confession since the entire verse centers on Christ Himself. Of course, the elements of this confession point to the central belief that Jesus is Lord. He is Lord because he was made flesh, died and rose again. The vindication of the Spirit is seen in Christ's being raised from the dead and ascending into heaven. Angels witnessed everything, as did the disciples who preached the Risen Christ to the nations. People who heard and believed this preaching, posited their faith in Jesus and became Christians. What a magnificent confession this is!

Later in the letter to Timothy, Paul wrote another crucial confession, almost a creed:

Take hold of the eternal life to which you were called when you made your good confession in the presence of many witnesses.

In the sight of God, who gives life to everything,
and of Christ Jesus, who while testifying before Pontius Pilate made the good confession,
I charge you to keep this command without spot or blame
until the appearing of our Lord Jesus Christ,
which God will bring about in his own time —
God, the blessed and only Ruler,
the King of kings and Lord of lords,
who alone is immortal and who lives in unapproachable light,
whom no one has seen or can see.

To him be honor and might forever. Amen. (1 Timothy 6:12b-16)

This is also a Christological confession and is also a *doxology*. A doxology is a statement of praise to God. Yet, at the same time, it is also almost a creed in many ways. It distilling many Christian doctrines into short, pithy statements. Through it, we learn that God is the life-giver, He is immortal, and He is the most exalted ruler. We also learn that Christ will return in God's appointed time and that we Christians must hold true to our confession until that day.

The question we must ask ourselves is whether today's Christians really know what they are confessing?

---

[1] Guthrie, Shirley C., Christian Doctrine. Atlanta, John Knox Press, 1968. pp. 31,32

3 THE DEVELOPMENT OF CREEDS

As we saw in the previous chapter, creeds were formed to meet two distinct needs. The first was to teach or be used as memory aids for major theological statements. The original creedal forms were probably in the forms of easily memorized hymns and baptismal formulas. The second reason was to counteract false teachings and beliefs that attempted to usurp the truth of the Bible.

The earliest quasi-creedal confessions were simple statements of the Godhood of Jesus, such as Paul's affirmations that "Jesus **IS** Lord":

That if you confess with your mouth, "Jesus is Lord," and believe in your heart that God raised him from the dead, you will be saved. (Romans 10:9)

...and every tongue confess that Jesus Christ is Lord, to the glory of God the Father. (Philippians 2:11)

It is this pronouncement that is central to Christianity, the concept around which everything revolves. If Christ is not Lord indeed, then in Him there can be no hope for our salvation.

The next creedal step is the procession to simple Binitarianism (two-in-one) stemming from the realization that Jesus and the Father are One, such as:

...yet for us there is but one God, the Father, from whom all things came and for whom we live; and there is but one Lord, Jesus Christ, through whom all things came and through whom we live. (1 Corinthians 8:6)

The so-called "Apostle's Creed" (developed later than the lives of the early apostles) shows a more completely outlined theology. It demonstrates a full list of non-negotiable theological beliefs that have been placed into a readily memorized form. As all can see, it also has developed the earlier Binitarianism towards Trinitarianism by incorporating the Holy Spirit's role.

I believe in God, the Father Almighty,
and in Jesus Christ His only begotten Son,
who was born of the virgin Mary,
was dead and buried.
On the third day he rose from the dead
and ascended into heaven,
and sits on the right hand of the Father,
whence he shall come to judge the living and the dead.
I believe in the Holy Spirit,
the holy Church,
the remission of sins,
the resurrection of the flesh,
and life everlasting.

Later forms of the creed developed slightly, replacing the simple phrase "was dead and buried" with the more expanded confession below.

...suffered under Pontius Pilate,
crucified, dead and buried;
He descended into hell,
rose again the third day.[1]

This entire creed was structured to counteract the subversive teachings of Gnosticism and its offshoots. It was first seen just before 400 AD. It outlines the key concept that there is one God Who is the Father, and His Son Jesus. The Son was conceived by a miracle of the Holy Spirit and was born a man and faced suffering and death. This is of great importance for us to grasp. Gnostics claimed that the Son was merely some form of apparition. According to their dualistic beliefs, nothing in the material world can be deemed good (not evil) and thus Jesus could not have been real flesh.

But if Jesus had not been real flesh, formed as a 100% man, then His suffering would merely been an apparition also! By their claims, the Gnostics contradicted the fundamental understanding of the Savior as outlined throughout Scripture and is so poignantly stated in Hebrews 2:

*Since the children have **flesh and blood**, he too **shared in their humanity***
so that by his death he might destroy him who holds the power of death—
that is, the devil—and free those who all their lives were held in slavery by

*their fear of death. For surely it is not angels he helps, but Abraham's descendants. For this reason he had to be made **like** his brothers **in every way**, in order that he might become a merciful and faithful high priest in service to God, and that he might make atonement for the sins of the people. Because he himself suffered when he was **tempted**, he is able to help those who are being tempted. (Hebrews 2:14-18, bold highlights are mine)*

The additions in the Gallican form of the creed only drive home the concept of the humanity of Jesus. He had to feel and be tempted to sin against the Father's will and choose His own just like we do. It is by His resistance of falling into sin that He was rendered into the perfect sacrifice undeserving of God's judgment of death.

One of the cornerstones of our faith is the Resurrection. We point with awe at an empty tomb and marvel at the work of the Father. The empty tomb is our guarantee of our certain future glory, as Peter indicated:

and this water symbolizes baptism that now saves you also—not the removal of dirt from the body but the pledge of a good conscience toward God. It saves you by the resurrection of Jesus Christ, who has gone into heaven and is at God's right hand—with angels, authorities and powers in submission to him. (1 Peter 3:21,22)

Because of its critical importance, the Resurrection also forms a pivot point in the Apostles' creed. It stresses its primacy because, without it, our faith is useless. See the Apostle Paul's words to the Corinthians.

*For what I received I passed on to you as of **first importance**: that Christ died for our sins according to the Scriptures, that he was buried, that he was raised on the third day according to the Scriptures, and that he appeared to Peter, and then to the Twelve....If there is no resurrection of the dead, then not even Christ has been raised. And if Christ has not been raised, our preaching is useless and so is your faith. More than that, we are then found to be false witnesses about God, for we have testified about God that he raised Christ from the dead. But he did not raise him if in fact the dead are not raised. For **if the dead are not raised, then Christ has not been raised either. And if Christ has not been raised, your faith is futile; you are still in your sins.** Then those also who have fallen asleep in Christ are lost. If only for this life we have hope in Christ, we are to be* *pitied more than all men. But Christ has indeed been raised from the dead, the firstfruits of those who have fallen asleep. (1 Corinthians 15:3-5,13-20, bold highlights are mine)*

If Christ were not truly living-and-breathing flesh, then there was no death. If there was no death, then there was no resurrection, and if no resurrection occurred, then there is no hope! The danger of the Gnostic heresy among believers was to spark a complete collapse of the hope brought by the gospel account of God's saving grace!

Therefore, the creed followed Biblical teaching and affirmed that Jesus was indeed made flesh and he did suffer crucifixion at the hands of Pilate. It also affirmed the death of Christ, His subsequent resurrection and His ascent into glory. Finally, it pointed to our ultimate hope, the return of Christ to take His place on His judgment seat. That judgment is portrayed wonderfully in Revelation where John wrote:

Then I saw a great white throne and him who was seated on it. Earth and sky fled from his presence, and there was no place for them. And I saw the dead, great and small, standing before the throne, and books were opened. Another book was opened, which is the book of life. The dead were judged according to what they had done as recorded in the books. The sea gave up the dead that were in it, and death and Hades gave up the dead that were in them, and each person was judged according to what he had done. Then death and Hades were thrown into the lake of fire. The lake of fire is the second death. If anyone's name was not found written in the book of life, he was thrown into the lake of fire. (Revelation 20:11-15)

As all can see, the creed itself covers much ground concerning the Person and work of Christ Jesus. However, while it mentioned the three persons of the Godhead, it was not a complete Trinitarian creed. It merely asserted belief in the Father, Jesus and the Spirit, along with belief in the Church (the bride of Christ), forgiveness of sins, and eternal life. By this lack of a strong statement of the Trinity, we may conclude that the concept of the Triune God ("Three in One") was not under strong attack at the time this creed developed. History bears this out. Gnosticism did not have much to say about the Trinity specifically. It primarily taught on a strict dualism of two distinct gods and a dualistic view of matter being all evil and spirit being all good. It was later on in its history that the Church had to refine its thoughts and statements on the unity of the Trinity when it faced the strong, heretical, anti-Trinitarian attacks of Arianism.

The creed which developed as a response to the Arian attack is the so-called "Nicene" creed. While it was structured similarly to the Apostle's Creed, it was more detailed, especially in regards to the Trinity. This creed was formulated during the period extending between the important Councils of Nicea in 325, and of Constantinople in 381. The most popularly quoted creed is known as the Niceno-Constantinople Creed since it is the form which was fully refined and completed at the latter council.

We believe in one God, the Father Almighty,
maker of heaven and earth, and of all things visible and invisible.

And in one Lord Jesus Christ, the only-begotten Son of God,
begotten of the Father before all ages,
light from light,
true God of true God,
begotten not made,
of one substance with the Father,
through whom all things were made,
who for us men and our salvation
came down from heaven,
and was incarnate from the Holy Spirit and the Virgin Mary
and became man,
and was crucified for us under Pontius Pilate,
and suffered and was buried,
and rose again on the third day according to the Scriptures,
and ascended into heaven,
and sits on the right hand of the Father,
and will come again with glory to judge the living and dead,
of whose kingdom there will be no end;

And in the Holy Spirit, the Lord and life-giver,
who proceeds from the Father,
who with the Father and the Son is co-worshipped and co-glorified,
who spoke though the prophets;
and in one, holy, catholic[2] and apostolic Church.

We confess one baptism for the remission of sins;
we look forward to the resurrection of the dead
and the life of the world to come. Amen.

This creed was highly developed when compared to the earlier creeds, yet the framework underlying the creed is the same basic confession as before. Most notable is the inclusion of extensive wording which both underlines and highlights the divinity of our Lord Jesus Christ, and the assertions that the Son and the Father are co-existent and co-eternal.

This takes a stance against the heresy of Arianism which claimed that Jesus, the Son of God, was merely a created being of the Father's. According to Arius and his followers, Jesus is a subordinate being under the Father and is based upon a misreading of John 14:28. As Jesus defined it, the Father is greater than Him because the Son chooses to defer to the Father and to do His will. Arius defined the passage that Jesus is physically less than the Father and thus assumed that Jesus must be a created being. Of course, with this misunderstanding of Scripture, Arianism irrevocably broke other fundamental statements such as John 10:30 in which Jesus stated clearly that *"I and the Father are one."*

The concept of the Trinity was developed more in this creed. This can be easily seen with the definition of the Son and the Father being co-substantial and the Spirit proceeding from the Father and Son. The entire Trinity is co-worshipped and co-glorified as One with three distinct Persons, each possessing a specific role within the Godhead.

In this chapter, we have seen how creeds and confessions have grown from the simple truth of *"One Lord, one faith, one baptism, one God and Father of all, who is over all and through all and in all"* in Ephesians 4:5-6 to the scripturally-sound Niceno-Constantinople creed. We have also learned how this growth in strict doctrinal definitions was spurred by the need to teach the basics of Christianity to converts who are under siege by heretical ideas and false or inaccurate teaching.

We are living in the time of the Big Lie. The spirit of Anti-Christ surrounds the Church today more than ever. The Christian is surrounded today by heresies that range from mainstream cults such as Mormonism and Jehovah's Witnesses, to occult spiritualism, to the Eastern-influenced New Age movement, to the post-modernistic mindset that all truth is relative.

It is imperative that we must not only believe what we know, but that we know what we believe and why!

The rest of this book is a study of Theology according to the Word of God. Its purpose is to strengthen the Christian in the faith. We will put aside the milk of infants and being to become mature and partake of the meat of our belief (see Hebrews 5:12-14).

---

[1] Gallican version of the Apostles' Creed (6th Century) as quoted in Moody, Dale <u>The Word of Truth</u>. Grand Rapids, William B. Eerdmans, 1983. p. 418

[2] Notice that the word "catholic" used here means "universal." There is one bride of Christ, regardless of denomination.

4 Understanding Theological Tension

The key to our understanding Christian Theology may be summed up in the word "tension." Many cornerstone beliefs must be held in perfect tension in order to have a proper and healthy theological position. Like the strings on a guitar, if it is not in perfect tension, the results derived from building upon them will be discordant and wrong. More on point, if one's understanding of Christian theological concepts are not properly balanced, the result will be at best a dimmed understanding of God's plan and work and at worst a heretical position that does not line up with the revealed Truth of Scripture.

Having said this, what exactly is the definition of theological tension? The best way to explain the concept of "tension" is to briefly examine a case study on concepts which we will explore in greater depth later on in our studies.

Let me ask you, first of all, to consider Jesus' nature, essentially attempting to answer Who He really is. I am starting with the assumption that you are already a believer who has met the risen Christ and given your life over to Him. Maybe you have already attended Bible studies, or heard sermons, or read books that have dug into this important theological position. Is Jesus' nature equal to God's nature or is His nature that of Man? A proper understanding of this will focus you on how He atoned for our sin, the herald angels' and His own claims of deity during His Earthly ministry, His preexistence, and His ongoing role in all eternity. An incorrect understanding of His nature will reduce Jesus to being a liar, eviscerate Scripture, undermine the Godhead, destroy the power of the Cross, and destroy Christ's role as King of Kings and Lord of Lords!

If you believe, for example, that Jesus' nature is *only* divine, then you can assert His Oneness with the Father and Spirit, His eternal existence without any beginning, His sinless character, and such. However, is His nature is only divine, then He could not have taken the sins of mankind on Himself by facing Adam's temptation to reject God and choose His own will yet refusing to do so out of love for God (see Luke 22:41-44).

As noble as the argument may sound, this position actually negates Scriptural passages such as Hebrews 4:15, "*For we do not have a high priest who is unable to sympathize with our weaknesses, but we have one who has been tempted in every way, just as we are—yet was without sin.*" How can I make this statement? Simply because were Jesus' nature totally divine, He would not be able to be tempted to sin since God's nature is sinless and perfect and thus can commit no sin. Believing this way opens the door to all sorts of heresy wherein Jesus only "played the part" of a man (such as the position taken by Gnosticism as discussed later) by imposing some sort of miraculous virtual reality on historical events and did not actually face temptation and death.

If you believe, on the other hand, that Jesus' nature is *only* human, then you negate His preexistence. If Jesus is only human then He is no different from you nor me. He was born at a specific time and then exists (like us) for all eternity. Taking this stance will negate the Scriptures such as John 8:54-59 where Jesus stated that *"...before Abraham was born, I AM,"* John 10:30 ("*I and my Father are one*"), and John 17:10-12. You will be able to err in the direction of historical Arianism (discussed later) in which Jesus is only a created being (which, incidentally, is the point-of-view taken by Jehovah's Witnesses today), or in the direction of Mormonism which teaches that mere men can become gods like a totally human-natured Jesus did because of mere obedience to God.

So, the tension begins in understanding that Jesus had *two* natures: a divine nature and a human nature. The human nature was imparted to Jesus at the time of the Incarnation (Matthew 1:18-23; Luke 1:26-38) as He humbled Himself and laid aside some of the prerogatives of being God (Philippians 2:6-8). It is within the parameters of His human nature that the Hebrews 4 passage is true and His overcoming temptation is achieved against the human nature to sin. It is His eternal divine nature that makes 1 Peter 1:18-21 hold true in that He was "*chosen before the creation of the world*" since He is a member of the Godhead and not merely a created being. Great! Now we can reconcile Scripture and Jesus' nature!

Almost, but not quite. Consider that the first stage of the tension can be resolved by ascribing both natures to Jesus but also of paramount importance is holding a tension on *how much* of each nature Jesus has. Was Jesus 10% human nature and 90% divine? How about 50:50 (like the Armenian Orthodox hold)? Was He 75% human and 25% God?

Without delving into this too deeply, the only valid answer is that Jesus held both natures 100% at the same time. If you were to dilute His divine nature, you start undermining His preexistent eternity as a member of the Godhead and lean towards Him being a created being. Therefore, He has to be 100% God. On the other hand, if you dilute the human nature given to Him at the Incarnation, then you start minimizing the power of His perfect, sinless sacrifice to atone for mankind's sin! Phil 2:6 reminds us that Jesus "*being in very nature God*" then "*made himself nothing taking the very nature of a servant*" (verse 7) and "*humbled himself and became obedient to death*" (verse 8). He laid aside aspects of His divine nature and appropriated (took) the human nature (nature of a servant). When He faced temptation to serve God or serve Himself, He did so with the complete nature that you and I have — He was not bolstered by some sort of super-human, God nature.

I know that this was a bit involved and maybe long, but this example outlines the theological concept of the Divine and human natures in the second Person of the Trinity. It is important to notice how tension is crucial in holding the proper view. The proper view dovetails with Scripture and holds true at all points. Hopefully now you can understand how variance from this view can lead to holding false and heretical views.

Such is the type of tension that is critical to many theological statements. This tension is prescribed by the Scriptural passages themselves, not by the human interpreters. Try to bear this in mind as you approach the many doctrinal positions that undergird Christianity.

5 AUTHORITY

Authority is essential. There must be an ultimate source which defines the "rules." We all know this to be true from experience because we know that a football game, or a tennis match, or an automotive race, or any other sport must conform with a standardized rulebook. It must be moderated by an authority which enforces the rules and resolves complaints. Without rules or with unfair application of the known rules, these endeavors rapidly degrade into chaotic anarchy.

Theologically speaking, understanding our sources of authority is also of paramount importance. The ultimate source of all authority, of course, is God Himself. He is Ruler over all eternity and the Creator and Sustainer of all His creation. Should this not be the case, then the entire theological model implodes upon itself and becomes something else entirely. True Christian theological efforts must start with God and acknowledge His ultimate authority.

If this is true, how can we know God? He has chosen to reveal Himself in the Creation ("general" revelation), through the Bible, and in a very special way through the Person of Jesus ("special" revelation). John 1:17 and 18 states, *"For the law was given through Moses; grace and truth came through Jesus Christ. No one has ever seen God, but the one and only Son, who is himself God and is in closest relationship with the Father, has made him known."* True. God, in all His glory and majesty, has never been seen by mankind. In this passage the two agents of special revelation can be clearly seen. The law is a manifestation of God's Word (Scripture or the Bible), a subject we will take up in a moment. Central to this passage is that the "one and only Son, who is himself God" who has indeed been seen by man.

The same disciple, John, who penned the passage above also wrote concerning Jesus: *"That which was from the beginning, which we have heard, which we have seen with our eyes, which we have looked at and our hands have touched—this we proclaim concerning the Word of life. The life appeared; we have seen it and testify to it, and we proclaim to you the eternal life, which was with the Father and has appeared to us. We proclaim to you what we have seen and heard, so that you also may have fellowship with us. And our fellowship is with the Father and with his Son, Jesus Christ."* (1 John 1:1-3)

Jesus, the Second Person of the Trinity, the Son of God, was made flesh through the miracle of the Incarnation and is indeed Immanuel ("God with us"). He has been given authority by the Father (Matthew 28:17; John 7:28,29; Philippians 2:9-11) and has delegated some of His authority to the Church. Paul stated *"That power is the same as the mighty strength he [the Father] exerted when he raised Christ from the dead and seated him at his right hand in the heavenly realms, far above all rule and authority, power and dominion, and every name that is invoked, not only in the present age but also in the one to come. And God placed all things under his feet and appointed him to be head over everything for the church, which is his body, the fullness of him who fills everything in every way."* (Ephesians 1:19b-23)

The authority of Jesus is shared with the Church. It is His Body which is focused on His agenda of salvation. His authority is mediated within both believers and the Church by means of the Third Person of the Trinity Who is just as much part of the One God as are the Father and the Son. As Jesus taught His disciples just before the Crucifixion, He said, *"[B]ut when he, the Spirit of truth, comes, he will guide you into all the truth. He will not speak on his own; he will speak only what he hears, and he will tell you what is yet to come. He will glorify me because it is from me that he will receive what he will make known to you. All that belongs to the Father is mine. That is why I said the Spirit will receive from me what he will make known to you." (John 16:13-15)* It is the Holy Spirit who extends God's authority into and through the Church.

Many try to lessen the Holy Spirit and thus do Him a disservice. He is an equal part of the Triune God Who, like the Father and the Son, executes a distinct role. Jesus described Him to His disciples as the Advocate who *"[W]hen he comes, he will prove the world to be in the wrong about sin and righteousness and judgment: about sin, because people do not believe in me; about righteousness, because I am going to the Father, where you can see me no longer; and about judgment, because the prince of this world now stands condemned."* (John 16:8-11) This description is rife with descriptions of authority. The Spirit proves, convicts, and judges.

Ultimately the reins of all authority are held by God. This authority is shared between the Persons of the Father, Son, and Holy Spirit as they are all One. Somehow, the Persons of the Trinity delegate aspects of authority to each other. Also, as stated earlier, Jesus delegates some authority to His Church through its indwelling by the Holy Spirit. This is clearly seen in the following passage:

"If your brother or sister sins, go and point out their fault, just between the two of you. If they listen to you, you have won them over. But if they will not listen, take one or two others along, so that 'every matter may be established by the testimony of two or three witnesses.' If they still refuse to listen, tell it to the church; and if they refuse to listen even to the church, treat them as you would a pagan or a tax collector.

Truly I tell you, whatever you bind on earth will be bound in heaven, and whatever you loose on earth will be loosed in heaven.

Again, truly I tell you that if two of you on earth agree about anything they ask for, it will be done for them by my Father in heaven. For where two or three gather in my name, there am I with them." (Matthew 18:15-20)

Again, we can see terms of delegated authority that we certainly cannot miss. Church discipline is something directly ordained by Jesus and which should be properly practiced when it is appropriate. The Apostle Paul emphasized this point while dealing with a case of incest within the Corinthian church in 1 Corinthians 5:1-13. His final point in verses 12 and 13 needs to be well heeded: *"What business is it of mine to judge those outside the church?* **Are you not to judge those inside?** *God will judge those outside. 'Expel the wicked person from among you.'"* See also 1 Timothy 5:19-21 and Jude 1:10-16 for some other direct admonitions for the Church to use its authority wisely to maintain discipline.

While all actual authority is God's, He has revealed His will and His commandments within the pages of the Holy Bible. The Scriptures represent the written record of God's authoritative words which have been revealed to mankind through the ages. In 2 Timothy 3:16, the Spirit-inspired Apostle Paul wrote that *"[A]ll Scripture is God-breathed and is useful for teaching, rebuking, correcting and training in righteousness..."* Once again, notice the language of authority in words such as "rebuking" and "correcting." It is plain that the Word of God is an important instrument that conveys God's authority within our midst.

There are many who attack the principle of the plenary, verbal inspiration of the Bible. A extraordinary number of these, unfortunately, are people within the Church itself. The principle states that God moved people supernaturally in order that the written word was perfect as He intended. Note that this does not eliminate the contributions, characters, and gifts of each of the co-authors. We can readily see them shine through their words. However, what it does mean is that the Biblical texts as they were originally written contained what God intended them to state.

Opponents of this principle range from those who, uncomfortable as they may feel about defending some parts of the Bible, have chosen to state that some passages are merely allegorical and not literal, through vehement revisionists who have chosen to decide upon their own "authority" which passages are truly holy and which ones can be ignored or even deleted! The problem with not accepting God's Word as it stands brings up the question of how can such a person know what God actually demands of them? As they parse the Bible, how can they be assured that they are not eliminating key commandments that will actually condemn them in the end?

I submit to you that each person has to make the step of faith and accept God's Word on God's own authority as being integral and complete for the purposes that He intended. It is only after this transaction has been accomplished in one's heart and it in turn births a mental determination that one will follow the Bible wherever it may lead, that a true, solidly-grounded Christian life can begin.

Several times, the evangelist Billy Graham has spoken and written about his battle within himself about the place of Scriptural authority. Here is an excerpt of his testimony:

In the summer of 1949, my team and I were preparing for the most intensive evangelistic mission we had ever attempted, a citywide outreach in Los Angeles, California. Although the press had ignored it, several hundred churches had come together to prepare and pray for the planned three-week-long event. We believed God had led us there, and many were praying He would use the meetings to bring many to Christ.

Just weeks before the mission was to start, however, I experienced a major crisis of faith—the most intense of my life. Some months before, a fellow evangelist whom I respected greatly had begun to express doubts about the Bible, urging me to "face facts" and change my belief that the Bible was the inspired Word of God. "Billy," he said, "you're fifty years out-of-date. People no longer accept the Bible as being inspired the way you do. Your faith is too simple." I knew from my own reading that some modern theologians shared his views.

For months doubts about the Bible swirled through my mind, finally coming to a boil during a conference at which I was speaking in the mountains east of Los Angeles. One night, alone in my cabin at the conference, I studied carefully what the Bible said about its divine origin. I recalled that the prophets clearly believed they were speaking God's Word; they used the phrase "Thus says the Lord" (or similar words) hundreds of times. I also knew that archaeological discoveries had repeatedly confirmed the Bible's historical accuracy.

Especially significant to me, however, was Jesus' own view of Scripture. He not only quoted it frequently, but also accepted it as the Word of God. While praying for His disciples, He said, "Sanctify them by the truth; your word is truth" (John 17:17). He also told them, "I tell you the truth, until heaven and earth disappear, not the smallest letter, not the least stroke of a pen, will by any means disappear from the Law" (Matthew 5:18). Shouldn't I have the same view of Scripture as my Lord?

Finally I went for a walk in the moonlit forest. I knelt down with my Bible on a tree stump in front of me and began praying. I don't recall my exact words, but my prayer went something like this: "O Lord, there are many things in this book I don't understand. There are many problems in it for which I have no solution. ... But, Father, by faith I am going to accept this as Thy Word. From this moment on I am going to trust the Bible as the Word of God."

When I got up from my knees, I sensed God's presence in a way that I hadn't felt for months. Not all my questions were answered, but I knew a major spiritual battle had been fought—and won. I never doubted the Bible's divine inspiration again, and immediately my preaching took on a new confidence. This was, I believe, one reason why our Los Angeles meetings had to be extended from three weeks to eight.[1]

Some branches of the Christian Church (for example, the Roman Catholics) also believe in authoritative pronouncements from one who they view as having been chosen by God to lead their church. Others also believe in the authority of contemporary prophets whom they perceive as speaking inspired by God in the vein of the Old Testament prophets. An example of this is found in Acts 21:10,11:

After we had been there a number of days, a prophet named Agabus came down from Judea. Coming over to us, he took Paul's belt, tied his own hands and feet with it and said, "The Holy Spirit says, 'In this way the Jewish leaders in Jerusalem will bind the owner of this belt and will hand him over to the Gentiles.'"

Agabus was clearly led by the Spirit for he testified the truth. The Apostle Paul did not change the course of his journey towards Jerusalem, not because he did not believe the prophesy, but because he had also received an authoritative message through the Spirit that said, as he told the Ephesian elders, *"And now, compelled by the Spirit, I am going to Jerusalem, not knowing what will happen to me there. I only know that in every city the Holy Spirit warns me that prison and hardships are facing me." (Acts 20:22,23)* Agabus' exercise of God's authority was to allow Paul and the believers assembled in Caesarea what awaited Paul in Jerusalem.

In keeping with this, note that the Apostle Peter wrote:

*We also have the prophetic message as something **completely reliable**, and you will do well to **pay attention to it**, as to a light shining in a dark place, until the day dawns and the morning star rises in your hearts. Above all, you must understand that **no prophecy of Scripture came about by the prophet's own interpretation of things.** For prophecy never had its origin in the human will, but prophets, though human, spoke from God as they were carried along by the Holy Spirit. (2 Peter 1:19-21, bold emphasis is mine)*

The prophetic voice is clearly a source of God's authority in action but a few warnings must be shared about it.

- The Church is admonished in 1 John 4:1, *"Dear friends, do not believe every spirit, but test the spirits to see whether they are*

from God, because many false prophets have gone out into the world." We are not to blindly follow any and every utterance. To be a prophetic word, it must be in perfect accordance with God's revealed word in the Bible and with Jesus, the Word who became flesh (John 1:14).
- Just as we saw in the passage from 2 Peter, the interpretation must be in accordance with God's Scripture and must not introduce some new principle that the prophet must then explain.
- Jesus taught that *"Watch out for false prophets. They come to you in sheep's clothing, but inwardly they are ferocious wolves. By their fruit you will recognize them....Thus, by their fruit you will recognize them."* (Matthew 7:15,16a,20) You must evaluate the prophet and determine if they exhibit and have exhibited the fruit of the Spirit for some time (Galatians 5:22,23) and a spirit of servanthood.
- Signs and wonders mean absolutely nothing insofar as validating the word of a prophet. Jesus warned that *"[For] false messiahs and false prophets will appear and perform great signs and wonders to deceive, if possible, even the elect."* (Matthew 24:24)
- The prophesy must be 100% accurate at all points. Deuteronomy 18:21,22 states, *"You may say to yourselves, 'How can we know when a message has not been spoken by the Lord?' If what a prophet proclaims in the name of the Lord does not take place or come true, that is a message the Lord has not spoken. That prophet has spoken presumptuously, so do not be alarmed."* Jeremiah 28:9 is also worth reading in this light.

All extra-Biblical authority such as pronouncements and prophesies need to pass the Scriptural litmus tests. God has stated through His prophet Samuel, *"He who is the Glory of Israel does not lie or change his mind; for he is not a human being, that he should change his mind."* (1 Samuel 15:29) God will **never** reverse His Biblical standpoint on any subject and any prophesy or pronouncement that is in direct opposition to it must be, by definition, a lie. Another consideration worth mentioning that should raise alarms on pronouncements is how Jesus responded to the Jewish Pharisees and Scribes who, many times, reverted to following their copious writings *about* Scripture rather than Scripture itself (see Matthew 12:1-14; 16:5-12; Mark 7:5-23; and Luke 11:46). In Jesus' own words concerning the burdensome writings and legalistic hair-splitting that they had wrought with their extra-Biblical expositions, he declared *"Woe to you experts in the law, because you have taken away the key to knowledge. You yourselves have not entered, and you have hindered those who were entering."* (Luke 11:52)

---

[1] Graham, Billy <u>The Journey: Living by Faith in an Uncertain World.</u> Thomas Nelson, Nashville, 2006. pp 108-110 (Quoted at http://www.billygraham.org/articlepage.asp?articleid=1313)

6 The Doctrine of God and His Revelation

The theological word "doctrine" means principle. Theologians refer to the principles surrounding an issue as the *doctrine* of that issue. As we examine each theological subject, we will indicate that we are studying the doctrine of the subject.

The purpose of our introducing the creeds originally was to use them as a model to guide our study of theology. Different theological writers take different approaches to defining theology, but invariably most, like the creeds, start with the Person of God. Without a solid grasp of God's character, existence, and transcendence, the rest of theology has no basis!

The starting point of the word "theology" is the *Theos* (the Greek word for God). In Him, we understand that all things hang together. Without Him, there is no need to discuss other issues. Sin is sin only because it is sin against God. Salvation is the result of God's action in Man's life. Man's existence, along with that of the Universe itself, depends entirely on God's creative powers, His sustenance, and His love. In Ephesians 4:6, Paul writes about the *"one God and Father of all, who is over all and through all and in all."*

Most theologians begin discussing God by arguing for His existence. We will not do this since we are already Christians and we already know that He exists and that He works mightily in our lives. We know and accept that:

For since the creation of the world God's invisible qualities—his eternal power and divine nature—have been clearly seen, being understood from what has been made, so that men are without excuse. (Romans 1:20)

God exists and has shown enough of Himself in the Creation[1] that His existence is plainly visible. We especially do not need to question God's existence in the least since we have met the risen Christ and have followed Him in faith. As Hebrews 11:6 states:

And without faith it is impossible to please God, because anyone who comes to him must believe that he exists and that he rewards those who earnestly seek him.

God exists. We believers are aware of this simple truth both within our minds and in our respective spirits. Our faith in this simple fact is what brought us to know Him, and so we need not waste precious time outlining and discussing philosophical proofs for His existence. If you are interested in pursuing this subject, there are a number of excellent theological texts that can help you. I warn you to be very careful and to choose something by a solid mainstream Christian theologian (ancient or modern) because there are a number that present non-Biblical arguments that can only serve to lead you astray.

The first of God's attributes that we should examine is His *revelation*. Our community of faith exists because God has chosen to reveal Himself in history. God has always been personal. He has always been the God of Abraham, of Isaac, of Jacob, of Moses, of David, of Isaiah, of Daniel, of Peter, of Paul, of me and of you! He is the One who personally walked in the Garden with Adam during the cool of the evening. This is one of the enigmas concerning God—how could He choose to have a personal relationship with each of us and still be so vast that the Universe itself is small and insignificant to Him?

The supreme revelation of God occurred when the Word of God was whispered into the silent darkness of the back streets of Bethlehem. John's gospel states:

In the beginning was the Word, and the Word was with God, and the Word was God....The Word became flesh and made his dwelling among us. We have seen his glory, the glory of the One and Only Son, who came from the Father, full of grace and truth. (John 1:1,14)

and also later:

No one has ever seen God, but God the One and Only Son, who is at the Father's side, has made him known. (John 1:18)

We will notice that the revelation of God is a threefold process: It happens within history, then within His written Word, and finally in the community of faith.[2] God revealed Himself through His mighty works in history such as the Creation, the calling of Abraham, the freeing of Israel from bondage in Egypt, and the suffering of His Son on a rough-hewn Roman cross at Calvary's stark hilltop. The acts are kept alive within the words of the Scriptures for subsequent generations to see God revealed though their history. Ultimately the community of faith that believes the Scriptures also experiences God's revelation within itself. God is alive and well and living within believers' hearts.

We must take a moment to grasp a very important point. God reveals Himself by showing His Person to us. He is not a smoke-and-mirrors magic show like the fabled "great and powerful Oz."[3] This fact has proven true in each revelation of Himself. It culminated in His supreme incarnate revelation in the broken, pierced, and agonizing body of His precious Son dying on our behalf.

We must also realize that by sharing Himself with each of us as He has chosen to do, He makes His revelation Person-to-person. In other words, He has never chosen to reveal Himself as some sort of philosophical concept nor does He treat us as such. We must each meet the risen Christ in our own individual "Damascus Road" experiences and come to know that He, indeed, is the Lord. It is because of this immediacy and nature of His revelation that we do not merely know *about* God but we truly know Him personally. As the hymn states, *"He walks with me, and He talks with me..."*[4]

We must concede that the Gospel is the record of God's revelation to all the ages. Paul declares that:

I am not ashamed of the gospel, because it is the power of God for the salvation of everyone who believes: first for the Jew, then for the Gentile. For in the gospel a righteousness from God is revealed, a righteousness that is by faith from first to last, just as it is written: "The righteous will live by faith." (Romans 1:16-17)

The theological author, Shirley Guthrie, in his book <u>Christian Doctrine</u>, has stated that God's revelation is words with action.[5] If we were to build on this concept we would realize that Jesus, as God's Word uttered into a world of sin, did not appear merely to be *heard* but also to *do* (see John

6:38). "Jesus is himself the Word of God. What God has to say to us is what he did among us and for us in this man."[6] Guthrie continued by pointing out the difference between the Word of God, the Person of Jesus Who is the ultimate revelation of God, and the Word of God, the Bible, which documents God's revelation. Clearly the incarnation of Christ is a superior revelation of God than the Scripture, but without the written Word we could not be lead to know the Person of the Word! Christians do not believe *IN* the Bible, they believe *THROUGH* the Bible which is our tool to discover God's special revelations in history!

Scripture in many places, as we would expect, bears witness to God's revelation. Through His revelation in Creation we have what is called **general revelation** which was mentioned earlier.

The wrath of God is being revealed from heaven against all the godlessness and wickedness of men who suppress the truth by their wickedness, since what may be known about God is plain to them, because God has made it plain to them. For since the creation of the world God's invisible qualities—his eternal power and divine nature—have been clearly seen, being understood from what has been made, so that men are without excuse. (Romans 1:18-20)

General revelation in the majesty, size, consistency, intricacy, the miracles of the Creation, and the intelligent design that underlies and sustains every part of that Creation all demonstrate that there is a God. This is not the kind of personal revelation that is capable of bringing a soul to complete salvation. Yet, what Paul stated in the passage above serves to illustrate that God has placed enough hints of His essence in Creation to make man know that there must be a God out there and begin searching for Him. However, there must be a transition from the words of the hymn...

In the stars His handiwork I see,
On the wind He speaks with majesty,
Though He ruleth over land and sea,
What is that to me?

...to these words which speak of a personal **special revelation** by the living, loving God:

Till by faith I met Him face to face
and I felt the wonder of His grace—
Then I knew that He was more
than just a God,
who didn't care,
that lived away out there.
And now He walks beside me day by day,
Ever watching o'er me lest I stray,
Helping me to find the narrow way—
He's everything to me.[7]

God is not satisfied by keeping men playing guessing games on Who He might be, as if He were some sort of philosophical concept around which men with astute minds attempt to wrap cute definitions. He dispels all doubts and questions hastily in the wonder of His presence. Men cower in awe before Him, cover their eyes, declare themselves unclean, and prostrate themselves in worship. In no way do they have any doubt that they have gained an audience with the Almighty of Ages. As Moses was sojourning in the land of Midian, tending his father-in-law's sheep in the wildernes of Horeb, there appeared the angel of the Lord before him...

...in flames of fire from within a bush. Moses saw that though the bush was on fire it did not burn up. So Moses thought, "I will go over and see this strange sight—why the bush does not burn up."

When the LORD saw that he had gone over to look, God called to him from within the bush, "Moses! Moses!" And Moses said, "Here I am."

"Do not come any closer," God said. "Take off your sandals, for the place where you are standing is holy ground." Then he said, "I am the God of your father, the God of Abraham, the God of Isaac and the God of Jacob." At this, Moses hid his face, because he was afraid to look at God. (Exodus 3:2-6)

There was not a shadow of a doubt on Moses' mind that he had come face to face with God Almighty! A similar experience is narrated concerning Joshua, who was busy contemplating the strategy to defeat Jericho and was surveying the battlefield when...

...he looked up and saw a man standing in front of him with a drawn sword in his hand. Joshua went up to him and asked, "Are you for us or for our enemies?"

"Neither," he replied, "but as commander of the army of the LORD I have now come." Then Joshua fell facedown to the ground in reverence, and asked him, "What message does my Lord have for his servant?"

The commander of the LORD's army replied, "Take off your sandals, for the place where you are standing is holy." And Joshua did so. (Joshua 5:13-15)

Joshua, just as Moses before him, had no doubt that he had come face to face with God. We do know that this was a manifestation of God and not an angel, since Joshua was permitted to worship Him. Angels (God's messengers) know that only God can be worshipped and enforce that rule. Joshua recognized God and gave Him the worship that He deserves, face down and submissive to His will. (Some theologians believe that this was a revelation of the pre-incarnate Christ, which is consistent with the name "Commander of the Army of the Lord," the image of Christ from Revelation 19:14.)

While Isaiah, a priest, was serving in the Temple at Jerusalem, he too came face to face with God.

In the year that King Uzziah died, I saw the Lord seated on a throne, high and exalted, and the train of his robe filled the temple. Above him were seraphs, each with six wings: With two wings they covered their faces, with two they covered their feet, and with two they were flying. And they were calling to one another: "Holy, holy, holy is the LORD Almighty; the whole earth is full of his glory."

At the sound of their voices the doorposts and thresholds shook and the temple was filled with smoke.

"Woe to me!" I cried. "I am ruined! For I am a man of unclean lips, and I live among a people of unclean lips, and my eyes have seen the King, the LORD Almighty."

Then one of the seraphs flew to me with a live coal in his hand, which he had taken with tongs from the altar. With it he touched my mouth and said, "See, this has touched your lips; your guilt is taken away and your sin atoned for."

Then I heard the voice of the Lord saying, "Whom shall I send? And who will go for us?" And I said, "Here am I. Send me!" (Isa 6:1-8)

In this very intense and special revelation, God allowed this man to gain a deeper glimpse into His very Being. He permitted Isaiah to see Him in His throne-room on high. Take note of the seraphs flying around Him and singing of His glory. In this instance, as in the others cited above, there was no difficulty in Isaiah discerning God as God. His instant response was one with which we all resound, "I am a man of unclean lips, and I live among a people of unclean lips...." This is the spontaneous confession of sin that any man would utter when faced with the awesome perfection of God.

Notice carefully that in the passage above God did not require Isaiah to perform some act other than the act of contrite confession. He Himself provided for the cleansing of Isaiah from his state of sin! Once free from the burden of sin, and having heard God call for someone to represent Him, the redeemed man's rejoicing heart exploded resoundingly with the words "Send me!" Once we have met God and receive His wonderful liberating, saving grace, we joyously want Him to use us in His work.

As mentioned previously, the supreme manifestation of God in history is through the Person of Jesus. This is mainly because it is in Jesus that all things reach fulfillment and through Him we are granted perfect access to the throne of God through His grace and our faith. For Jesus was...

...chosen before the creation of the world, but was revealed in these last times for your sake. Through him you believe in God, who raised him from the dead and glorified him, and so your faith and hope are in God. (1 Peter 1:20,21)

Jesus' own admission is that He is the revealer of the Father:

...no one knows the Father except the Son and those to whom the Son chooses to reveal him. (Matthew 11:27b)

Paul (then Saul) who was the chief Jewish persecutor of the early Church, also met God face to face through the Person of Jesus Christ. He was traveling to Damascus with permission from the high priest to take any Christians that he might have found there back to Jerusalem as his prisoners, when...

...suddenly a light from heaven flashed around him. He fell to the ground and heard a voice say to him, "Saul, Saul, why do you persecute me?"

"Who are you, Lord?" Saul asked.

"I am Jesus, whom you are persecuting," he replied. "Now get up and go into the city, and you will be told what you must do." (Acts 9:3b-6)

Paul instantly knew that he was dealing with Almighty God and immediately referred to Him as Lord. Imagine his chagrin when he discovered that the Lord was the same Jesus whose followers he had been attempting to wipe from the land! This personal special revelation was with the risen Christ, the revelation to which all of us Christians aspire (even though rarely with such a cosmic light-show as Saul enjoyed).

We will examine one more passage that illustrates God's Person-to-person revelation:

On the Lord's Day I was in the Spirit, and I heard behind me a loud voice like a trumpet, which said: "Write on a scroll what you see and send it to the seven churches: to Ephesus, Smyrna, Pergamum, Thyatira, Sardis, Philadelphia and Laodicea."

I turned around to see the voice that was speaking to me. And when I turned I saw seven golden lampstands, and among the lampstands was someone "like a son of man," dressed in a robe reaching down to his feet and with a golden sash around his chest. His head and hair were white like wool, as white as snow, and his eyes were like blazing fire. His feet were like bronze glowing in a furnace, and his voice was like the sound of rushing waters. In his right hand he held seven stars, and out of his mouth came a sharp double-edged sword. His face was like the sun shining in all its brilliance.

When I saw him, I fell at his feet as though dead. Then he placed his right hand on me and said: "Do not be afraid. I am the First and the Last. I am the Living One; I was dead, and behold I am alive for ever and ever! And I hold the keys of death and Hades. (Revelation 1:10-18)

Just as in Saul's Damascus Road meeting with God, the disciple John had an encounter centered on the resurrected and glorifed Lord Jesus Christ. Now that Jesus had been revealed to the world, *all* encounters with God are mediated through Him, the second Person of the Trinity.[8]

God, in the Person of the Father, outlines and exercises His will in Heaven. He is Supreme Ruler of the Eternal Realm. This fact is underlined especially in the relationship between the Son and the Father in the New Testament. In Galatians 1, Paul opened with a blessing that states:

Grace and peace to you from God our Father and the Lord Jesus Christ, who gave himself for our sins to rescue us from the present evil age, **according to the will of our God and Father***, to whom be glory for ever and ever. Amen. (Galatians 1:3-5, bold emphasis is mine)*

In the Garden of Gethsemane, again the Son prayed to the Father saying, "*Father, if you are willing, take this cup from me; yet not my will, but yours be done.*" (Luke 22:42) The Father defines His will and the Son executes it faithfully and brings glory to God the Father. In another prayer, Jesus said, "*Father, the hour has come. Glorify your Son that your Son may glorify you.*" (John 17:1) Again, the same idea is brought forth in the Christological hymn of Philippians 2:6-11:

And being found in appearance as a man, he humbled himself by becoming obedient to death—even death on a cross! Therefore God exalted him to the highest place and gave him the name that is above every name, that at the name of Jesus every knee should bow, in heaven and on earth and under the earth, and every tongue acknowledge that Jesus Christ is Lord, to the glory of God the Father. (Philippians 2:8-11)

The Son delights in doing the will of the Father and the Father delights in the Son. Isaiah prophesied that God stated, "*Here is my servant, whom I uphold, my chosen one in whom I delight; I will put my Spirit on him, and he will bring justice to the nations*" (Isaiah 42:1) which was fulfilled in Jesus (see Matthew 12:18) In speaking about Jesus, the Apostle Paul stated that *"God was pleased to have all his fullness dwell in him, and through him to reconcile to himself all things, whether things on earth or things in heaven, by making peace through his blood, shed on the cross."* (Colossians 1:19,20) Such a reconciliation of everything will be to restore all things to the Father's control at the end of time. Again, look at what Scripture states about the Son laying everything at the Father's feet:

The last enemy to be destroyed is death. For he "has put everything under his feet." Now when it says that "everything" has been put under him, it is clear that this does not include God himself, who put everything under Christ. When he has done this, then the Son himself will be made subject to him who put everything under him, so that God may be all in all. (1 Corinthians 15:26-28)

Through these passages, we have gained a bit of an understanding of the Father's rule and caught a glimpse into the Trinity in action. We will deal with the Trinity in its own chapter and touch more on both the Person of the Son and the Person of the Holy Spirit in subsequent sections.

---

[1] This is what is called *General Revelation*. The entire Creation speaks of the majesty of the Creator. This is in contrast to *Special Revelation* which occurs when God reveals Himself in a special fashion, such as through Scriptures, as the "Angel of the Lord" to the Old Testament participants, or in the most important instance of *Special Revelation*, as Jesus the Messiah.

[2] Guthrie, Shirley C., <u>Christian Doctrine</u>. Atlanta, John Knox Press, 1968. p. 72

[3] L. Frank Baum <u>The Wonderful Wizard of Oz</u>. Chicago, George M. Hill Co, 1900. Better known by most in the MGM's 1939 adaptation to the screen, *The Wizard of Oz*, in which the wizard appears to be some great and awe-inspiring fantasy but is really a man behind a curtain controlling the machinery.

[4] C. Austin Miles, *"In the Garden."* Written in 1912.

[5] Guthrie, <u>Christian Doctrine</u>, p. 75.

[6] Guthrie, <u>Christian Doctrine,</u> p. 76.

[7] Carmichael, Ralph, *"He's Everything to Me"*. Copyright 1964.

[8] Do note that this statement does not preclude the fact that all previous encounters with God during Old Testament times may also have been mediated through pre-incarnate Christ, that is the Second Person of the Trinity before "He became flesh." A strong argument can be made that references to the "Angel of the Lord" are references to the Son and not the Father. Take for example the encounter with Moses at the burning bush where God identified Himself as "I

AM" (Exodus 3:14). Jesus told the Pharisees that "before Abraham was born, I am!" (John 8:58). This is in keeping with the basic character of Christ, the Son who does His Father's will. We will see more about this when we discuss the Trinity.

7 "What is Truth?"

As the Roman procurator Pontius Pilate asked this question (John 18:38), he must have leaned forward expectantly to hear the Lord of the Universe provide the answer. After all, this is the question of the ages that has entertained every person's mind at some time or another. While it may have been defined by philosophers, lawyers, teachers, kings, princes, and paupers and yet, none of them truly grasps its full implication. Truth is elusive to the human mind and yet it is truth that will either set one's worldview on a collision course with God's reality or set it on track.

Today, we live in the post-modernistic world where the mindset is that there is no objective and knowable truth. Cultural relativism is based upon the fallacious assumption that what is right and true for me is not so for someone else. Unfortunately, this taints one's worldview and sets up many insurmountable contradictions. These should be alarming to each of us post-modern men and women if we would stop long enough to examine the ramifications of these assertions. Unfortunately, most of us don't. So the end result is that this mindset is not only found in the world at large but has also seeped insidiously into the pews and the pulpits of many of our churches.

The Barna Group published a survey on "God, Jesus Christ, the Holy Spirit, Satan, and demons" in 2009. [1] This was done on a pool of self-described *Christians* from different denominational backgrounds.

- Of the group, 40% agreed that "Satan is not a living being but is a symbol of evil" and 39% believed that "Jesus Christ sinned when he lived on earth" (22% strongly and 17% somewhat). Incredibly, 6% of the respondents had no opinion on if Jesus sinned or not!
- Almost 2/3 of the pool did not believe that the Holy Spirit is a living force, 38% strongly and 20% somewhat in agreement.
- In terms of God being the "all-powerful, all-knowing Creator of the universe who rules the world today" almost 1/5 of the responders responded otherwise. Only 55% strongly agreed that

"the Bible is accurate in all the principles it teaches" while 5% are unsure of what to believe. On this last topic, 22% disagreed with the statement.
- In answering the question if "the Bible, the Koran and the Book of Mormon are all different expressions of the same spiritual truths," 41% of these Christians agreed somewhat or strongly while 40% disagreed. This left a group of 19% who were unable to commit either way.
- The final statistic of interest was that 59% indicated that their faith had transformed their lives and 29% agreed that it had been helpful even if not transformational. A whopping 9% polled that their faith had not made a difference in them or their living.

In her book, Total Truth, Nancy Pearcey quoted several points from a survey by sociologist Christian Smith[2] at the University of North Carolina conducted among Christians in the latter half of the 1990s. The question of if absolute moral standards exist elicited the following percentages of responses of "Yes:

75% of evangelicals
65% of fundamentalists
55% of mainline Protestants
34% of liberal Protestants
38% of Catholics

Furthermore, when asked how important defense of a biblical worldview is in intellectual circles, half or more of the different Protestant groups responded that it was very important. However, the "bad news is that when asked to articulate a biblical worldview perspective on issues in the public square, no one could do it. Not *one person* in the entire survey. Respondents spoke strictly in the language of individual morality and religious devotion; they seemed unable to express a Christian philosophy of business, politics, or culture."[3]

In his book, The Faith, Chuck Colson quoted another Barna study and stated "The majority of evangelicals—whom Barna calls 'born-again Christians'—do not believe in absolute truth. Sixty percent of Americans can't name five of the Ten Commandments; 50 percent of high school seniors think Sodom and Gomorrah were married."[4]

These shocking numbers are the vital statistics that present a picture of anything but a thriving Church. It appears that the majority of those in our church pews are not transformed by the gospel; they merely "do" religious activities to appease their consciences. How could they be transformed if they don't accept the gospel as being true, Jesus as being sinless, or Satan being a real entity who is out to do harm to the whole human race? The answer comes down the question that Pilate asked Jesus, "What is truth?"

We all make the mistake at some point of our lives of thinking that truth is an object, something that can be derived by introspection and philosophical musing. If this remains the standard by which we will measure truth, then we will be sucked into the moral relativism of our age. Even if we tend to approach truth as a framework created by God and interwoven into the Creation, we are likewise in peril of deriving the wrong answer to the age-old question. The only true answer to the question is not a what but a Who. The Truth is spelled with a capital T and resides in God Himself:

*Thomas said to him, "Lord, we don't know where you are going, so how can we know the way?" Jesus answered, "I am the way and **the truth** and the life. No one comes to the Father except through me. **If you really know me, you will know my Father as well.** From now on, you do know him and have seen him." (John 14:5-7, bold emphasis is mine)*

Jesus responded using definite articles (the) and not indefinite ones (a, an). He is THE way and THE truth and THE life. Pilate was asking the Truth to define truth when the Truth was staring him in the face. "Truth itself cannot be stated. Truth simply is, and what it is, the good with the bad, the joy with the despair, the presence and absence of God, the swollen eye, the bird pecking the cobbles for crumbs. Before it is a word, the Gospel that is truth is silence, a pregnant silence in its ninth month, and in answer to Pilate's question, Jesus keeps silent, even with his hands tied behind him managed somehow to hold silence out like a terrible gift."[5]

With this understanding, one can understand why those *outside* of the family of God might not comprehend truth but there is certainly no excuse for those who are inside the Church. If one is a Christian having allegedly met and accepted Jesus Christ as Lord and Savior, then how can such a person claim that there is not absolute truth? Truth is wrapped up in the Godhead and thus must, by definition, be absolute because God is absolute! Truth is also knowable because God has revealed Himself, in "general" revelation, in "special" revelation through Scripture, and most eminently in the Person of Jesus. We, who are called by His Name, must believe in the existence of Jesus Himself and through this we must also believe in an absolute and knowable Truth. According to the formula in John 14:6, the following assertions are true:

>   Jesus = The Way
>   Jesus = The Truth
>   Jesus = The Life

To assert anything other than this as a believer contradicts all that a believer *is*. How many ways are there to God? The answer is: "One." Is there absolute and knowable truth? The answer is: "Certainly." Is having Jesus as Lord and Savior the only way to life eternal? The answer is a resounding "Yes!" Any other position denies the Word, claims Jesus to be a liar, and ultimately breaks down the Doctrine of God. If this is your propensity, then (pardon my frankness) you would do better to live the life of the world and don't waste your time in the Church. This may seem a bit harsh to some but if you follow the logic to its logical conclusion, it makes sense. Quoting the Apostle Paul, for "[i]*f only for this life we have hope in Christ, we are of all people most to be pitied.*" (1 Corinthians 15:19)

The entire discussion in this book hinges upon the fact that God exists and that He is the source of knowable and absolute truth. Upon this hangs the authority of the Scripture, the Oneness of God, the Trinity, the Creation and God as Creator, the existence of Sin, the concepts of Salvation and Atonement, the Church, and the hope of Heaven, and so on. If there is the slightest wavering in one's core theology that God is, that He is almighty and all-powerful, that He is incapable of lying, and that He has revealed Himself through Scripture in its entirety, then the proverbial baby has been thrown out with the bathwater. The foundations upon which your Christian faith is set must be integral and without a single crack.

Anyone who claims that they can parse the Scriptures for what is truth and what they can safely ignore is self-deluded, at best. Imagine, for example, the quandary that would ensue if I could argue that John 3:16 is God's truth but John 3:18 is not. Upon what basis (other than personal opinion) could I make this assumption? Another could argue the opposite situation and be equally "true." At that point, all Scripture is suspect and only a fool could move forward hoping somehow that there be a god and that he or she could extend favor or eternal life. There can be no hope when one has a flawed foundation! Either all of Scripture is, as it claims, *"God-breathed and is useful for teaching, rebuking, correcting and training in righteousness, so that the servant of God may be thoroughly equipped for every good work"* (2 Timothy 3:16,17) or it is not. Either *"God is not human, that he should lie, not a human being, that he should change his mind. Does he speak and then not act? Does he promise and not fulfill?"* (Numbers 23:19) or you must claim that He does lie. There is no gray area or wiggle room available on these points. Either God is Who He claims to be and the Bible is His Word or not.

Only when a person has come to the conclusion that they choose to take God at His Word then the life of faith can begin. Ultimately, the human will must enter into the picture by choosing what to believe or not. (Consider that even an atheistic assertion that there is no god requires faith, arguably misplaced faith, but faith none the less.) Therefore, when one hears about God, maybe through a preacher, a missionary, a pamphlet or tract, a radio preacher heard in the dark of a night, a family member, or a friend, there must be a **conscious** acceptance of the spoken word.   Paul stated under God's inspiration in Romans 10:17, *"[c]onsequently, faith comes from hearing the message, and the message is heard through the word about Christ*." Following up on this, Hebrews 11:6 states that *"[and] without faith it is impossible to please God, because anyone who comes to him must believe that he exists and that he rewards those who earnestly seek him*."

A Christian's worldview must derive from the acceptance that God is absolute truth and makes it known. God does not exist in isolation from the world at large; He is in control of all of Creation and is all-powerful and all-knowing. As God, He has called us to a life of faith and to live according to His righteousness. He specifically has said, *"Be holy because I, the Lord your God, am holy."* (Leviticus 19:2b)

A believer cannot engage in segmenting his or her life into a Christian part and a secular part. God's rule over each of us extends at all times and in all places. It is not possible to put on some sort of Christian "hat" and participate in Church for an hour or two a week and then put on a crude, worldly, do-whatever-pleases-me "hat" for the bulk of the week mediated by of one's lack of the God-centered worldview. Unfortunately, many Christians' lives today are built on the poor foundation of relativistic truth and they do exactly this. The net result is that the name of Jesus is trampled on by those who think that all Christians are moralistic phonies at best and outright hypocrites at the worst!

Of course, this is not a problem confined to the post-modernistic world. It has more to do with human nature and the power of temptation than on any philosophical take on truth. Even as the Church was being established in the first century, the Apostle Paul admonished the Ephesians (who lived in a morally decadent and idolatrous city) to:

***Follow God's example**, therefore, as dearly loved children and walk in the way of love, just as Christ loved us and gave himself up for us as a fragrant offering and sacrifice to God.*

*But among you there must **not be even a hint** of sexual immorality, or of **any kind** of impurity, or of greed, because these are improper for God's holy people. Nor should there be obscenity, foolish talk or coarse joking, **which are out of place**, but rather thanksgiving. For of this you can be sure: No immoral, impure or greedy person—such a person is an idolater—has any inheritance in the kingdom of Christ and of God. Let no one deceive you with empty words, for **because of such things God's wrath comes on those who are disobedient**. Therefore do not be partners with them.*

*For you were once darkness, but now you are light in the Lord. **Live as children of light** (for the fruit of the light consists in all goodness, righteousness and truth) and find out what pleases the Lord. **Have nothing to do with the fruitless deeds of darkness, but rather expose them**. It is shameful even to mention what the disobedient do in secret.* (Ephesians 5:1-12, bold emphasis is mine)

It is clear that, under the guidance of the Holy Spirit, Paul was admonishing the Ephesians, and consequently all believers in all ages, that their daily life must reflect God's light. We are saved by the grace of God, not to sink back into the same life we used to live, but to live a new and holy life. At the center of this new life is a Christian worldview which has God and His absolute Truth as the hub around which everything rotates.

If you are not convinced yet, then see what the Apostle Paul wrote to Timothy in 1 Timothy 3:14,15: "*Although I hope to come to you soon, I am writing you these instructions so that, if I am delayed, you will know how people ought to conduct themselves in God's household, which is the church of the living God, the pillar and foundation of the truth.*" In other words, the Church at large resonates with the character of God and that manifestation is as the foundation of **the** truth. Again, just as was seen in Jesus' statement we examined earlier, we are not manifesting simply "a" truth or one of many truths. The Church bears witness to and is founded upon the one and only Truth. This makes perfect sense because the Church belongs to Christ (as we will see in another chapter). Thus, if Jesus is The Truth and the Church is founded upon Him, then it certainly has The Truth as its foundation.

We who are called by the name of Christ need to return to the crucial understanding that only by being anchored to a solid and correct central axis (pillar in the passage above) of absolute Truth can we ever hope to make proper sense out of life. With God and His Word front-and-center everything else will fall into its rightful place. Who we are relative to Creation is measured by who we are relative to God. The effect of our choosing sin over righteousness can only be assessed relative to our walk with God. The way we choose a spouse, raise a family, treat our neighbors and co-workers, speak to one another, save and spend money, accomplish our work, act with integrity and honesty, spend our leisure time, and every little detail of our existence must grow out of the character of God's Truth. How we face tomorrow either is dominated by the worldly panic of "what ifs" or it is faithfully released and entrusted to the One who said "[but] seek first his kingdom and his righteousness, and all these things will be given to you as well. Therefore do not worry about tomorrow, for tomorrow will worry about itself. Each day has enough trouble of its own." (Matthew 6:33,34)

---

[1] http://www.barna.org/barna-update/article/12-faithspirituality/260-most-american-christians-do-not-believe-that-satan-or-the-holy-spirit-exis

[2] Smith, Christian, Michael Emerson, Sally Gallagher, Paul Kennedy, and David Sikkink <u>American Evangelicalism: Embattled and Thriving.</u> University of Chicago Press, Chicago, 1998

[3] Pearcey, Nancy Total Truth: Liberating Christianity from Its Cultural Captivity. Wheaton, Crossway Books, 2005. pp. 70,71
[4] Colson, Charles The Faith. Grand Rapids, Zondervan, 2008. p. 28
[5] Buechner, Frederick Telling the Truth: The Gospel as Tragedy, Comedy & Fairy Tale. New York, Harper and Row, 1977. p. 16

8 THE BIBLE: THE WRITTEN WORD OF GOD

As we discuss theological issues, it is important to understand the sources that we use in developing these truths. We already mentioned that God has partially revealed Himself through the Scriptures so we need to spend a while speaking about the authority and the history of the Holy Bible.

There is almost no subject that causes greater friction among Christians than the discussion of the Bible: each denomination, indeed in some cases each congregation, has its sacredly held views on the authority and the place Scripture has in its beliefs. Some hold views about only a specific version of the Bible being inspired and others relegate Scripture to the same level (or maybe even slightly lower) as learned pronouncements of its Church leaders! It is with great trepidation that I will plot a course through these minefields of dogma and attempt to lay out the simple statement of belief that underpins this entire book.

The one and only authority that is used in discussing *these* theological issues in this book is that of the Protestant Bible, that is the 66 books that include the 39 Old Testament books of the Hebrew TANAKH (Torah, Nevi'im, and Kethuvim) and the 27 books of the New Testament. It is not my intention to argue meaninglessly about other sources of revelation and their place in theology...it is plain that any authority that is not bound in conjunction with the Word of God is in error. As the Apostle Paul states in Galatians 1:8, *"But even if we or an angel from heaven should preach a gospel other than the one we preached to you, let him eternally be condemned!"*

In other words, if any word that is preached is contrary to the Gospel, it must be rejected and the preacher of said errant word should be dismissed from your presence.

THE WRITTEN WORD OF GOD: WHAT IT IS.

The written Word that we hold in our hands today is a remarkable document with a miraculous history. Much of it was originally spoken words, words handed down by word of mouth over generations before finally being written down. Consider these points:

- The book of Genesis clearly was maintained in an oral form for many generations until the Israelites settled down in a place where Moses (and maybe others) could concentrate on documenting the experiences of the patriarchs.
- Some of Exodus through Joshua may show the evidence of oral tradition: the stories that were lovingly told over and over from generation to generation to preserve the history of the Israelites being led out of bondage in Egypt and into the promised land by the love of the Lord.
- The gospel accounts (Matthew through John) were written later than most of the rest of the New Testament (Paul's epistles were written first) and recorded the memories of those who actually walked with Jesus at some time prior to their deaths.

In some cases, the Word of God was delivered as word pronouncements. The prophetic formula, "This is what the Lord says..." introduces much of God's direct Word to be spoken to the people as He spoke through the prophets (see, for example, 2 Samuel 7:5, Jeremiah 7:1,2, Ezekiel 7:1,2 , Joel 1:2, Hosea 4:1, Amos 1:3, Micah 2:1). In other cases, the Word of God was given to the writer to be written in exact form that it was delivered (e.g. Daniel 12:4, Revelation 19:9, and see Revelation 10:3,4 for an instance of the converse, where the writer was **not** permitted to write some detail).

Regardless of one's position concerning the different methods of Biblical critical studies, one point must be stressed. The books of the Bible have been transmitted to us and preserved for our use by God's grace and miraculous works and as they stand today, they represent our spiritual "marching orders" which we dare not disobey.

The purpose of the written Word of God is described in 2 Timothy 3:16,17:

"All Scripture is God-breathed and is useful for teaching, rebuking, correcting and training in righteousness, so that the man of God may be thoroughly equipped for every good work."

It is important that we understand that the purpose of God's written Word is to demonstrate the following key points about the Lord and His relationship with us:

- A. He is God,
- B. He is Creator,
- C. He has outlined His standards of holiness and righteousness,
- D. Man, through disobedience, is sinful and bound to eternal destruction,
- E. God is loving and gracious and gave His only-begotten Son to pay the price on Man's behalf,
- F. Man needs to only accept the gift of grace from God and accept Christ as Savior to be saved, and
- G. Man's salvation will result in an eternity of life as co-heirs with Christ.

While many attempt to use Scriptures to prove any and every situation in life, this only ends up holding God's Word up to ridicule. This is no different than someone attempting to build a rocket using only a medical textbook on human anatomy as their guide! While God's written Word addresses many subjects outside of God's character and the history of redemption, it is not meant to be forced into every nook and cranny.

THE WRITTEN WORD OF GOD: CANONIZATION.

The most striking detail of the Protestant Bible that most people notice is the fact that it is divided into two sections, the Old Testament and the New Testament. The Old Testament is based entirely on the standard Hebrew Scriptures known as the TANAKH (that is: the Torah (Law such as Genesis, Exodus and Leviticus), the Nevi'im (Prophets such as Isaiah, Amos, Jonah and Micah), and the Kethuvim (Writings such as Psalms, Proverbs, etc.) which deals with the Israelite experiences with God from the dawn of human history until about 400 B.C. The New Testament deals exclusively with the period extending from Jesus' birth through the early Church (a period from 4 B.C. through around 90 A.D.).

The process of canonization (that is, the acceptance of the final form as official scripture) of the Bible as we have it began before the time of Christ. It is obvious from references within Scripture itself that the Torah was the first section that was somewhat accepted as the binding Word of

God at the reign of Josiah (640 B.C.). In 2 Kings 22:8 we have the following:

Hilkiah the high priest said to Shaphan the secretary, "I have found the Book of the Law in the temple of the Lord." He gave it to Shaphan who read it.

The "book of the Law (or Covenant)" was clearly recognized as God's authoritative Word. The response to the reading of this recognized Word of God is described in 2 Chronicles 34:29-32:

Then the king called together all the elders of Judah and Jerusalem. He went up to the temple of the Lord with the men of Judah, the people of Jerusalem, the priest and the Levites – all the people from least to the greatest. He read in their hearing all the words of the Book of the Covenant, which had been found in the temple of the Lord. The king stood by his pillar and renewed the covenant in the presence of the Lord – to follow the Lord and keep his commands, regulations and decrees with all his heart and all his soul, and to obey the words of the covenant written in this book. Then he had everyone in Jerusalem and Benjamin pledge themselves to it; the people of Jerusalem did this in accordance with the covenant of God, the God of their fathers.

Most scholars believe that the Torah was canonized by about 400 BC and that the writings of the Prophets (the early prophets (Judges through Chronicles) and the later prophets (Isaiah, Jeremiah, Ezekiel, Daniel and the twelve minor prophets)) were formally accepted as Scripture sometime around 200 BC.

It is clear that the concept of Scripture meant the *Torah* (Law) and *Nevi'im* (Prophets) during the time of Jesus. When He delivered the Sermon on the Mount, he stated that:

Do not think that I have come to abolish **the Law** *and* **the Prophets***; I have not come to abolish them but to fulfill them. I tell you the truth, until heaven and earth disappear,* **not the smallest letter, not the least stroke of a pen, will by any means disappear from the Law until everything is accomplished***. (Matthew 5:17,18, bold highlights are mine)*

By His pronouncement, He unequivocally told His audience was that He was there to fulfill Scripture as it was known at the time (Law and

Prophets). He also indicated, by his exclusion of anything contradicting either the Law and Prophets as they stood, *that they were indeed the Word of God and that He was to fulfill them exactly as they were written.* In essence, He was placing God's seal of approval on the Scripture in its current form!

After the destruction of Jerusalem in 70 A.D., the Jews found themselves once again in a situation of exile and without a centralized place of worship. There was the pressure to formalize the religious heritage of Israel even without a central Temple which had served to bring all Jews together at some point in their lives. The leading rabbis of Judaism set the final canon of the Scriptures.[1] It included the Torah and the Nevi'im from before, but also finally introduced the Kethuvim (the writings) such as the Psalms, Proverbs, Song of Solomon, etc.) as Scripture. The accepted structure of the Hebrew Scriptures has not changed since that date.

It is logical that the early Christian Church would adopt the Hebrew Scriptures as part of their sacred writings since Jesus Himself had indicated that He had come to confirm and to uphold the Law and the Prophets. Christianity is solidly bound in Judaism and shares the same heritage. However, Christianity also extended itself beyond Judaism since the advent of Christ and His declaration of the gospel message. The Son of God spoke and acted according to the prophesies of the Old Testament and introduced new and complete understandings of what had been open-ended prophetic mysteries. These sayings and understandings needed to be captured in written form especially when the early believers came to the realization that maybe Jesus was not returning immediately to ransom His Church!

The New Testament probably started with copies of the original letters Paul wrote to individual churches. It was actually encouraged by Paul that the churches should exchange letters with each other:

After this letter has been read to you, see that it is also read in the church of the Laodiceans and that you in turn read the letter from Laodicea. (Colossians 4:16)

As alluded to earlier, the early Christians believed that Jesus was going to return immediately, and so no significant efforts were made to keep a written account of His life and His teachings. The eyewitnesses of Jesus,

His disciples and closest followers, still lived within the membership of the early Church and they taught the next generation of believers from their rich memories of Jesus and His teaching. Hence the first writings were the letters in which different Christian subjects were discussed. It was not until these original witnesses started to die off from both natural causes and persecution that an actual effort was made to record the life of Christ.

For you know very well that the day of the Lord will come like a thief in the night. (1 Thessalonians 5:2)

It is strongly believed that the gospel of Mark was the first of the gospels and many scholars are convinced that it represents the gospel of Peter as told to John Mark:

She who is in Babylon, chosen together with you, sends you her greetings and so does my son Mark. (1 Peter 5:13)

As this greeting indicates, Peter was probably in Rome (viewed as the new Babylon) as a prisoner of the Roman government and Mark was his able assistant. It makes perfect sense that he would have recounted his eyewitness stories to Mark who eventually wrote them down in the first gospel account sometime after Peter was executed. This also explains why Mark is the most concise of the gospel accounts. It was just an accounting of the facts. Biblical commentators believe that Mark may also have been an eyewitness to the arrest of Jesus due to the inclusion of the detail of the young man in Mark 14:51,52.

As the gospel of Mark began to be circulated (sometime around 60 A.D., 30 years after Jesus was crucified and resurrected), the gospel of Matthew took form. There are strong similarities between the two gospels, so much so that it is believed that Matthew used Mark as his template and fleshed in details seemingly missed by Mark's short gospel account (around 65 A.D). At around the same time, Luke began work on what became a two-volume work, the gospel of Luke and the book of Acts. This assumption is based upon the introduction to both books which are addressed to a "person" named Theophilus:

Many have undertaken to draw up an account of the things that have been fulfilled among us, just as they were handed down to us by those who from the first were eyewitnesses and servants of the word.

Therefore, since I myself have carefully investigated everything from the beginning, it seemed good also to me to write an orderly account for you, most excellent Theophilus, so that you may know the certainty of the things you have been taught. (Luke 1:1-4)

In my former book, Theophilus, I wrote about all that Jesus began to do and to teach until the day he was taken up to heaven, after giving instructions through the Holy Spirit to the apostles he had chosen. (Acts 1:1,2)

Scholars are unsure if Theophilus actually was actually the name of a person or just a Greek play on words: Theo+philus is a combination of the Greek words that means "the one who loves God". If it were to be the latter, these books would thus have been addressed to us, the Church.

It is believed that Luke was completed around 70 A.D. Based upon the specific details he outlined it seems that Luke had a great deal of input from Jesus' mother and/or members of His earthly family (such as his half-brothers James and Jude who both became leaders in the Church) as he wrote his account. His was the last gospel account to surface until around 90 A.D. when a totally different gospel account was written. Unlike Matthew and Luke, the gospel of John was not based on the gospel of Mark and thus it provides a totally different view of Jesus from the eyes of the "disciple that Jesus loved," one of those who was close to Him at all points in His ministry, one who had walked for over 50 years as a follower of Jesus, and who had suffered great persecution for His name's sake.

All of these works were circulated among the early churches and were tediously hand-copied and carefully maintained. These writings were slowly collected and finally accepted and canonized in 397 A.D. at the Synod of Carthage. Hence our Holy Scriptures are based on the Hebrew canon of Scripture (called the Old Testament) and the New Testament canon approved at the Synod of Carthage.

THE WRITTEN WORD OF GOD: ITS LANGUAGES AND TRANSLATIONS.

It is important when discussing the written Word of God to have a solid understanding of the role of language in its presentation. The language of the Old Testament is primarily Hebrew with the exception of a large part the book of Daniel and a couple sections of Ezra which were written in

Aramaic. The language that encapsulates the New Testament is *Koine* (pronounced as "coin-ay") Greek, the common Greek tongue of all of the Greek Empire. This empire was later absorbed into the Roman Empire.

It is also important to realize the marvelous miracle which was done to permit these documents to live through the years. Parts of the Scriptures began their lives nearly 3500 years ago! Sadly, not many Christians today try to imagine how the Scriptures were copied and preserved; we tend to take the wonder of the printing press for granted. Prior to the 1440s, before Gutenberg invented the process of printing with moveable metal type, all manuscripts had to be laboriously copied by hand. Many of the earliest texts were not even written initially. They were passed from generation to generation by word of mouth. Even with all of this, God ensured that His Word remained intact and capable of achieving its goals.

The importance of many historical documents such as the Dead Sea Scrolls, the Septuagint (the authorized Greek translation accomplished in the 200s B.C containing Hebrew writings which included the Old Testament.), and early New Testament fragments of text is underestimated or even ignored by most Christians. However, they are extremely crucial since they form a system of checks to determine how accurate the current-day Biblical text is relative to the original (oldest known) manuscripts. The accuracy rate has proven to be extremely high especially when one considers the repeated hand copying of the Bible. These are also important in deciding what the original text was if later copies show any differences. The Bible is one of the most ratified books on the planet and it demonstrates consistent accuracy throughout all the archeological finds.

All good translations need to start with a solid copy of the original language texts. Any reputable text sometimes has one or more variant readings, segments that vary slightly in phrasing or wording. Good translations will optimally show these variants as footnotes that indicate the readings as "or..." or "some reliable ancient manuscripts have...." The best translations are achieved by committees of top-notch translators who peer-review each stage of the translation. Every translation needs to accurately convey the dynamic Word of God as expressed in its original tongue to the reader in a readily understandable form. It must attempt to bring out the subtle nuances of those underlying languages to each of us who read it in our modern tongues.

THE WRITTEN WORD: FACTUAL OR ALLEGORY?

Earlier in this book, we touched upon the subject of Authority and discussed the fact that the written Word is God's revelation to mankind and as such has His full authority behind it. We also explored the principle of the plenary, verbal inspiration which indicates that the writers of the Bible were inspired by God. Their message, although written with their style and character, was precisely what God had ordained it to be. The Biblical journey was one in which God and man collaborated to produce His message. This is so succinctly outlined in the writings of Peter:

*Above all, you must understand that no prophecy of Scripture came about by the prophet's own interpretation of things. For prophecy **never had its origin in the human will**, but prophets, though human, **spoke from God as they were carried along by the Holy Spirit**. (2 Peter 1:20,21, bold emphasis is mine)*

We saw in Matthew 5:18 that Jesus emphatically stated that the entire Word stood as written and was to be fulfilled in its smallest detail. The Apostle Paul in 2 Timothy 3:16 demonstrated that the Scriptures were inspired by God by literally compounding the words "God" and "breathed" to describe the process. Thus, it is obvious because of His diligent care in preparing it that God's intention for the Bible is for it to be the unquestioned sourcebook of our faith.

There are those among the membership of the Church who claim that parts of the Bible are merely allegories and may even relegate them to the level of myths. They parse the Scriptures and attempt to decipher what is "true" and what is "allegorical." They have problems with the likes of the Creation narrative, the Fall narrative with Adam and Eve, the Flood narrative with Noah's ark, the destruction of Sodom and Gomorrah, the crossing of the Red Sea, Jonah and the big fish, the sun standing still in Joshua, the feeding of the five thousand, the Pentecostal outpouring of the Spirit, and so on. In their eyes, God cannot be so big and powerful that He can will and accomplish such feats that defy their understanding of science and logic.

The problem with this approach is that faith is sacrificed at the altar of reason and intellect. These two now become a false god that has takes the place of the Lord and is in defiance of the First Commandment: *"I am the Lord your God, who brought you out of Egypt, out of the land of slavery. You shall have no other gods before me."* (Exodus 20:2,3) If God is in the place of primacy and is accorded full authority, and with the Biblical assertion that God is incapable of lying, it follows that His Word is also completely authoritative and accurate for His plans.

A troubling concern is the underlying reason for allegorizing the Biblical narratives in the first place. If one claims to be a believer anchored in Christ, how can it be that he or she cannot accept the Flood narrative or the separation of the Red Sea at face value? If these are relegated to the level of myth, and can't be swallowed as reality, then how in the world can a person accept the miracle of the Incarnation where God Himself became man? Likewise, if these narratives are allegorical, then how can one have faith in the Resurrection wherein Jesus bodily and physically was raised from the dead by the Father's hand? I am sorry to be blunt here but I can't help but wonder upon what such a person bases their hope!

This was the Apostle Paul's point while addressing the believers in the Corinthian church during the middle of the first century. There were those in that church who had fallen under the spell of some false teachers who had preached that the resurrection was anything but literal and physical. Paul's response is the same as my response to anyone who claims the name of Christ and yet denies the complete, literal accuracy of the Scriptures:

*But **if it is preached that Christ has been raised from the dead**, how can some of you say that there is no resurrection of the dead? If there is no resurrection of the dead, then not even Christ has been raised. And **if Christ has not been raised, our preaching is useless and so is your faith**. More than that, **we are then found to be false witnesses about God, for we have testified about God that he raised Christ from the dead**. But he did not raise him if in fact the dead are not raised. For if the dead are not raised, then Christ has not been raised either. And **if Christ has not been raised, your faith is futile**; you are still in your sins. Then those also who have fallen asleep in Christ are lost. **If only for this life we have hope in Christ, we are of all people most to be pitied**.* (1 Corinthians 15:12-18, bold emphasis is mine)

The point is that, even if something Biblical is hard to swallow, faith requires us to leave it within God's realm. There is not some principle in which demands that we must understand the *how* that God works within the heavenly and physical realms. We must simply know and trust that God is all-powerful and authoritative. Our faith is in Him, not in our five senses or in the canyons of our intellectual prowess. Either we will choose to trust Him entirely or we will not.

This latter statement is the crux of the First Commandment. God is to be enthroned supremely over all other aspects of our lives and these must be made subject to His authority. Faith is trust, plain and simple. We must make a conscious effort to entrust our doubts and our lack of understanding to His Lordship. Should we choose to parse His Word, then we have absolutely no hope and, as Paul stated, our faith is futile and we should be pitied for "wasting our time."

Dallas Willard wrote that "[T]he Bible is, after all, God's gift to the world through his Church, not to the scholars. It comes through the life of his people and nourishes that life. Its purpose is practical, not academic. An intelligent, careful, intensive but straightforward reading—that is, one not governed by obscure and faddish theories or by a mindless orthodoxy—is what it requires to direct us into life in God's kingdom."[2] With this in mind, let us consider the fact that the Bible does nothing for us unless it is read.

THE WRITTEN WORD OF GOD: MY HUMBLE OPINION.

As you have already discovered, I am using the New International Version (NIV) for the quotes in this book. There are a number of solid reasons why I mostly use this version, some of which I will share with you.

1. It is readable. Since the primary purpose of the Bible is to demonstrate man's sin and God's perfect plan of redemption, it makes sense to make this as understandable as possible for the short period of time that I might have to tell someone about God's Good News.
2. It is International: The translators of the NIV set the important goal of ensuring that the translation would be easily understood by all English language speakers: American, Canadian, English, Australian, New Zealanders, and any of inhabitants of the many other English-speaking countries of the world.

3. It is well done: The translators attempted to keep the feel of the underlying language structures through the use of "dynamic equivalents," language idioms that translate concepts in a meaningful way rather than in a word-for-word stilted manner.

Even so, I have more than one committee translation at my disposal and use them regularly. These include the New King James (NKJV), New American Standard (NASB), the Revised Standard Version (RSV), and the King James Version (KJV). Also I have the Greek and Hebrew texts available and use them for critical study.

An important point of all of this is that all translations are in some way or another based on consensus of opinions. It makes sense in critical passages to get a good feel for the wider range of these opinions and then let the Holy Spirit guide you through to the meaning that He wishes you to have at the time. A translation is only a tool, and as a tool exists only to be used in constructing something, so is your translation. *Your Bible will do nothing for you if it is not read regularly.* Likewise, its words will do nothing if the Holy Spirit is not invited in to interpret the meaning. Finally, it will do nothing without being applied to your life prayerfully *"so that the man of God may be thoroughly equipped for every good work."* (2 Timothy 3:17)

In my personal use of the Bible, I prefer to purchase a translation of my choice, one with rather wide margins for making short notes. Each time through a passage, I attempt to highlight crucial new truths with different colors of highlighter. This permits me years later to see how many different ways the same passages have spoken to me over all of the readings and to grasp how far the Holy Spirit may have moved me in understanding a portion of God's Word. I also believe that after many years (about 10 or so), it is not a bad idea to reevaluate translations to determine if anything better has come along, and even if not, to purchase a new Bible and start the process over again. It is a wonderful experience to occasionally look back at your old Bible and see the different truths that you had seen in a passage and read the notes that you had made back then.

Recently, with the advent of tablet computing, another option for Biblical study has presented itself. I, like many, have purchased Bible software for my tablet that permits me to enjoy reading the word using any of several versions including ones in other languages. I have found that I prefer using my tablet when travelling by air because it is more convenient to use on airplanes, in airports, and in hotels than my full-sized Bible. Additionally, it spares my daily Bible the rigors of travelling and protects it from being creased, bent, and damaged by being shoved mercilessly into luggage. However, I would *never* consider substituting my tablet with its planned obsolescence and its frailty for an actual printed Bible![3]

The Word of the Lord is dynamic and fills you more and more as you read it. New Christians, or Christians who have never learned about Scriptural order would be advised to get hold of The Narrated Bible[4] or The Daily Bible[5] (which is also available on many tablets) and read these to get a feel for the chronology of Biblical events. Once again, these are not replacements for your actual Bible but are just another tool to help you to understand the broad brush strokes of God's written Word. Another important skill to pick up is to learn the names and order of the books of the Bible. There are several tools on the Internet that can help you achieve this very critical skill and learning this will help you enjoy the Word even more.

Let me close this chapter by urging you to let the Word of the Lord speak to you richly through your time spent in it. Do not let the truths that you discover be forgotten: highlight key verses and write notes. A good Bible highlighter will leave no damage (I prefer dry highlighters) and notes can be made neatly with a sharp pencil or special fine-tipped Bible marker. You will be truly amazed when, one day during a Bible study, you might turn to one of these passages and be able to share a truly marvelous testimony on how Scripture spoke to you on one special occasion!

---

[1] For many years, it was taught that the rabbinical School at Jamnia convened a council in 90 AD and that it was at this so-called the Council of Jamnia this canonization occurred. This has been challenged on several fronts over the last few decades.

[2] Willard, Dallas The Divine Consipiracy. New York, Harper One Publishers, 1997. p. xvi

[3] See the Appendix "Choosing and Using a Bible" for more information.

[4] The Narrated Bible in Chronological Order edited by F. LaGard Smith, Harvest House Publishers

[5] The Daily Bible edited by F. LaGard Smith, Harvest House Publishers

9 God's Character and His Nature

Having revealed Himself through Personal special revelation and through His speaking through Scripture, God has been able to teach mankind about Himself. His character and nature are fully revealed for us to properly know Him.

One of the most immediate aspects of God's nature that we learn is that of His **holiness**. It is His holiness which sets Him apart from His creation. We must learn to have an appreciation of the difference between the holy and the profane. As Dale Moody states in Word of Truth, "Religious thought requires the distinction between the sacred and the profane, Those who regard all things as sacred usually end up treating things as profane."[1]

Without an appreciation for God's holiness and what renders it different from our profanity, how can we treat Him with the deference that He requires? On the other hand, we must not let His holiness engulf His other attributes (such as His love) that we make Him unapproachable and inaccessible! As with all things religious, there is a tension between God's perfect holiness and our ability to access Him through our mediator, Jesus Christ. We must take neither His holiness nor His love for granted as many Christians have in the past. Either they worship a perfectly holy God who is aloof and isolated from corrupt creation, or they tend to trivialize God into the "friend next door" who can be treated in a fickle fashion. We must draw our example from Jesus, who being a member of the Godhead and sharer of God's holiness, was still perfectly humble before the Father in prayer and in His life (see Phil 2:6-8)!

An understanding of God's holiness is essential to understand other divine attributes such as His **wrath** and His **righteousness**. His holiness presents itself within the context of His revelation. In Exodus 3, Moses was told to take off his sandals because the ground upon which he stood was holy. In Isaiah 6, Isaiah's lips were cleansed and his sins atoned to purify him to be in the presence of Holy God.

Holiness is not only an attribute of God's nature but it is something that He can impart to places and to objects. The contents of the Temple were made holy as were the offerings and bread which were placed on the altar. In 1 Sam 21:1-6, David and his followers were hungry as they came to the Tabernacle. Picking up at verse 3, let's follow the narrative where David was speaking...

"Now then, what do you have on hand? Give me five loaves of bread, or whatever you can find."

But the priest answered David, "I don't have any ordinary bread on hand; however, there is some consecrated bread here—provided the men have kept themselves from women."

David replied, "Indeed women have been kept from us, as usual whenever I set out. The men's things are holy even on missions that are not holy. How much more so today!"

Without delving too deeply into the desperate subterfuge that David used as he began running for his life from the enraged and crazy King Saul, we can at least pause and notice several interesting attributes about holiness:

1. Men can be made holy for some undefined period of time.
2. Objects can be made holy.
3. Objects that have been made holy can be used by men who have been made holy.
4. Holy objects cannot be used by profane (unholy) people.
5. People following the commands of Holy God can opt to render objects holy even if not required by that specific situation.

David and his (assumed, yet fictitious) men had performed a prescribed ritual to render and keep themselves holy. The bread of the Presence had also been rendered holy through prescribed ritual. Ahimelech the priest had no difficulty with David and his men consuming the holy bread as long as they had been rendered holy. The converse situation is implied, that if the men were not holy then they could not partake of the holy bread.

While David's reply to the priest was meant to set Ahimelech at ease, it also demonstrated that it appeared to be routine for David's warriors to consecrate their possessions regardless of if such consecration was required or not. What a concept! How often do we dedicate our possessions to God and consecrate them to His use? Do we cling to our possessions, our gifts, and our lives, preferring to keep them profane instead of consecrating them to God and rendering them to His holy use?

Consider also that God's holiness keeps Him separated from the profane. To Isaiah He said,

For this is what the high and lofty One says—he who lives forever, whose name is holy: "I live in a high and holy place, but also with him who is contrite and lowly in spirit, to revive the spirit of the lowly and to revive the heart of the contrite." (Isaiah 57:15)

Another aspect of God's holiness is that it is not limited to Him but is also bestowed upon those who meet His favor. The Lord is not only in the high and holy place but also indwells a contrite soul, one that has made itself lowly for Him and has therefore been prepared to be made holy.

The subject of God's holiness is visited on many occasions in prophetic writings. Take for example the following passage from Ezekiel:

"This is what the Sovereign LORD says: When I gather the people of Israel from the nations where they have been scattered, I will show myself holy among them in the sight of the nations. Then they will live in their own land, which I gave to my servant Jacob." (Ezekiel 28:25)

Two other attributes of God which go hand-in-hand are His **righteous anger** and His **justice** (or **wrath**). If God's holiness is His set-apartness, then His righteous anger and justice/wrath are the agents of His holiness. It is His righteous anger which maintains the barrier between the profane and His holiness. It is His just wrath which burns against the profane and destroys evil. We will lump the two attributes together for the purpose of this study and call the collective concept His wrath. In this passage from Jeremiah, God associates several attributes to Himself including justice and righteousness:

"Let not the wise man boast of his wisdom or the strong man boast of his strength or the rich man boast of his riches, but let him who boasts boast about this: that he understands and knows me, that I am the Lord, who exercises kindness, justice and righteousness on earth, for in these I delight," declares the Lord. (Jeremiah 9:23,24)

The apostle Paul touched upon the wrath of God in his excellent summary of history that introduces the book of Romans. He stated that...

[T]he wrath of God is being revealed from heaven against all the godlessness and wickedness of men who suppress the truth by their wickedness (Romans 1:18)

But because of your stubbornness and your unrepentant heart, you are storing up wrath against yourself for the day of God's wrath, when his righteous judgment will be revealed. God "will give to each person according to what he has done." (Romans 2:5,6)

God's wrath is and will be unleashed upon those who deny Him and to those who deliberately keep knowledge of Him from others. The wrath of God has two distinct phases: the *ongoing* wrath which is "being revealed" and the *final* wrath at the end of time, the "day of God's wrath" (see "The Eternal Realm" chapter for more on this final day).

God's wrath is His holy response to evil. Like acid and base (alkali) react violently in the presence of each other, God's holiness reacts violently to sin. The two cannot mix. There is no middle ground. God's wrath burns against sinful individuals (Achen in Josh 7), against evil cities (e.g. Sodom and Gomorrah in Gen 18:20 and Gen 19), sinful nations, and will culminate at the end of time in the Final Judgment (Revelation 20:11-15). An interesting concept of the wrath of the Lamb is brought forth in Revelation. The wrathful Lamb is Jesus:

They called to the mountains and the rocks, "Fall on us and hide us from the face of him who sits on the throne and from the wrath of the Lamb! For the great day of their wrath has come, and who can stand?" (Revelation 6:16,17)

The juxtaposition of the world's most timid creature (a lamb) and extreme wrath is important. The underlying thought here is that the Lamb has had it with the iniquity of the world and its rejection of His atonement. The door to salvation has closed and history is drawing to a rapid end. The love that has held the wrath at bay for so long and has been extended to everyone for all of this time is now held in check and the day of reckoning is here. Perfect holiness in the Lamb reacts to the evil of the world. The wheat is separated from the chaff according to this criterion.

No one who is born of God will continue to sin, because God's seed remains in him; he cannot go on sinning, because he has been born of God. This is how we know who the children of God are and who the children of the devil are: Anyone who does not do what is right is not a child of God; nor is anyone who does not love his brother. (1 John 3:9,10)

Another attribute of God is that He is **forever eternal.** He has neither beginning nor end. Time and space start and end within Him. The book of Psalms has this to say:

Before the mountains were born
or you brought forth the earth and the world,
from everlasting to everlasting you are God. (Psalm 90:2)

The same concept is also found in Isaiah where God reveals to us:

For this is what the high and lofty One says—
he who lives forever, whose name is holy: (Isaiah 57:15a)

Also to John in Revelation, God described Himself:

"I am the Alpha and the Omega," says the Lord God, "who is, and who was, and who is to come, the Almighty." (Revelation 1:8)

The indisputable fact is that God exists forever. He has always been and always will be the great "I Am" which is the name by which He indicated to Moses his timelessness. Who is God? He IS! He is in history and outside of history. He described Himself to humans the only way He could (Exodus 3:14) as the present continual tense of the verb that denotes existence! God's eternity is something that we must just accept; our finite brains cannot wrap themselves around the concept of eternity.

Since God is eternal, it is logical that everything that came into being did so from His will. Let us briefly explore the concept of God as Creator. The first words of the Bible start with an affirmation that God created. It does not debate God's existence, He just is!

In the beginning God created the heavens and the earth. (Genesis 1:1)

The Genesis 1 account proceeds to ascribe all of creation to God using a formula as follows: "And God said 'Let there be x...' and it was so and God saw that it was good." The long and the short of the creation is that at first there was **nothing**, and then God made **everything**. The Psalmist wrote:

By the word of the LORD were the heavens made,
their starry host by the breath of his mouth. (Psalm 33:6)

The concept of creation is echoed elsewhere in the Psalms. In Psalm 104 God and His creative power are described:

O LORD my God, you are very great;
you are clothed with splendor and majesty.
He wraps himself in light as with a garment;
he stretches out the heavens like a tent
and lays the beams of his upper chambers on their waters. (Psalm 104:1b-3a)

He set the earth on its foundations;
it can never be moved.
You covered it with the deep as with a garment;
the waters stood above the mountains.
But at your rebuke the waters fled,
at the sound of your thunder they took to flight;
they flowed over the mountains,
they went down into the valleys,
to the place you assigned for them. (Psalm 104:5-8)

How many are your works, O LORD!
In wisdom you made them all;
the earth is full of your creatures. (Psalm 104:24)

In the Book of Job, we can "hear" the Lord speaking from within a storm and asking Job some simple questions (Well, simple if you were the Agent of Creation, that is):

"Where were you when I laid the earth's foundation?
Tell me, if you understand.

Who marked off its dimensions? Surely you know!
Who stretched a measuring line across it?
On what were its footings set,
or who laid its cornerstone—
while the morning stars sang together
and all the angels shouted for joy? (Job 38:4-7)

There is no doubt in this passage that God is the Creator, a fact which is reiterated in many places throughout Isaiah:

I am the LORD, and there is no other.
I form the light and create darkness,
I bring prosperity and create disaster;
I, the LORD, do all these things. (Isaiah 45:6c-7)

For this is what the LORD says—
he who created the heavens, he is God;
he who fashioned and made the earth, he founded it;
he did not create it to be empty, but formed it to be inhabited—he says:
"I am the LORD, and there is no other. (Isaiah 45:18)

I am the LORD,
who has made all things,
who alone stretched out the heavens,
who spread out the earth by myself (Isaiah 44:24b)

In Jeremiah 27, God sent a message to the kings of the lands around Judah. In this word of prophesy, He defined Himself as Creator and also as the rightful title-holder of all of Creation, including their kingdoms:

Then send word to the kings of Edom, Moab, Ammon, Tyre and Sidon through the envoys who have come to Jerusalem to Zedekiah king of Judah. Give them a message for their masters and say, "This is what the LORD Almighty, the God of Israel, says: 'Tell this to your masters: **With my great power and outstretched arm I made the earth and its people and the animals that are on it**, *and* **I give it to anyone I please.** *Now I will give all your countries into the hands of my servant Nebuchadnezzar king of Babylon; I will make even the wild animals subject to him.'" (Jeremiah 27:3-6, bold emphasis is mine)*

That God is the Creator does not surprise us who are believers and is not really open to question. This is because the last word on Creation was not spoken until the New Testament. It is only after we have been introduced to Jesus and His work, that we are informed that it was the Son of God Who was the agent of Creation. From the confession in John's gospel where the Word is described as:

Through him all things were made; without him nothing was made that has been made. (John 1:3)

to the apostle Paul's statements that:

He is the image of the invisible God, the firstborn over all creation. For by him all things were created: things in heaven and on earth, visible and invisible, whether thrones or powers or rulers or authorities; all things were created by him and for him. He is before all things, and in him all things hold together. (Colossians 1:15-17)

These passages state conclusively that Jesus is the Person of the Trinity who was responsible for the Creation! It is fascinating that it is only in the light of the New Testament that we can make sense of God's use of the word "us" when He stated:

"Let us make man in our image, in our likeness..." (Genesis 1:26a)

In the middle of Eternity, God decided to create time, space, and matter. He opened a gap in Eternity, designed all of the natural laws, created the wondrous Universe with His own hands, created a special place in Earth, and then created man and woman to be His companions!

Every natural law exists because He designed it. The constant of gravitation which keeps us planted on the Earth's surface, which keeps the Earth revolving around the Sun, and which keeps the galaxies in place is in His control. The unvarying speed of light, the rule that force is equal to mass times acceleration, the strong force of the nucleus of the atom which holds protons and neutrons together, the constants of magnetism: all of these and more were designed by Him and are held in place by Jesus Himself:

He is before all things, and in him all things hold together. (Colossians 1:17)

Consider also how God stated this truth in the Old Testament. Jeremiah was prophesying a message of hope from God to the people of Judah. God would keep His promises to bring them back from exile in Babylon, the punishment He was bringing on them for their constant idolatry. He stated:

"This is what the Lord says: 'If you can break my covenant with the day and my covenant with the night, so that day and night no longer come at their appointed time, then my covenant with David my servant—and my covenant with the Levites who are priests ministering before me—can be broken and David will no longer have a descendant to reign on his throne.'" (Jeremiah 33:20,21)

*"This is what the LORD says: 'If I have not **established my covenant with day and night and the fixed laws of heaven and earth**, then I will reject the descendants of Jacob and David my servant and will not choose one of his sons to rule over the descendants of Abraham, Isaac and Jacob. For I will restore their fortunes and have compassion on them.'" (Jeremiah 33:25,26, bold emphasis is mine)*

God created the natural laws that surround this universe, and lets these laws guide His actions. Under exceptional conditions, He will work signs and miracles around those laws. It is the miracles which totally violate the laws of nature that demonstrate who holds the reins of this universe. When the world was flooded, the seas parted, a fish was commanded to protect and transport a prophet, the sun stood still or reversed, the dead were raised to life, and a widow's flour and oil were not exhausted, the implication is that He who controls all is none other than God, the Lord Almighty!

Consider also that secular scientists have identified at least 20 conditions that have to be met in order that life might be sustained on a planet. All of these conditions are met on Earth and the chances of life occurring anywhere else are astronomical (a trillionth of a trillionth of a percent!).[2] God created this vast universe with one thing in mind, mankind!

The final attribute of God which we will discuss, the one which in many ways holds the other attributes at bay (such as His wrath), is His **selfless love**. This affirmation is plainly stated as:

God is love. Whoever lives in love lives in God, and God in him. (1 John 4:16b)

God's love is the major theme throughout all of Scripture. His love has been the major motivator in His revelation as He has always attempted to reach out to sinful man and tempered His justice with mercy and kindness. The ultimate demonstration of the love of God was Jesus at Calvary, the act of selflessness through which we all are granted access to God's love and salvation.[3]

But God demonstrates his own love for us in this: While we were still sinners, Christ died for us. (Romans 5:8)

This quote forms one of the underlying themes in Romans. Paul's message therein was that God loves all mankind with a self-sacrificial love that led to the cross. Jesus said to His disciples:

My command is this: Love each other as I have loved you. Greater love has no one than this, that he lay down his life for his friends. You are my friends if you do what I command. (John 15:12-14)

We are all His friends by extension. Jesus loved us with the love of God because He laid down His life for all. Earlier, we learned that He decided to lay down His life even before the foundation of the world itself (1 Peter 1:19,20). In other words, even before Jesus created the world, He purposed that we were His friends! It has been said that it was God's love and not the Roman nails that held Jesus pinned to the cross.

In the Book of Exodus, there is a passage where God has permitted Moses to remake the stone tablets of the commandments which were broken during the incident of the golden calf. When they were complete, God appeared in a cloud before Moses and:

And he passed in front of Moses, proclaiming, "The LORD, the LORD, the compassionate and gracious God, slow to anger, abounding in love and faithfulness, maintaining love to thousands, and forgiving wickedness, rebellion and sin. (Exodus 34:6-7a)

This love of God is steadfast. It permits Him to continue holding on to us regardless of our propensity to wander astray from His commands. God, through this steadfast love, remains the constant of our lives. He is always there waiting for us and loving us in spite of ourselves. Nothing demonstrates this fact more vividly than the book of Hosea.

I will betroth you to me forever;
I will betroth you in righteousness and justice,
in love and compassion.
I will betroth you in faithfulness,
and you will acknowledge the LORD. (Hosea 2:19,20)

In Matthew's gospel, there is a very personal picture of Jesus and His steadfast love lamenting over Jerusalem just days before He knew that the people of Jerusalem were going to turn their backs on Him. It is the picture of God who has constantly loved a people which has rejected Him:

"O Jerusalem, Jerusalem, you who kill the prophets and stone those sent to you, how often I have longed to gather your children together, as a hen gathers her chicks under her wings, but you were not willing." (Matthew 23:37)

The tear-streaked face of the Savior serves as a wonderful illustration of God's steadfast love. Repeatedly through history God has come back to renew the covenant relationship with His people. Just as often, His people have rejected Him and chased after their false gods. Even so, He has never allowed Himself to be swayed. It is His steadfast love for us that culminated in the sacrifice of His Son on a rough hewn cross in the place called Golgotha. It is His steadfast love that still keeps the doors of salvation open to "whosoever will." (see Revelation 22:17)

How the heart of such a loving God is pierced when we continue to reject Him by rejecting His gift of everlasting life! It is His unfathomable love which holds His wrath in check and which grants us access to His majestic presence. God's love is strong as it overrides the other attributes of wrath and righteous anger for now. When are we people going to realize that the day is coming when His love will be made complete to those who have lived by faith, and His wrath will be revealed against the godlessness in this world? Oh, the anguish of facing the wrath of the Lamb!

---

[1] Moody, Dale The Word of Truth. Grand Rapids, Wm B. Eerdmans, 1981. p 95.

[2] Ross, Dr. Hugh The Fingerprint of God, 2nd Ed. Orange, Promise Publishing Co., 1991, pp. 128-132.

[3] Editor's note: The ultimate demonstration of the love of God was indeed Jesus' sacrifice at Calvary. However, it was the entire passion of His life beginning with shedding His Deity throughout His life on earth and culminating during the entire week of His Passion when He suffered betrayal, beatings, and humiliation. His ultimate separation from His Father, and then finally in an act of obedience, love, and complete surrender He exchanged His life for ours. Through this selflessness we are all granted access to God's love and salvation.

10 The Doctrine of the Trinity

One of the more difficult theological doctrinal concepts to comprehend is that of the Trinity.[1] It has served as one of the most controversial subjects in Christian history and has served to split the Church. These woes are linked to the fact that it is hinted at in Scripture but never is completely laid out in the pages of the Bible. Because of this, many people are inclined to disregard it. After all, if God did not define the Trinity explicitly in His Word, then what difference could it make?

The problems that arise from not having a fleshed-in theology of the Trinity can come from one of two directions. Before we touch on these, it is worth mentioning that the one's understanding of the Trinity must be well balanced between God's Threeness-in-One AND His Oneness-in-Three at the same time. As discussed in an earlier section, this forms a theological tension and must be dealt with very carefully to not corrupt Scripture or our understanding of God Himself. Any emphasis of either of these positions over the other leads to heresy[2] and a degrading of God's personhood!

One possible avenue of attack is to overstress God's Threeness-in-One to the point that each member of the Godhead is a totally independent of the others. What this leads to is a belief in three distinct gods, an accusation that Islam lodges against Christianity. Do we actually serve three gods? No! We serve one God.

Hear, O Israel: The LORD our God, the LORD is one (Deuteronomy 6:4)

On the other side of the fence, what happens when one overstresses God's Oneness-in-Three? Imagine that God is really One (as claimed above) but that somehow He puts on one of three different faces depending upon which "character" is needed to fit the bill at any particular moment. The extreme of this view presents God as an actor with three distinct masks and He wears the appropriate mask when He confronts different situations. This actually was the heresy that was introduced by the second-century Monarchians who claimed that since God was unity, He presented different modes of His being.

Any adherent of this viewpoint eliminates the ability for God to simultaneously coexist as Father, Son, and Holy Spirit. Thus, anyone sacrificing God's Threeness-in-One would have to state that when Jesus prayed, He was merely talking to Himself. They would also have to claim that when Jesus was raised from the dead, He merely switched masks or modes and walked out of the tomb (which brings up the additional problem of could He really have died on the cross in the first place). This view totally undermines the death-burial-resurrection of Christ! It also contradicts Scripture wherever it presents multiple members of the Godhead working simultaneously.

When all the people were being baptized, Jesus was baptized too. And as he was praying, heaven was opened and the Holy Spirit descended on him in bodily form like a dove. And a voice came from heaven: "You are my Son, whom I love; with you I am well pleased." (Luke 3:21,22)

As stated earlier, God is Three-in-One and One-in-Three at the same time. Both concepts must be firmly grasped and held in perfect tension to prevent one's theology from being undermined.

Let us turn our attention to Scriptural references to the Trinity. In Matthew 3:16,17, Mark 1:10,11, and Luke 3:22 (quoted earlier), one can clearly see all three members of the Trinity working simultaneously. In Isaiah 63:16 it states:

But you are our Father, though Abraham does not know us or Israel acknowledge us; you, O LORD, are our Father, our Redeemer from of old is your name.

One can also see that this idea is repeated in Isaiah 64:8:

Yet, O LORD, you are our Father. We are the clay, you are the potter; we are all the work of your hand.

The definition here is that God is Father of Israel. Jesus indicated that acceptance of Him is tantamount to acceptance of the Father in John 13:19,20 and 14:6,7,9-14. This teaching of the unity of the Father and the Son is also found in John 10:14-18:

"I am the good shepherd; I know my sheep and my sheep know me—-just as the Father knows me and I know the Father—and I lay down my life for

the sheep. I have other sheep that are not of this sheep pen. I must bring them also. They too will listen to my voice, and there shall be one flock and one shepherd. The reason my Father loves me is that I lay down my life— only to take it up again. No one takes it from me, but I lay it down of my own accord. I have authority to lay it down and authority to take it up again. This command I received from my Father."

More of the same Binatarian[3] concept of Father/Son unity can be found in John 6:37-40,46,57.

In John 17:1,2 we find Jesus on His knees praying:

After Jesus said this, he looked toward heaven and prayed: "Father, the time has come. Glorify your Son, that your Son may glorify you. For you granted him authority over all people that he might give eternal life to all those you have given him."

In John 5:19,20 we can learn that Jesus the Son works under His Father's orders. John 12:47-49 teaches that Jesus spoke for the Father. Yet, in John 10, Jesus taught that the Father and the Son are One:

Jesus answered, "I did tell you, but you do not believe. The miracles I do in my Father's name speak for me, but you do not believe because you are not my sheep. My sheep listen to my voice; I know them, and they follow me. I give them eternal life, and they shall never perish; no one can snatch them out of my hand. My Father, who has given them to me, is greater than all; no one can snatch them out of my Father's hand. I and the Father are one." (John 10:25-30)

"Do not believe me unless I do what my Father does. But if I do it, even though you do not believe me, believe the miracles, that you may know and understand that the Father is in me, and I in the Father." (John 10:37,38)

Look at Matthew 12:30-32 for an interesting teaching concerning blasphemy. In this teaching, there is a glimpse at the unity of the Spirit and the rest of the Trinity. John 14:26 demonstrates an interworking between the Father, the Spirit, and the Son. This is more pronounced in 14:15-20 and 16:12-16.

The Father entrusts all judgment to the Son as we can see in the following passages which would make no sense without the separate Persons within the Godhead.

Moreover, the Father judges no one, but has entrusted all judgment to the Son, that all may honor the Son just as they honor the Father. He who does not honor the Son does not honor the Father, who sent him. (John 5:22,23)

...that at the name of Jesus every knee should bow, in heaven and on earth and under the earth, and every tongue confess that Jesus Christ is Lord, to the glory of God the Father.(Philippians 2:10,11)

I saw heaven standing open and there before me was a white horse, whose rider is called Faithful and True. With justice he judges and makes war. His eyes are like blazing fire, and on his head are many crowns. He has a name written on him that no one knows but he himself. He is dressed in a robe dipped in blood, and his name is the Word of God. The armies of heaven were following him, riding on white horses and dressed in fine linen, white and clean. Out of his mouth comes a sharp sword with which to strike down the nations. "He will rule them with an iron scepter." He treads the winepress of the fury of the wrath of God Almighty. On his robe and on his thigh he has this name written: KING OF KINGS AND LORD OF LORDS. (Revelation 19:11-16)

We earlier discussed the early conceptual principle of Binitarianism which was developed on the way to an understanding of the Trinity. This is clearly seen in the passages quoted above as well as in 1 Corinthians 8:6 and 1 Timothy 2:5. In these passages the roles of two of the Persons with each other is indicated. Likewise, Scripture contains passages that define Trinitarian formulas, with each Person having a definite role. For example, consider these passages:

There are different kinds of gifts, but the same **Spirit***. There are different kinds of service, but the same* **Lord***. There are different kinds of working, but the same* **God** *works all of them in all men. (1 Corinthians 12:4-6)*

Praise be to the **God and Father** *of our Lord Jesus Christ, who has blessed us in the heavenly realms with every spiritual blessing in Christ. For he chose us in him before the creation of the world to be holy and blameless* *in his sight. In love he predestined us to be adopted as his sons through* **Jesus Christ**, *in accordance with his pleasure and will—to the praise of his glorious grace, which he has freely given us in the One he loves.... In him we were also chosen, having been predestined according to the plan of him who works out everything in conformity with the purpose of his will, in order that we, who were the first to hope in Christ, might be for the praise of his glory. And you also were included in Christ when you heard the word of truth, the gospel of your salvation. Having believed, you were marked in him with a seal, the promised* **Holy Spirit**, *who is a deposit guaranteeing our inheritance until the redemption of those who are God's possession—to the praise of his glory. (Ephesians 1:3-6,11-14, bold emphasis is mine)*

A pre-Trinitarian blessing can be seen in the pattern Jude 20,21:

But you, dear friends, build yourselves up in your most holy faith and pray in the **Holy Spirit**. *Keep yourselves in* **God's** *love as you wait for the mercy of our* **Lord Jesus Christ** *to bring you to eternal life. (Bold emphasis is mine)*

In Galatians 4:6, the Trinitarian formula can be seen clearly in the God/Father, Son, and Spirit working independently: *"Because you are his sons, God sent the Spirit of his Son into our hearts, the Spirit who calls out, 'Abba, Father.'"* The Great Commission in Matthew 28:19,20 expresses a completely fleshed-in Trinitarian pattern as Jesus tells the disciples:

"Therefore go and make disciples of all nations, baptizing them in the name of the **Father** *and of the* **Son** *and of the* **Holy Spirit**, *and teaching them to obey everything I have commanded you. And surely I am with you always, to the very end of the age." (Bold emphasis is mine)*

Take the time to also read 1 Peter 1:2-12. This passage lays out the Trinity in verse 2, then deals with each person and His respective role. The Father is described in verses 3-5, the Son in verses 6-9, and the Spirit in verses 10-12.

The doctrine of the Trinity is supported throughout Scripture, from the moment of Creation when the Godhead said, "Let **us** make man in our image, in our likeness..." in Genesis 1:26 and all the way through to Revelation. It is important for believers to have some understanding of the Triune Godhead and to not allow heretical beliefs undermine it. It is a difficult concept to completely grasp.

Since the concept is so difficult, there are many analogies for describing the Trinity. It was St. Patrick who taught the new Irish converts during the 5th century that the Trinity was like a Shamrock leaf: one leaf but with three distinct lobes. One is three and three is one. My brother-in-law, James Day, uses another an analogy that I like. "The Trinity is like a cup of coffee," he says, "Coffee, milk, and sugar." They are all one and it is not easy to parse them back into their respective parts. Where does the milk start and the sugar end? Where does the coffee end and the sugar start? One is three and three is one.

May the reader beware, though. While these may be nice conceptual aids that might help someone grasp the basic concept, but it is very important to realize that any analogy, no matter how clever it may be, will fail to adequately model the special relationship of the Trinity. The model will break down because God is not created (like a Shamrock or the elements of coffee) and one could make arguments on how each can be separated (which is not possible with the Godhead).

As mentioned before, it is important that we keep the basic concept of the Holy Trinity front and center in our theological understanding. History has proven time and again that variation from understanding the Oneness in Threeness and the Threeness in Oneness simultaneously coexisting in perfect balance leads to heretical stances. Most cults break this tension and lean one way or the other and then build their faulty theologies upon this broken rock. The key principle that we each must appropriate and which must guide our every understanding of theology can be boiled down to:

Every word of Scripture must harmonize with every other word; every concept in Scripture must be in accordance with every other concept.

In other words, each part of Scripture hinges upon every other part. God does not change (Num 23:19), so thus everything must be consistent.

To avoid being misled, the believer must ensure that he or she knows their Bible inside out and back to front. The same God who declares that He is One (Deut 6:4) also revealed that He is Father and Son in John 1:14 and Father, Son, and Spirit in Gal 4:6. Only a sound understanding of the

Trinity can reconcile these concepts, and I propose that only a sound understanding of the Trinity can serve to keep a believer from being taken captive by false teaching.

Anytime someone preaches or teaches anything that breaks the Godhead apart or anything that renders God as acting in three different roles (Father one moment, then Son another, for example), I warn you to be very careful! My advice is for you to walk away from that situation because if someone does not maintain a healthy balance of Who God really is, can they *truly* understand the Scriptures written by God Himself? I believe that the Apostle Paul said it right:

Evidently some people are throwing you into confusion and are trying to pervert the gospel of Christ. But even if we or an angel from heaven should preach a gospel other than the one we preached to you, let them be under God's curse! (Galatians 1:7b-8)

Indeed, such a person is trying to subvert God's very Person in order to confuse and to mislead.

The Trinity is all-encompassing. The Godhead is, among His other qualities, eternal, boundless, creator, sustainer, righteous, loving, just, all-powerful, ruler of all, ever-present, all-knowing, judge, and savior. The existence of the Three co-eternal and co-substantial Persons allow for voluntary delegation of roles: the Father wills, the Son submits to His will, and the Spirit proceeds and works. Within the Trinity is the perfect example of total accord where total selfless love maintains unity.

Jesus, as He prayed over His disciples on the night He was betrayed said, *"I pray also for those who will believe in me through their message, that all of them may be one, Father, just as you are in me and I am in you. May they also be in us so that the world may believe that you have sent me. I have given them the glory that you gave me, that they may be one as we are one—I in them and you in me—so that they may be brought to complete unity. Then the world will know that you sent me and have loved them even as you have loved me." (John 17:20b-23)*

Chuck Colson summed up the Trinity by stating, "The Trinity enables us to better understand the scriptural teaching that God is love. Love cannot exist without someone to love, which is why Allah and any unitary understanding leads to a cold, impersonal god. The essence of the God of the Bible is His intertwined triune nature of Father, Son, and Holy Spirit. The three continuously pour out love to one another and receive love in return. The Trinity exists as a perfect community of self-giving."[4] Precisely! The Trinity's Oneness is maintained by pure agape (selfless) love and the self-submissive attitudes in the Threeness provides the perfect demonstration of the power of that selfless love in action.

---

[1] An apocryphal story from an anonymous source states that a "man of God" was struggling to understand the doctrine of the Trinity. He decided to go for a walk on the beach where he saw a little boy digging a hole in the sand with a seashell. The boy then ran off to the ocean, filled the shell with water, and rushed back to pour it into the hole he had made.

"What are you doing, my little man," the man asked.

"I'm trying to put the ocean into this hole," the boy replied.

The "man of God" suddenly realized that this was precisely was he was trying to do in order to fit the great mysteries of God into his mind.

[2] Heresy can broadly be defined as beliefs that are in conflict with orthodox, commonly accepted Christian viewpoints. I prefer the narrower definition of beliefs that are not in conformance with the overall Scriptural definitions of religious topics.

[3] Binatarianism is an understanding that God exists in two Persons. It is an early step towards Trinitarianism, based upon direct statements such as Jesus' that "I and my Father are One." (John 10:30).

[4] Colson, Charles <u>The Faith</u>, Grand Rapids, Zondervan, 2008. p. 105

11 The Doctrine of Man

Before we can discuss Jesus and His work of atonement, we must discover the doctrine of sin. Before we can fully understand the doctrine of sin, we need to understand man for he lives entwined within a constant state of sin. Listen to the cry of the Psalmist:

O LORD, what is man that you care for him, the son of man that you think of him? (Psalm 144:3)

We too must ask this same question. What do we know doctrinally about ourselves? Why are we so important in God's plans?

We know that God created man as the crowning achievement in creation. Genesis 2 states that God created man (*adam* in Hebrew) from the dust (*adamah* in Hebrew) of the ground. Dale Moody, in his systematic theology text, demonstrates an interesting interplay of words here: "A*dam* came from the *adamah*, and it is the *adamah* which *adam* tills until the toils of life are over and he returns to the *adamah* again."[1]

Once God had created the Universe and the Earth, the fish, birds, and animals, He turned His attention to the creation of man.

Then God said, "Let us make man in our image, in our likeness, and let them rule over the fish of the sea and the birds of the air, over the livestock, over all the earth, and over all the creatures that move along the ground."

So God created man in his own image, in the image of God he created him; male and female he created them.

God blessed them and said to them, "Be fruitful and increase in number; fill the earth and subdue it. Rule over the fish of the sea and the birds of the air and over every living creature that moves on the ground." (Genesis 1:26-28)

Unlike everything else which He created by command, man was created by His very hand and He deliberately blew the breath of life into his nostrils. Man was God's crowning creation at the end of the entire process. From the moment of His creation of man, God's person-to-person, face-to-face approach to us can be clearly seen.

The LORD God formed the man from the dust of the ground and breathed into his nostrils the breath of life, and the man became a living being. (Genesis 2:7)

But for Adam no suitable helper was found. So the LORD God caused the man to fall into a deep sleep; and while he was sleeping, he took one of the man's ribs and closed up the place with flesh. Then the LORD God made a woman from the rib he had taken out of the man, and he brought her to the man. (Genesis 2:20b-22)

The inspired writer of the Genesis accounts indicated that God considered the creation of man and woman special, events worthy enough to be personally done by His own hand. God had created the Universe for man's inhabitation, since man is the crown of Creation. In Isaiah, God reveals this fact:

For this is what the LORD says—
he who created the heavens, he is God;
he who fashioned and made the earth, he founded it;
he did not create it to be empty, but formed it to be inhabited—
he says: "I am the LORD, and there is no other. (Isaiah 45:18)

After God created the universe, He created man and woman. He then gave them explicit directions on their place in nature:

God blessed them and said to them, "Be fruitful and increase in number; fill the earth and subdue it. Rule over the fish of the sea and the birds of the air and over every living creature that moves on the ground." (Genesis 1:28)

God's supreme commandment to man is to "subdue nature." The word translated "subdue" here does not imply destruction, but rather it indicates stewardship. Stewardship is the tending or management of someone else's property. This makes perfect sense since..."[T]he Earth is *the Lord's, and everything in it*" as the Psalmist wrote in Psalm 24:1. We are all given the charge of tending and developing it. Every time man invents something, discovers a cure for a dreaded disease, or saves some species from extinction, he is merely following the commandment of God to manage/tend/subdue nature.

Carefully consider our assigned responsibility towards nature. It must be well-balanced. Moody states, quite correctly, that "the blessing of God upon man's dominion has been perverted in two directions (1:28). Too much emphasis on replenishing the earth leads to overproduction and overpopulation, and too much emphasis on subduing the earth leads to exploitation and the rape of natural resources. In any case, man remains the lord of creation. It is only when he forgets that his dominion is exercised under the dominion of God that disaster follows. Technology without theology leads to tyranny over God's good creation."[2]

As good stewards over what God has entrusted us we must always be on our guard to not destroy it. The ecologically-minded Christian will always maintain a *balance* on usage of resources. On the one hand man must survive and continue to develop, but on the other hand man must neither permit or participate in the wanton destruction of the world nor apply his efforts in a way that violates God's laws. There is no experience that is more humbling than to walk amidst the majestic giant redwoods lining the Northern California coast and to realize that some of these trees were alive before Christ was even born! It is their majestic beauty that causes man to fall to his knees and to cry out from the depth of his being, "*O God, what is man that you mindful for him, the son of man that you care of him?*" (Psalm 8:4). We should all spend some time in pristine nature to contemplate the wonders of our magnificent Lord's creative power. We must also wisely seek to administer everything placed in our control as good stewards since this task remains as God's first commandment to man!

Liberal thinkers always attempt to subjugate man to nature and therefore they warp the Biblical view of mankind. God's point of Creation is that the universe exists for mankind. This is not to make man self-important but because God planned from the very beginning that nature was to exist under man's stewardship. Every time you look up at the sky and see the Milky Way, or see a beautiful mountain scene or a perfectly shaped tree, or contemplate the force of waves dashing against rocks, or dwell on a truly awe-inspiring sunrise or sunset, you should thank God that He made this especially for you!

Animal life is described in Scripture as being living "souls" (*nephesh* in Hebrew). Man shares this attribute with all animal life. Look at Ecclesiastes 3:18-21. Both the animals and mankind share the same fate of living and dying. However, man also has the image of God embedded in his being according to Genesis 1:26,27. Thus, man is a living being created differently from other living animals because man not just flesh and blood but **is** also an eternal soul. Each person who has ever lived, or who will ever live, has been created specifically by God. He accounts for their entire lifetimes (see Psalm 139:13-18) and man's spirit returns to God at death (Ecclesiastes 12:7 and Psalm 104:29,30).

A word of caution needs to be raised here. Each and every man and woman is a combination of a fleshly body and an eternal spirit. The two might be separated conceptually, but theologically man is both body and spirit. When we die, our bodies may return to the ground from which they came (Genesis 3:19, Job 7:21, Ecclesiastes 3:20, Psalm 146:4) but within God's plan, each man's spirit will be reunited with its body in His presence. He will miraculously resurrect each body and simultaneously transform it into a heavenly, eternal body. Take careful note of Hebrews 9:27, 1 Corinthians 15:35-54, 1 Thessalonians 4:16,17 and Revelation 20:12-13.

We must avoid the danger of *dualism*, that is, believing that one's body is "evil" but one's spirit is "good" so that God cannot love our bodily forms, or believing that Christ could not have been in the form of "evil" flesh, or (even worse) that we can indulge our bodies in sin with impunity thinking that they will perish but our spirits will be saved (see, for example, Galatians 5:13-25).

What is meant by the "image and likeness of God?" This phrase has sparked much theological debate over the centuries among both Hebrew and Christian scholarship. Some theologians have argued that it is something which man had but it was lost in the Fall. Others claim that it is something which man never lost and present as proof the different attributes of man such as reason, spirituality, creativity, and conscience as being the components of the "image of God." While we are not going to enter into this debate, let us touch on some thought-provoking ideas on the issue.

Moody argues in <u>The Word of Truth</u> that it is clear that the Fall did not take away the image of God in man.[3] His assertion is based on the passage in Genesis 9 wherein God made a covenant with Noah after the flood:

"And for your lifeblood I will surely demand an accounting. I will demand an accounting from every animal. And from each man, too, I will demand an accounting for the life of his fellow man. Whoever sheds the blood of man, by man shall his blood be shed; for in the image of God has God made man." (Genesis 9:5,6)

Other scholars have concluded that this passage indicates that the "likeness of God" has been lost since only the image is mentioned here. I personally believe that this assumption is very thin and based upon over-parsing the words. An intriguing passage can be found in James' epistle where he discusses why believers should avoid cursing one's fellow men, since:

With the tongue we praise our Lord and Father, and with it we curse men, who have been made in God's likeness. Out of the same mouth come praise and cursing. My brothers, this should not be. (James 3:9,10)

The insinuation is that by cursing fellow men, one essentially is cursing God because of His likeness or image within them! If we take this concept farther, we might see why God is so insistent on loving one another. Jesus, when confronted by the Pharisees who asked Him what is the greatest commandment, replied:

Jesus replied: "'Love the Lord your God with all your heart and with all your soul and with all your mind.' This is the first and greatest commandment. And the second is like it: 'Love your neighbor as yourself.' All the Law and the Prophets hang on these two commandments." (Matthew 22:37-40)

Likewise, love of fellow man is used as one of the criteria to separate the people into two groups during the Judgment. The Lord will say to the righteous:

'Come, you who are blessed by my Father; take your inheritance, the kingdom prepared for you since the creation of the world. For I was hungry and you gave me something to eat, I was thirsty and you gave me

something to drink, I was a stranger and you invited me in, I needed clothes and you clothed me, I was sick and you looked after me, I was in prison and you came to visit me.'

"Then the righteous will answer him, 'Lord, when did we see you hungry and feed you, or thirsty and give you something to drink? When did we see you a stranger and invite you in, or needing clothes and clothe you? When did we see you sick or in prison and go to visit you?'

"The King will reply, 'I tell you the truth, whatever you did for one of the least of these brothers of mine, you did for me.'" (Matthew 25:34b-40)

The image of God resides in each of us regardless of our state of sin. When we demonstrate love to each other, we somehow demonstrate love to God also and when we hate one another, we also demonstrate hatred to God.

Moody states that since the likeness and image of God was in Adam, it was something passed to his progeny. In Genesis 5:3 we find,

When Adam had lived 130 years, he had a son in his own likeness, in his own image; and he named him Seth.

Thus, using this passage he argues, "[t]he image and likeness of God in creation is now transmitted to Seth through human procreation and divine creation working together."[4]

In examining Genesis 1:26 closely, it appears that the phrase "in our likeness" is parenthetical to "in our image." It seems to be more of an explanation of the preceding phrase than as a separate item. The two thoughts are not linked with the conjunction *and*. It reads, "Let us make man in our image, in our likeness, and let..." and not "Let us make man in our image and our likeness" as so many theologians attempt to read it. To quote Moody once again, "The basic meaning of the image of God appears at the very beginning when 'after our likeness' is added by way of explanation. Likeness to God is the image of God, but one's view of determines the view one holds of the image. In the context of Genesis 1:1-2:4a the central concept of God is that of the Creator who rules not only over nations, as in Isaiah 40-55, but over all creation. Man is the crown of creation, and, under the dominion of God the Creator, man has dominion over all other creatures: fish and birds, cattle and creeping things (1:26)."[5] In other words, God has delegated some of His authority to mankind.

The 20th century Swedish theologian, Gustaf Aulén, approached the understanding of the "image of God" in terms of destiny due to the fact that "the purpose of God is for man to have a life characterized and defined by his will and love, and that consequently this is a God-given destiny. That man has this destiny is the meaning of the idea that he is created in the image of God."[6]

Jesus, who Paul described as the second Adam in Romans 5:5ff and 1 Corinthians 15:45ff, is the one man who is not in rebellion to God. He shows the true incarnation and full potential of the image and likeness of God in man. It is through Him that we see "that to be truly human, to be man in the image of God, is not to possess some intellectual or spiritual or moral qualities in oneself, but to be man-in-relationship, man-in-community, or man-in-encounter. We cannot be human by ourselves, in ourselves, independently and self-sufficiently. Only as we discover our very existence in relatedness to God and to fellowman can we be truly human."[7] Man truly becomes man within community; after all, God said that it was not good for the man to be alone. We can summarize this in the words of Guthrie: "as God himself is spontaneously and freely with and for men, so he created human beings to be like himself–spontaneously and freely with and for one another."

None of these views are mutually exclusive. In fact, they probably all approach the truth simultaneously. Let us enumerate the points that have been made:

1. God exists in community within His Being (the Trinity), a property which he extended to man also. He created woman to be man's companion because it was not good for man to be alone. Also, God created man to be in fellowship with Him. Witness the fact that God was in daily fellowship with Adam and when Adam and Eve hid from His presence, He sought them calling "Where are you?"
2. God created man and provided for his every need. He even provided them eternal life through the Tree of Life in Eden. His

will demanded few things of them, merely to rule the earth and not to eat of the Tree of Knowledge of Good and Evil. God's image in man meant that they would willingly comply to His will and experience His love through fellowship.
3. God is ruler over all Creation. As ruler, He created man to share in the responsibility of tending Creation. His image is that of an incorruptible and loving ruler whom man is meant to emulate while tending the Earth.

The apostle Paul summarized the creation of man and the purpose of mankind when he addressed the Athenians at the Aeropagus (Mar's Hill):

"The God who made the world and everything in it is the Lord of heaven and earth and does not live in temples built by hands. And he is not served by human hands, as if he needed anything, because he himself gives all men life and breath and everything else. From one man he made every nation of men, that they should inhabit the whole earth; and he determined the times set for them and the exact places where they should live. God did this so that men would seek him and perhaps reach out for him and find him, though he is not far from each one of us. 'For in him we live and move and have our being.' As some of your own poets have said, 'We are his offspring.'" (Acts 17:24-28)

Thus, God created man and continues to do so by giving all men "life and breath" in order that they would seek Him and interact with Him. God wants men and women to be social companions not only with each other but also with Him. Suffice it to say also that God created man with a free will because it is His desire that man voluntarily choose (with his mind) to love Him (with his emotions) and to serve and obey Him (with his will). We will deal with this more when we discuss the Doctrines of Sin and Atonement.

Guthrie also made a very valid point on gender and race distinctions based on the Genesis creation narrative. In my opinion, he has really nailed the problem once and for all and his point is worthy of consideration. "To be a human being in the image of God is first of all to have something in common with all the other animals – sexuality. Every human being is a male or female. Sex is not just something we 'have,' but something we are – as creatures in the image of God. (Perhaps it is worth noting here that the only distinction mentioned as fundamental to man's humanity is the sex distinction. We see here that animals are created according to 'kinds' or 'species,' but not man. The attempt to find some essential distinction between men in terms of race or 'kind' is to dehumanize and make animals out of both ourselves and other men.)"[8] Mankind's sexuality is special and created by God for many specified purposes, primarily for the special companionship of a committed marriage relationship. A man's or woman's race is inconsequential before God. God's Word has been warped enough by those who have attempted to force a racist bent into it.

No discussion on the creation of mankind would be complete without discussing the creation of woman. Woman was created to be a companion to man. She was created primarily for social reasons. If there are any doubts about this, look carefully at God's reasoning prior to her creation:

The LORD God said, "It is not good for the man to be alone. I will make a helper suitable for him." (Genesis 2:18)

When no suitable helper was found among the animals, God created woman (Genesis 2:19-23) as a social partner for the man, not merely to be a sexual object! Notice the emphasis that both man and woman are created in God's image:

So God created man in his own image, in the image of God he created him; male and female he created them. (Genesis 1:27)

Another point worthy of mention is that man was put into a deep sleep while woman was being made to prevent him from being a spectator to the miracle. John Stott made a tantalizing comment by stating that "[A] special work of divine creation took place. The sexes became differentiated....According to Genesis 1 Eve, like Adam, was created in the image of God. But as to the matter of her creation, according to Genesis 2, she was made neither out of nothing (like the universe), nor out of 'the dust of the ground' (like Adam, v. 7), but out of Adam."[9] Moody states that "She is a person, not a thing."[10] He also indicates that the naming of the animals in Genesis underlines the language barrier between man and animal since animals are objects to which man's language points. On the other hand, language serves as the tool for social relations between man and woman. "The man-woman relation is falling apart when they no longer talk to each other."[11]

Throughout recent history, there has been much discussion about man-woman relationships and whether man is over woman, or vice-versa, or if man and woman are equal partners. Scripture has some indication that the latter is true under most conditions (other than within the envelopes of marriage and the Church). The apostle Paul states in numerous locations that men and women are equal in God. Here are some examples:

There is neither Jew nor Greek, slave nor free, male nor female, for you are all one in Christ Jesus. (Galatians 3:28)

In the Lord, however, woman is not independent of man, nor is man independent of woman. For as woman came from man, so also man is born of woman. But everything comes from God. (1 Corinthians 11:11,12)

There is a sense of man and woman complementing each other. Note carefully that there is not a hint that woman is to be **as** man or vice-versa. God created a man with attributes that make him a man and He created a woman with feminine attributes. These attributes are not to be subjugated but must be cultivated so that within a marriage the man and the woman properly complement each other's attributes. It is on this point that the entire women's movement has erred. Women are told to become more masculine and men are urged to develop their "feminine side." Within God's perfect plan, man's "feminine side" is his helper, his wife! What is supposed to result when a man develops his "feminine side" and a woman develops her "masculine side" and then they have to work together? Is there any wonder that there is so much gender confusion and strife-filled marriages today?

Man and woman are equal in the Lord, but they are not equal in attributes and duties before Him. It is in regards to this that Paul addressed the Ephesians concerning the marriage relationship:

Wives, submit to your husbands as to the Lord. For the husband is the head of the wife as Christ is the head of the church, his body, of which he is the Savior. Now as the church submits to Christ, so also wives should submit to their husbands in everything.

Husbands, love your wives, just as Christ loved the church and gave himself up for her to make her holy, cleansing her by the washing with water through the word, and to present her to himself as a radiant church, without stain or wrinkle or any other blemish, but holy and blameless. In this same way, husbands ought to love their wives as their own bodies. He who loves his wife loves himself. After all, no one ever hated his own body, but he feeds and cares for it, just as Christ does the church— for we are members of his body. (Ephesians 5:22-30)

This passage has been bent horribly out of shape through the centuries to justify that man has complete dominion over womankind which is quite contrary to the intent of this passage. A wife must submit to the husband's will, however the husband is commanded to love his wife. How can a husband with true, selfless love make egocentric or despotic decisions to which he expects his wife to submit? Substitute the definition of love from 1 Corinthians 13:4-8a below for the word "love" in the command to husbands. Would there be a wife who would have a problem submitting to decisions made by a husband who makes them out of true love?

Love is patient, love is kind. It does not envy, it does not boast, it is not proud. It is not rude, it is not self-seeking, it is not easily angered, it keeps no record of wrongs. Love does not delight in evil but rejoices with the truth. It always protects, always trusts, always hopes, always perseveres. Love never fails.

This is quite opposite of an image of a man dragging his wife by her hair to his cave, isn't it? How many of us married men live to this lofty standard? I am prepared to say that there are not many, so is there any wonder that wives are not submissive? Did Paul demand wives to submit to brutishness and boorishness? No, he asked them to submit to the will of a Christ-seeking husband, a husband who out of love would selflessly give even his very life for her as Christ did for His bride, the Church!

One more point must be made before we leave the subject of man-woman relationships. Procreation has God's blessing and, in fact, it is *commanded* of men and women. In Genesis 1:28, God blessed man and woman and commands them to "be fruitful and increase in number." Sexuality is a normal part of the male-female relationship with each other within the guidelines established at the Creation.

Another key point that must be emphasized is that while males and females can have social companionship with others of the same gender (such as the friendship of David and Jonathan), "the Genesis narrative makes the normal companion of male a female. God did not create Adam as male and male as some homosexual anthropology would suggest. Homosexuality is always unnatural (Romans 1:26f)."[12] In this day of extreme homosexual activism, we must not cave in to the rhetoric of its sympathizers but rather we must stand firm in the knowledge that God rejects such relationships and blesses heterosexuality within the context of marriage.[13] On the other hand, we must not join the bandwagon of hatred of homosexuals but must seek to reach out with the gospel of freedom. Jesus died for all sinners and He offers the power to break any sin.

When does God create each of us? When does He know us? The Old Testament is rife with statements such as:

"This is what the LORD says—your Redeemer, who formed you in the womb (Isaiah 44:24a)

For you created my inmost being; you knit me together in my mother's womb. I praise you because I am fearfully and wonderfully made; your works are wonderful, I know that full well. My frame was not hidden from you when I was made in the secret place. When I was woven together in the depths of the earth, your eyes saw my unformed body. All the days ordained for me were written in your book before one of them came to be. (Psalm 139:13-16)

Even before conception, God knows each person. The Psalmist and Isaiah concurred in stating that God is the agent of creation of each individual, that He takes a hand in forming the developing fetus. In Jeremiah, God states:

"Before I formed you in the womb I knew you, before you were born I set you apart; I appointed you as a prophet to the nations." (Jeremiah 1:5)

There is no doubt that God is aware of each and every life conceived and that He takes an active role in forming the new adam (man) and breathing the breath of life into his nostrils. Not only this, from the passage above, we can see that God even sets a plan for life even before birth. Isaiah described man as clay that the Lord shapes:

Yet, O LORD, you are our Father.
We are the clay, you are the potter;
we are all the work of your hand. (Isaiah 64:8)

Job made the point that all of humanity is formed by the work of God's almighty hands:

"If I have denied justice to my menservants and maidservants
when they had a grievance against me,
what will I do when God confronts me?
What will I answer when called to account?
Did not he who made me in the womb make them?
Did not the same one form us both within our mothers?" (Job 31:13-15)

This is also reflected in Job 10:8-12. God is shown to be the active agent in creation working even within the womb.

"Your hands shaped me and made me.
Will you now turn and destroy me?
Remember that you molded me like clay.
Will you now turn me to dust again?
Did you not pour me out like milk and curdle me like cheese,
clothe me with skin and flesh and knit me together with bones and sinews?
You gave me life and showed me kindness, and in your providence watched over my spirit."

In Zechariah, the prophet introduced God as follows:

*This is the word of the Lord concerning Israel. The Lord, who stretches out the heavens, who lays the foundation of the earth, and **who forms the spirit of man within him**, declares... (Zechariah 12:1, bold emphasis is mine)*

There are biological rules which originally God created which enables the development of a child. Scripture indicates that individuality is God-given. He knows each of us before we are even conceived and forms us in the womb. Since each and every life is known by Him and is planned before conception (as we saw in Psalm 139 and Jeremiah 1 above), there is no question about the origin of life in a fetus. It is clear that individual life begins at or before conception and that God is aware of that individual. Where does that place abortion in God's will? It relegates it to an act of murder, the shedding of man's blood.

How does God feel about the young (and arguably, the unborn)? In Jeremiah, as the prophet relays words of condemnation and coming judgment to the people of Judah, God's word said:

From the day it was built until now, this city [Jerusalem] has so aroused my anger and wrath that I must remove it from my sight. The people of Israel and Judah have provoked me by all the evil they have done—they, their kings and officials, their priests and prophets, the men of Judah and the people of Jerusalem. They turned their backs to me and not their faces; though I taught them again and again, they would not listen or respond to discipline. They set up their abominable idols in the house that bears my Name and defiled it. They built high places for Baal in the Valley of Ben Hinnom **to sacrifice their sons and daughters to Molech, though I never commanded, nor did it enter my mind, that they should do such a detestable thing and so make Judah sin.** *(Jeremiah 32:32-35, bold emphasis is mine)*

Consider this passage juxtapositioned against the words of Jesus, the Second Person of the Trinity, as He referred to children:

Jesus said, "Let the little children come to me, and do not hinder them, for the kingdom of heaven belongs to such as these." (Matthew 19:14)

Why are children so important to God? They are each eternal beings, adults in formation, made in God's likeness and image. Each has a destiny and an eternal soul that is priceless in God's sight. This worth is bestowed even in the womb, most likely from the moment of conception. There is something more than a simple biological process that drives the creation of each human being. The biology describes the formation of flesh and bone but cannot account for the "spirit of man" (Ecclesiastes 3:21 and Zechariah 12:1) that is created and imbued to each of us.

The rights of the unborn must be considered and held sacred by each Christian. Each fetus is a person, created in the image and likeness of

God, and thus is subject to the same consideration before being born as one would afford them after birth.

---

[1] Moody, Dale <u>The Word of Truth</u>. Grand Rapids, Wm B. Eerdmans, 1981. p. 171
[2] Moody, <u>The Word of Truth</u>. p. 226-7
[3] Moody, <u>The Word of Truth</u>. p 227
[4] Moody, <u>The Word of Truth</u>. p. 227
[5] Moody, <u>The Word of Truth</u>. p. 226
[6] Aulén, Gustaf <u>The Faith of the Christian Church</u>. Philadelphia, Fortress Pres, 1960. p. 236
[7] Guthrie, Shirley C., <u>Christian Doctrine</u>. Atlanta, John Knox Press, 1968. p 192
[8] Guthrie, <u>Christian Doctrine.</u> p. 193.
[9] Stott, John <u>Same-Sex Partnerships</u>? Grand Rapids, Fleming H. Revell, 1998. pp. 33,34
[10] Moody, <u>The Word of Truth</u>. p. 213
[11] Moody, <u>The Word of Truth</u>. p. 213
[12] Moody, <u>The Word of Truth</u>. p. 222
[13] The reader is urged to pick up a copy of the short book by the late John Stott called <u>Same-Sex Partnerships</u> mentioned above. This is a well-written and concise exposition on why the homosexual lifestyle is against God's created order and it corrects the mishandling of Scripture that has been done on both sides of the debate. He stresses a loving approach of dealing with homosexual sin and reminds us all that sexual sins such as adultery, pre-marital sexual encounters, and such *are all against God's established order* and must be dealt with.

12 The Doctrine of Sin

The childhood nursery-rhyme goes as follows:

Humpty Dumpty sat on a wall.
Humpty Dumpty had a great fall.
And all the king's horses and all the king's men,
cannot put Humpty Dumpty together again.

From a Theological perspective, all mankind exhibits the characteristics of Humpty Dumpty in our natures. Due to the problem of sin, we all fall and are rendered hopelessly broken. Yet, we consistently attempt to put ourselves and others back together. We advocate self-help and peer-assistance groups, attempt to make ourselves more righteous by doing good works, but in all truth we cannot really change ourselves. We may deceive ourselves and others for short periods of time but the truth shows us up eventually. We all exhibit the cracks of our brokenness through the layers of hastily applied paint and plaster.

The Doctrine of Atonement is central to Christianity. We will approach this concept in a later chapter and will discover that it is tightly intertwined with the nature and person of Jesus Christ. The Godly concept of the Atonement is the only true repair solution to fix Humpty Dumpty permanently. Only through the atoning blood of Jesus Christ can a man or woman be finally brought into a state of true peace with God. In fact, the word "atonement" is the Anglo-Saxon melding of *at-one-ment* which was used to describe a state in which there is no discord or strife within a relationship.

The Doctrine of Sin is indelibly wrapped with that of the Atonement. Without sin, there would be no need for atonement at all. These next few chapters will be very involved, so hang on tight and let us venture boldly into the seedy world of sin and then break out into the beautiful state of God's boundless grace!

It is important to realize that, in the beginning, when God created mankind, He created us to be sinless. Read Genesis 1:26-31. All of God's creation, including man, was made "very good." As we set the stage for the discussion on sin, we must realize that sometime prior to, or simultaneous with, the Creation, heaven was rocked by a rebellion that gave birth to evil. In order to understand sin and why there is evil in the world, we must grasp the details of this rebellion in the heavenly realm.

Bear in mind that Satan and his demons are all created beings, originally created as the guardian Lucifer and other good angelic beings who subsequently fell. To gain an understanding of who they were and how they ended up where they are today, we must read Ezekiel 29:11-19 and Isaiah 14:12-15. Notice that both of these references appear to be directed to rulers (the King of Tyre in Ezekiel and the King of Babylon in Isaiah) however their contexts indicate that God is speaking to the "power behind the throne" who is Satan. This understanding can be derived from internal evidence within the passages themselves.

In Ezekiel 29:17, the subject of that passage is described as being thrown to earth (from heaven), a description that certainly does not jive with the King of Tyre. In Isaiah 14:12, the subject is described as "morning star." Flip quickly over to Job 38:4-7 where God is describing the Creation. He indicated that *"the morning stars sang together"* and paralleled that statement with *"the angels shouted for joy."* In other words, the morning stars were the angels praising God as they do night and day.

Additional passages that we need to put into the hopper include Luke 10:18 (where Jesus stated to His disciples, *"I saw Satan fall like lightning from heaven."*) and Revelation 12:3,4,7-9. Finally, we must read Job 1:6-9 and Zechariah 3:1 and parallel them with Revelation 12:10.

With our minds primed with this material, let us now extract some truths concerning Satan. Scripture indicates that he was created as an angel. He was not just any angel, but rather appears to have been the guardian angel of the throne of God (Ezekiel 29:14), the head angel so to speak. He was created to be most beautiful (Ezekiel 29:13,17). However, he became infected with pride and ambition (Ezekiel 29:17a and Isaiah 14:13,14) and wanted to not just serve God, but to *be* God. The basis of his pride is laid out in the five ambitious "I will" statements in the Isaiah passage.

Since Satan wanted to become a god and to control it all, he led an angelic rebellion in heaven (Revelation 12:7) which was quashed by Michael and the rest of the faithful angelic host. In Revelation, he is described as the dragon who also in 12:2,3 "*swept a third of the stars from the sky*" and then attempted to kill the Baby Jesus to thwart God's plans of salvation. Of special interest here is the reference to one third of the "stars from the sky." It appears that this refers to the fact that one third of the angelic host were convinced by Satan to participate in the rebellion and to fight on his side. God's angels mounted a counteroffensive and overcame the rebels. The result of the quashed rebellion is that Satan and his minions were cast out of heaven and into the time/space continuum of the Creation (see Ezekiel 28:17b, Isaiah 14:12b,15, Luke 10:18, Revelation 12:4a,8-9a).

Before everyone panics, there are two realities which we must know about concerning Satan. First of all, Satan still has limited access to the throne room of God where he goes to accuse God's people (see Job 1:6-9, Zechariah 3:1 and Revelation 12:10). Second, and more importantly, his days are numbered and therefore his days of terrorizing Earth is finite (see Revelation 20:10).

Let's play a game for a moment, the game of "Opposites." Name the opposite for the following words. Up...down. Correct. Left...right. Good. Cold....hot. Right. Heaven....hell. Yep. God....? Nope, it is not Satan. There are not two distinct gods, one of good and one of evil. There is only One, holy God. Satan does not possess the attributes of divinity.

Our views of (what is called) cosmic dualism (good and evil) are, by definition, limited because of our finite perspective. What we do know is that even though evil exists within the world, God (who is ultimate Good) will conquer all evil at the end of time and reconcile everything to Himself (see Psalm 1:5, Matthew 25:41, Romans 8:18-25, and Revelation 20:7-10; 21:4). Therefore, evil exists here temporarily as a "pocket" that is both limited to, and subject to, the reign of time.

Just as crucial to understand is that God is not a god who dabbles both in good and in evil. He is not impressed with evil and does not condone it. He does not have a cosmic split personality! The Bible states:

You are not a God who takes pleasure in evil; with you the wicked cannot dwell. (Psalm 5:4)

See also Psalm 11:5 for another example. In other words, evil arises *outside* of God's throne room and for now is not quenched. This is actually an act of His grace, as the Apostle Peter writes:

But do not forget this one thing, dear friends: With the Lord a day is like a thousand years, and a thousand years are like a day. The Lord is not slow in keeping his promise, as some understand slowness. He is patient with you, **not wanting anyone to perish, but everyone to come to repentance.** *But the day of the Lord will come like a thief. The heavens will disappear with a roar; the elements will be destroyed by fire, and the earth and everything in it will be laid bare. (2 Peter 3:8-10, bold emphasis is mine)*

It is also important to grasp the fact that Satan and his demonic host were originally created as part of the angelic host. They fell into evil because of their lust for power. Now, they may attempt in their new fallen positions to thwart God's holy plans but they are severely hampered. They don't possess God's character and nature and thus they are not all-knowing (omniscient) and they are not omnipresent like He is. They may have great powers but those powers are limited and cannot even begin to match those of God Himself.

However, Satan is real and present. It is always a danger, whether out of fear or out of ignorance, to close one's eyes and ignore his presence. Peter warned:

Be self-controlled and alert. Your enemy the devil prowls around like a roaring lion looking for someone to devour. Resist him, standing firm in the faith, because you know that your brothers throughout the world are undergoing the same kind of sufferings. (1 Peter 5:8,9)

As we live in the temporal plain on Earth we can be blissfully unaware of anything going on except for the fact that evil befalls us. There are pestilences, storms, earthquakes, illnesses, and wars which, many times, claim the lives of the "innocent." Any attempt to explain this from what we can detect with our five senses is bound to be incomplete because we are totally unable to discern the spiritual world in our natural state. It is only through Scripture that we come to understand that what we see happening here and now is an offshoot of a greater battle within the Spiritual realm. The Apostle Paul stated this succinctly in Ephesians 6:10-13 when he commanded Christians to:

Finally, be strong in the Lord and in his mighty power. Put on the full armor of God so that you can take your stand against the devil's schemes. For our struggle is not against flesh and blood, but against the rulers, against the authorities, against the powers of this dark world and against the spiritual forces of evil in the heavenly realms. Therefore put on the full armor of God, so that when the day of evil comes, you may be able to stand your ground, and after you have done everything, to stand.

The Book of Job demonstrates the worldly approach of trying to deal with the problem of evil without understanding the fact that this is a symptom of something much larger and vaster. Job's friends and wife all were limited in their understanding of the causes of Job's misfortunes and were hasty to blame him for something he had done. We, the readers, are led behind the curtain and are shown that what befell Job was an outcome of Satan battling his will with God's (Job 1:1-2:8). The Apostle Paul also alluded to this spiritual battlefield in Ephesians 2:1-5.

So, the bad news is that Satan and his minions have lots of power but the good news to Christians is that "*...the one who is in you is greater than the one who is in the world.*" (1 John 4:4) As someone is reputed to have said, "Don't worry...I have read the last chapter, and we win!"

Now that we understand what happened in the heavenly spaces to birth evil, let us examine the Fall of man carefully. In the Creation narrative (as you recall from our earlier discussion), God created everything and finalized by making man, His crowning achievement. Genesis 2:8-17 outlines God's plans for mankind. Scripture states that there was a garden, Eden, that had been formed specially for man (2:8,15). In the center of this garden were *TWO* trees (2:9). We tend to remember the one but conveniently forget the second. The first of the trees was the <u>Tree of Life</u> and the other was the <u>Tree of the Knowledge of Good and Evil</u>. In verses 16 and 17, God set the parameters of man's occupancy of Eden:

"You are free to eat from any tree in the garden; but you must not eat from the tree of the knowledge of good and evil, for when you eat of it you will surely die."

With this knowledge in hand, turn the page to the account of the Fall in Genesis 3:1-24. Notice how Satan appeared in the form of a serpent to do what he does best: stir up trouble. (How do we know that this is Satan and not some random serpent? Look at Revelation 20:2 for the answer.) The question that the serpent asked in verse 1 was phrased to provoke. Literally the intent was to state, "Who is God to prevent you from eating from any tree in the garden? You have your rights!" The question was craftily phrased to cause a self-centered reflection in Eve.

In verse 2, the woman demonstrated that God was either not of primary importance in her life, or rapidly shifted from being in the first place on her priority list. Her answer was inaccurate, similar in nature to that of a child who cares only about knowing enough to stay out of trouble and not knowing enough to truly please a parent! From the beginning, God desired that man would choose to eat from the Tree of Life and obediently scorn the Tree of the Knowledge of Good and Evil. Instead, Adam and Eve somehow had rejected *both* trees to avoid any sort of problem. They did not care enough to know the difference between the trees and thus to be able to choose the right one. An inexact and insecure relationship with God always provides a perfect opportunity for Satan to attack.

Satan immediately jumped into the breach created by the woman's uncertainty (v 4) and recast the role of the Tree of the Knowledge of Good and Evil. After all, the deceiver claimed, its fruit serves to make men into God! His insinuation was that God preferred to keep man "dumb and happy," a grossly unfair condition that the woman could easily remedy by reaching out and plucking one of its fruit.

The woman (who had already demonstrated that her relationship with God was lacking a solid foundation of trust) turned to the tree and surveyed its fruit in the new light shed upon it by the serpent (v 6). She looked at it from every point of view except God's! The fruit was pretty. It had a great color and luster. It looked fleshy and probably would be mighty filling. She determined (by sight alone) that the "fruit was good for food." She *never* looked at the fruit as the single thing that a loving Father knew was so harmful to man that He had prohibited its consumption solely out of His love for them! Without a second's thought, she ate it and gave it to her husband, Adam (v 6b). Together, within mere minutes, they had broken God's only prohibitive commandment to them.

In verses 7-12 we can see the immediate consequences of sin. There is a realization of a change in state that sin creates (v 7), a voluntary separation of man from God's presence (v 8), a shifting of the blame (v 12), and an overall feeling of dirtiness and inadequacy (v 10). Notice, nothing had actually changed in Adam's or Eve's situation between verse 1 and verse 12 except for the commission of the sin! Yet something compelled them to hide their nakedness and hide from God. Natural, unrepentant man lives a life that is a constant effort to flee from God and to hide from His presence!

Verses 13-24 then take us through the longer term consequences of sin but they also demonstrate God's grace. The first curses fall upon Satan as the tempting serpent (v 14,15). Satan will never rest secure knowing that all mankind is tainted – he and his minions will constantly slave to keep mankind down. On the other hand, there is the certain promise that the woman will bear Satan's ultimate enemy. Notice that the enmity will be between "your offspring and hers" and not *their offspring*. The Virgin Birth of the Savior was a future blessing that is concealed in this verse. This Savior will be bruised by the serpent but He will crush the serpent's head. Satan's death blow was going to be dealt by this special offspring.

In the curses pronounced upon Adam (v 17-19) we see that man's lot in life is cast. Instead of resting satisfied in God's blessings, man would now have to toil the land by the sweat of his brow. It will no longer cooperate and will provide thorns and thistles (hardships) in response to man's hard and endless work. Man will slave and return eventually to the ground in the sleep of death. Additionally, since then, the frustrations of man's earthly life serve to mask his view of his own eternity. It takes all of his effort to get through each day.

Finally, in verses 22-24, God expelled man from the garden so that he could not grab the fruit of the Tree of Life. Man will never again be able to come to the Tree of Life under his own effort or under his own conditions. From now on, **all** access to the Tree of Life will only be through God's grace.

Speaking of grace, verses 20 and 21 contain two instances of grace in action. In verse 20, Eve was named thus because Adam realized that God's pronouncement in verse 15 was a sure thing. The woman would bear the source of all life as her offspring. Man-in-sin is dead but she would one day bear the One who is the Way, the Truth, and the Life (Jesus) and thus become the mother of all the living!

The final act of grace that we need to extract from this passage is that God met man's immediate need. What was Adam's complaint to God in verse 10? He complained that he was ashamed because he was naked. God clothed him in verse 21. Notice that in order to meet man's need, the first blood sacrifice was made. Man's nakedness could not be adequately covered by leaves (which signified man's own self-righteous attempt to cover his own shame in verse 7). It needed a divinely-provided garment composed of the skins of animals. Man's sin required the shedding of innocent blood.

Dale Moody stated that "the state of sin is described as expulsion from the presence of the Lord God."[1] He also indicated that "sin is a state of spiritual death that leaves man without access to the tree of life. Men are indeed 'alienated from the life of God because of the ignorance that is in them' (Ephesians 4:18)."[2]

Every man and woman experiences the Fall anew within themselves (see the discussion of Original Sin below). Our sinfulness arises from our own individual self-aggrandizing quest to serve ourselves, to enthrone our desires instead of God. Look at Romans 7:7-25. We know better and yet we voluntarily choose to ignore God and his perfect commandments to enthrone our own lusts (see 2 Peter 2:18,19). Romans 3:23 can therefore state the truth that ALL have sinned. The words of A. W. Tozer so eloquently state mankind's problem: "There is within the human heart a tough fibrous root of fallen life whose nature is to possess. It covets 'things' with a deep and fierce passion. The pronouns 'my' and 'mine' look innocent enough in print, but their constant and universal use is significant. They express the real nature of the old Adamic man better than a thousand volumes of theology could do....Things have become necessary to us, a development never originally intended. God's gifts now take the place of God and the whole course of nature is upset by the monstrous substitution."[3]

We need to grasp another essential truth about sin. Sin is always directed against God. Gustav Aulén stated that, "there is no sin which is not sin against God. It is meaningless to talk about sin if it has no relation to God...From the viewpoint of Christian faith it would be meaningless to divide 'sins' into two classes: sins against God and sins against the neighbor. There is no sin against the neighbor which is not sin against God. The sin against the neighbor becomes sin because it is sin against

God. If we were to talk about sins which are not sins against God, the concept of sin would have lost its meaning. It would have moved outside of the religious sphere."[4]

All mankind is like Adam in their respective natures. As we just saw, Romans 3:23 states it plainly: "*For all have sinned, and fall short of the glory of God.*" Turn over to Romans 5:12-14 to realize the plight of every man and every woman. These verses lay out an indictment upon all mankind. All of mankind has sinned and because of this fact all mankind faces death, not the death that returns their bodies to the dust, but **DEATH** (in capital letters and wrapped in purple gift wrap and sealed with black ribbons) which is the eternal separation from God's love! Need more proof? Look also at Isaiah 59:2-8. Face it, mankind is doomed. Or is he? What we are going to discover in a later chapter is that God's grace reaches deeper than man's sin possibly can, and He opens a special way back to the Tree of Life for us.

One important point must be extracted from the God's actions in the Garden of Eden in Genesis 3. Do you recall that God sacrificed animals to provide the covering that man needed in Genesis 3:21? This leads us to a crucial concept which is articulated in Hebrews 9:22: "*...and without the shedding of blood there is no forgiveness.*" This concept is also found in Leviticus 17:11, "*For the life of a creature is in the blood, and I have given it to you to make atonement for yourselves on the altar; it is the blood that makes atonement for one's life.*" As we will see, Jesus' blood today covers and removes all sin.

The cost of sin, any sin, is the eternal life of the person who commits it. The atonement for sin is the ransom of that life. Each act of each man's or woman's sin requires blood. Actually, it demands his or her own life blood to atone for it! This produces quite a quandary which can only be answered by a loving God. It is not within mankind's power to atone for our sins because just one sin, by right, requires our very life! This is a crucial principle that leads us to the understanding that we can *never* work for our salvation because we do not know the actual cost of a sin. Likewise, we do not have enough lives to pay the price for every sin we have committed and will commit! It follows logically that since we cannot adequately atone for our own sins, we likewise cannot atone for the sins of others.

There is another point that must be stated. Sin has effects that ripple within our very society and affect our future generations. "Western Christianity, both Catholic and Protestant, has rightly looked upon sin as a disruption of the perpendicular relationship with God, but this horizontal human disruption should not be neglected. Anti-social behavior is an index of man's relation to God (see 1 Jn 3:10b-12)."[5] Sin *destroys* the relationship between man and God and also corrupts the relationship between man and fellow man. Therefore, sin is all-pervasive, destructive, and viral in nature. It is the cancer that eats away at each person and consumes society. Satan and his minions are alive and well and regenerating the temptations of the Garden of Eden every moment of every day.

A doctrine that springs directly from that of sin is the Doctrine of Original Sin and is worthy of mention here. Original Sin is, as discussed above, the fact that all mankind sins and thus is in need of redemption. In Catholic theology which dates back to the teaching of St. Augustine, Original sin is viewed as being a physical condition that is transferred from generation to generation through the seed of a man. Upon this view, they have built their theological stances on the Virgin birth rendering Jesus free of Original Sin and of christening babies.

On the other hand, Protestant theology views Original Sin as man's propensity to choose against God. All mankind will develop a strong will and will choose to go their way at some age of reason and understanding. This view negates the Catholic assertion that Jesus was somehow free of the propensity of Original Sin because this contradicts the assertion of Hebrews 2:16-18:

*For surely it is not angels he helps, but Abraham's descendants. For this reason he had to be made **like** his brothers **in every way**, in order that he might become a merciful and faithful high priest in service to God, and that he might make atonement for the sins of the people. Because **he himself suffered when he was tempted**, he is able to help those who are being tempted. (Emphasis is mine)*

According to the Protestant theological viewpoint, babies and those who are severely mentally challenged are saved by the fact that they have not formed a conscious thought to reject God. In other words, mankind is born innocent and then, like Adam, sins deliberately against God by choosing the way that they know is against the rules which are imprinted in their very spirit. The Apostle Paul stated this as:

*All who sin **apart** from the law will also perish apart from the law, and all who sin under the law will be judged by the law. For it is not those who hear the law who are righteous in God's sight, but it is those who obey the law who will be declared righteous. (Indeed, when Gentiles, who do not have the law, do by nature things required by the law, they are a law for themselves, **even though they do not have the law**, since they show that **the requirements of the law are written on their hearts**, their consciences also bearing witness, and their thoughts now accusing, now even defending them.) This will take place on the day when God will judge men's secrets through Jesus Christ, as my gospel declares. (Romans 2:12-16, bold emphasis is mine)*

The Protestant position concerning Original Sin also dovetails with the assertion that "*all **have** sinned and fall short of the glory of God*" which is stated in Romans 3:23. This denotes an active state, a decision at some point in one's personal history when sin enters into one's life in the same manner that it did at the Fall.

Sin is the great divider. It serves to separate man from God, to separate man from Heaven, and to separate man from man. Chuck Colson wrote, "When asked the same question I asked the inmates [of the California Rehabilitation Center], 'What's wrong with the world?' G. K. Chesterton, a delightful British writer, answered, 'I am.' The problem is sin! My sin. The evils we do — theft, murder, adultery, greed, arrogance, folly — all of these evils come from inside. The problem of sin is not what goes into us but what comes out of us."[6]

Consider God's words through the prophet Isaiah spoken to the sin-stained and rebellious nation of Judah: *"But your iniquities have separated you from your God; you sins have hidden his face from you, so that he will not hear."* (Isaiah 59:2) Isaiah then continued to outline a litany of Judah's sins in the following verses. Paul the Apostle wrote to the Romans and said, "*...just as sin entered the world through one man, and death through sin, and in this way death came to all people, because all sinned...*" (5:12) and reminded them that "*...the wages of sin is death...*" (6:23a). Sin is totally and completely destructive!

So, if the problem is that of Sin, and if man has a naturally fallen sin-nature, what can be done to save the human race from such warranted destruction? The news seems bleak. As Paul stated, *"What a wretched man I am! Who will rescue me from this body that is subject to death?"* (Romans 7:24)

The answer to this perplexing question lies in the tremendous an immeasurable love of the very same all-powerful God against Whom we sin. The answer is wildly exciting, unprecedented, and unexpected. It is, in fact, the Good News of the Gospel. God's response in answer to Paul's question above is found in Romans 7:25: *"Thanks be to God, who delivers me through Jesus Christ our Lord!"* The only answer to the problem of Sin is not in a process, or a procedure, or in some rite of passage, but the Answer is a Person. The Answer is none other than Jesus, the Second Person of the Trinity, the Son of God. Scripture tells us that *"[S]alvation is found in no one else, for there is no other name under heaven given to mankind by which we must be saved."* (Acts 4:12)

The next chapter will introduce us to Him...

---

[1] Moody, Dale The Word of Truth, Grand Rapids, Wm B. Eerdmans, 1981. p 272
[2] Moody, Dale The Word of Truth, p 272
[3] Tozer, A. W. The Pursuit of God. Harrisburg, Christian Publications, Inc., 1948, Kindle e-book, location 181 of 1179.
[4] Aulén, Gustaf The Faith of the Christian Church, Philadelphia, Fortress Press, 1960. p 232
[5] Moody, Dale The Word of Truth, p 273
[6] Colson, Charles The Faith, Grand Rapids, Zondervan, 2008. p 76

13 THE PERSON OF JESUS

A sob pierces the air and He bows His head. In this one moment of time we capture a poignant visible snapshot of the heart of God. A large, hot tear of grief courses down His cheek. It reflects His long-lived sadness at the human condition that was introduced by the Fall. Jesus' heart is tugged by the pathos of the moment, the outpouring of love by Lazarus' sisters and friends, their sense of loss underscored by the gulf of death. He knows that the human problems of pain, separation, hatred, and death all originate from man's rejection of God's lordship. The rebellion dates back to the Garden of Eden.

Jesus wept.[1] The warm tears flowed in sequence, streaking the face of the One Who had chosen to be the perfect sacrifice for all mankind's sin, from even before the foundation of the world. He Himself had created us for eternal fellowship with Him. Yet, mankind had become nothing more than fuel for the fires of Hell. He Who is "God with us"[2] weeps with us over our human condition, and then moves heaven and earth to save us all.

What makes Jesus so wonderful is that He makes the invisible and intangible God visible to our limited vision. Before the dawning of the days of the New Testament, God's Person and His character was conceptual, but when the Word, Who is God, "became flesh and made his dwelling among us," (John 1:1;14) we could finally know God in a new and intimate way. We could now literally see, hear, and touch Him. (1 John 1:1-3) It is through Jesus that we can finally have the depth of God's love register, not only in our mind's eye, but through our God-created senses. From Jesus, we can hear the voice of the Great "I Am" proclaim God's judgment and also declare God's love and grace. Jesus is the God-Man, flesh and blood, who "too shared in [our] humanity so that by his death he might break the power of him who holds the power of death--that is the devil--and free [us] who all [our] lives were held in slavery by [our] fear of death." (Hebrews 2:14,15)

His tears and anguished cries of pain cannot be hidden from our eyes (Hebrews 5:7-10). Jesus is completely authentic in every way. His heart is

God's heart. His desires are God's desires. His anguish is God's anguish. His love is God's love. He is the Second Person of the eternal Trinity; God made flesh; Immanuel; God with us; the Suffering Servant; the way, the truth, and the life. He is our peephole into Heaven itself for it is through Him that we can glimpse all of eternity. He is the way to Heaven having paved the road of salvation with His body, built the bridge over the gulf that separated man from God with the wood of His Cross, and sealed it all with His precious blood that was spilled for the atonement of mankind's sins (Romans 3:25).

Who exactly *IS* this Jesus? Could He really have been Who He claimed to be? Many in the world throughout history have accepted Him at His word and have been saved. Likewise, many have chosen to deny Him and consider Him more a figment of story-telling, or a poor deluded soul, than believing Him to be the Son of the Living God. How you decide to look at Jesus will have a profound effect on your life, on your worldview, and on your Eternity.

Jesus first appeared in the scope of human history sometime around 4 BC as documented in the birth narratives of Matthew and Luke. "For many, including Joseph, the doctrine of the Virgin Birth is hard to accept. But the God who could speak the universe into being, who could create human life, could certainly choose to make Himself known by the power of the Holy Spirit through a virgin...Only a totally sinless savior could take our sins upon Himself, which mean God, and only God, could be His Father."[3] The Son of God was born into the world as a simple, helpless baby yet this was not His starting point. *"In the beginning was the Word, and the Word was with God, and the Word was God...The Word became flesh and made his dwelling among us,"* said John in his gospel account (John 1:1,14). In this simple sequence of words, he described one of the greatest miracles God has wrought since the Creation: the Incarnation. God becoming flesh. God giving up the prerogatives of Godhood and taking upon Himself the status of man (see Philippians 2:5-8).

In Luke 1:35, the Angel Gabriel described this miracle as, *"the Holy Spirit will come on you, and the power of the Most High will overshadow you. So the holy one to be born will be called the Son of God."* Strange and bewildering words they were to a young Jewish virgin girl, and equally so to us "scientific" minds today. Through some special miraculous process, the God-Man Jesus was conceived. Shirley Guthrie wrote, "The incarnation of God in the man Jesus does not mean that Jesus is half God and half man. To put it bluntly, 'conceived by the Holy Ghost' does not mean that the Holy Spirit is a substitute for the human male in the conception and birth of Jesus. The church has never held that the Spirit is the 'father' of Jesus….'Conceived by the Holy Ghost' really means not that the Spirit is the father of Jesus, but that according to his human existence Jesus had no father at all. This phrase is not a biological explanation of the two natures. It means there is no biological explanation, that the Word became flesh purely by the will and word of God."[4] What it means is that the Son of God, the Second Person of the Trinity, became clothed with flesh in Mary's womb and was born to walk among us!

Jesus breathed the air of this world for about thirty-three years. Apart from the narratives of His Incarnation and birth, precious little is known about His childhood. We know that there was a purge in the land instigated by the paranoid and egomaniacal King Herod in which he attempted to kill off the "one who has been born king of the Jews" that the Magi had announced (Matthew 2:1-18). Herod, surely under Satan's influence, ordered countless baby boys senselessly killed in order to protect his kingdom but God had protected Jesus by directing Joseph to take his family to Egypt. We also know that after Herod's death soon thereafter, God called them back out of Egypt and they settled in Nazareth, a small town in the hilly regions of northern Israel.

We also know that Joseph and Mary then had some children of their own (see Matthew 12:46, 13:55; Mark 3:31, 6:3; Luke 8:19; Acts 1:14) including James and Jude who ranked among the leadership of the early Church and who both wrote epistles that are included in the New Testament. We also know that Joseph was out of the picture after Jesus' ministry started when He was about 30 years old so it is presumed that he had died (for proof of this, see Jesus' request to His disciple in John 19:26,27 – in Jewish tradition, the oldest son is in charge of taking care of his widowed mother). The only other snapshots of Jesus' childhood that God permits us is found in Luke 2:21-51. Of these, the narrative of the twelve-year-old Jesus at the Temple paints a picture that He was fully engaged and dedicated to serving God the Father. It also shows that the years of scratching out a living and raising a family had dulled Mary's and Joseph's memories of the excitement of God's activities in their lives before Jesus' birth:

"Why were you searching for me?" he asked. "Didn't you know I had to be in my Father's house?" But they did not understand what he was saying to them. (Luke 2:49,50)

This is a reminder that regardless of how close we are to God and His revelations, any of us can let our lives become so *"choked by life's worries, riches and pleasures"* that our spiritual maturity can be eroded (Luke 8:14). We must constantly petition that God will kindle the lamp of our lives so that we may not forsake our first love (Revelation 2:4,5)! In fact, from this passage and the ones quoted above (e.g. Matthew 12:46ff) it appears that even though Mary remembered the acts and recounted them to Luke years later (e.g. Luke 2:19), sometime before His crucifixion and resurrection occurred she had lost sight of the reason her son had been born.

In Nazareth, Jesus *"grew and became strong; he was filled with wisdom, and the grace of God was on him"* (Luke 2:40). He was obedient to His mother and Joseph (v 51) and grew "in favor with God and man." It is assumed by most that He picked up the trade of Joseph, the one chosen by God to help raise Jesus, and who was assumed to be His father by neighbors and family members. Needless to say, the question of the conditions surrounding His birth must have caused Him to be ostracized throughout His formative years. The contempt the Nazareth community showed Him comes through in Matthew 13:53-57a:

When Jesus had finished these parables, he moved on from there. Coming to his hometown, he began teaching the people in their synagogue, and they were amazed. "Where did this man get this wisdom and these miraculous powers?" they asked. "Isn't this the carpenter's son? Isn't his mother's name Mary, and aren't his brothers James, Joseph, Simon and Judas? Aren't all his sisters with us? Where then did this man get all these things?" And they took offense at him.

In spite of all the bitter pills that Jesus had to swallow, His walk was sinless and under God's favor. The book of Hebrews emphasizes that Jesus *"has been tempted in every way, just as we are—yet he did not sin."* (Hebrews 4:15) Regardless of the hatred that might have been thrown His way, He refused to hate. As He grew up and faced the temptations that besiege young men, He refused to fall before them and sin. In facing the pains of this life, He did not sin by crying out in curses or entertaining despair in

His heart. Even though He may have been out of sight of the rest of the world, His life still played out before the Father and the God-inspired word in Scripture testifies that He lived sinlessly.

Jesus next appeared on the scene when He was about 30 years old and started His Earthly ministry. He approached John the Baptist and was baptized, not because He had sinned and needed remission, but according to Him it was to *"fulfill all righteousness"* (Matthew 3:15), to assume the role of complete submission to the Father's will. It was at this moment in time that the Trinity appeared, each Person individually acting at the same time as has previously been discussed. It was the moment in which the road to the Cross began in earnest and the Father announced for all to hear that *"This is my Son, whom I love; with him I am well pleased."* (Matthew 3:17) With this Divine blessing upon His ministry, Jesus then faced the first of at least three major temptations to side-step the Cross. He was driven by the Spirit *"into the wilderness to be tempted by the devil"* (Matthew 4:1) after a fast of forty days and nights. In each of the three attempts that Satan launched against Him, He remained sinless by quoting the Word of God. Satan left him alone until *"an opportune time."* (Luke 4:13)

The temptation to avoid the Cross came up again a few years later from the mouth of Peter, one of His trusted disciples. Just after Peter had made the incredible God-revealed confession of Jesus being the Messiah, the Son of the living God (see, for example, Matthew 16:16), Jesus started to teach His closest friends that *"he must go to Jerusalem and suffer many things at the hands of the elders, the chief priest and the teachers of the law, and that he must be killed and on the third day be raised to life."* (16:21) Peter took Him aside from the other disciples and rebuked the One he had just identified as the Messiah, and told Him that such a thing would never befall Jesus (v 22). This second temptation, maybe even more beguiling than before since it involved kind-sounding and caring words from a friend's lips, was met instantly by Jesus' wrath. He did not let Himself become entrapped and compromise His mission! *"Get behind me, Satan! You are a stumbling block to me; you do not have in mind the concerns of God, but merely human concerns."* (v 23) He then turned that event into a teaching moment and taught that the Cross could not be avoided, neither for Him nor for those who choose to follow Him (vv 24-27).

The third time that Satan raised His head into Jesus' ministry and attempted to make Him choose against the Cross was in the Garden of Gethsemane. The tempter wove his snare of fear around the Son of God and attempted to appeal to the flesh of His human nature. He was in *"anguish"* (Luke 22:44), *"sorrowful and troubled"* (Matthew 26:38), *"overwhelmed with sorrow to the point of death"* (Mark 14:34), and prayed *"earnestly [till] his sweat was like drops of blood falling to the ground."* (Luke 22:44) Satan raised His anxiety level as God the Son contemplated the reality of this foreign subject of Death which faced Him in the next few hours. He prayed ever more intently, time after time after time *("Father, if you are willing, take this cup from me...")*, until He won the battle for His mission by subjecting His will to that of the Father *("Yet not my will, but yours be done.")* As prophesied in Genesis 3:15, the head of the Serpent was definitively crushed by the Son's faithful submission to the Father's will!

The "historic Jesus" is described in the gospel narratives. His is the story of a man born in Bethlehem's stall, Who preached the news that the *"kingdom of God has come near"* (Matthew 4:17), suffered on the Cross at Golgotha, was buried in Joseph of Arimathea's tomb, Who was miraculously raised from the dead, and Who ascended into Heaven ten days before Pentecost. He was the Word who *"became flesh and made his dwelling among us"* (John 1:14), Who taught multitudes, Who healed the sick, Who cast out demonic forces from crippled lives, and Who fed the thousands. The decision each of us has to face is if He really is Who He said He is. After all, He made bold proclamations such as *"I have come down from heaven not to do my will but to do the will of him who sent me"* (John 6:38), *"I and the Father are one"* (John 10:30), *"the Son of Man came to seek and to save the lost"* (Luke 19:10), and *"I want you to know that the Son of Man has authority on earth to forgive sins"* (Matthew 9:6).

Shirley Guthrie stated, "Why is Jesus the Son of God? Because he speaks with the authority of God himself and does mighty works which are God's works. 'Son of God' expresses his oneness with God and his consequent divine majesty and power."[5] It is certain that He spoke with authority. Gospel accounts indicate that *"[T]he people were amazed at his teaching, because he taught them as one who **had** authority, not as the teachers of the law."* (Mark 1:22) Whenever He spoke or acted, it was underscored with the authority of God Himself. John Stott declared, concerning the question whether Jesus was truthful, that the "evidence is at least threefold. It concerns the claims he made, the character he displayed, and his resurrection from the dead. No single argument is conclusive by itself. But these three strands weave together and point clearly to the same conclusion."[6]

Probably one of the more famous quotes concerning the question of Jesus' being God or not is found in C. S. Lewis' <u>Mere Christianity</u> in which he claimed, "A man who was merely a man and said the sort of things Jesus said would not be a great moral teacher. He would either be a lunatic — on the level with the man who says he is a poached egg—or else he would be the Devil of Hell. You must make your choice. Either this man was, and is, the Son of God, or else a madman or something worse. You can shut him up for a fool, you can spit at him and kill him as a demon or you can fall at his feet and call him Lord and God, but let us not come with any patronising nonsense about his being a great human teacher. He has not left that open to us. He did not intend to."[7] In fact, his position was that, "it seems to me obvious that He was neither a lunatic nor a fiend: and consequently, however strange or terrifying or unlikely it may seem, I have to accept the view that He was and is God."[8] Ultimately this is the decision that we must all make under conviction and in faith.

During all of His days of ministry Jesus was heading towards the Cross. Remember, He had chosen to come to pay the price for sin, *"before the creation of the world."* (1 Peter 1:20) He is described in Luke 9:51, *"as the time approached for him to be taken up to heaven, Jesus resolutely set out for Jerusalem."* This reflects the prophesy of Isaiah which stated, *"Because the Sovereign Lord helps me, I will not be disgraced. Therefore have I set my face like flint, and I know I will not be put to shame."* (Isaiah 50:7) He was resolute and taught from day one that the Son of Man had come to suffer and die. This was His mission (see Matthew 16:21; 17:12; Mark 9:12; Luke 9:22; 17:25; 22:15,26), the reason for His historical human existence.

As much as we know Jesus through the historic record of the Gospel, we also need to grasp His pre-existence. Remember from our discussion about God and the Trinity that Jesus is the Second Person of the Trinity and thus He has all of the rights, privileges, and characteristics of the Godhead. Many heretical cults attempt to make Jesus a mere creation of God's, someone who appeared before or at the Incarnation. Others try to reduce Him to a mere figment of mythology or into someone led by delusion and insanity. Yet, there is something totally different about Jesus and His claims to divinity. John Stott took up the subject and stated: "There have of course been many pretenders to greatness and to divinity. Psychiatric hospitals are full of deluded people who claim to be Julius Caesar, the prime minister, the president of the United States or Jesus Christ. But no-one believes them. No-one is deceived except themselves. They have no disciples, except perhaps their fellow patients. They fail to convince other people for the simple reason that they don't actually seem to be what they claim to be. Their claims are not supported by their character. Now the Christian's conviction about Christ is greatly strengthened by the fact that he really does appear to be who he said he was. There is no inconsistency between his words and his deeds. There is no doubt that he would need to be a very remarkable character in order to authenticate his extravagant claims. But Christians believe exactly that. His character doesn't prove his claims to be true, but it does strongly confirm them. His claims were exclusive. His character was unique."[9]

His claims to be both pre-existent and One with the Father either would fall flat at the Crucifixion or would be confirmed by the Resurrection. Many poor deluded or idealistic individuals go to their graves, sometimes in painful ways as Jesus did on the Cross. However, not one of them was raised from the dead victoriously. The proof of all of Jesus' claims to Who He really is rests upon the empty tomb with the empty and collapsed grave clothes. "This is the great choice every human being has to make. Is the resurrection account true or only a myth?"[10]

The Atonement will be discussed in a separate chapter but we must discuss briefly what happened at the Cross before we step over and examine the Resurrection. Jesus became a *substitutionary* sacrifice for all mankind's sin as the Apostle Paul pointed out in 2 Corinthians 5:21. *"God made him who had no sin to be sin for us, so that in him we might become the righteousness of God."* The sinless Son of God who was unworthy of death (the penalty of sin) was put to death on the Cross. Through this out-of-balance transaction the wrongs were righted and "His blood can make the foulest clean."[11]

Jesus suffered intensely on the Cross, both physically in His full humanity and spiritually in His full divinity. As He assumed all of mankind's sin He was increasingly separated from the Father Who could not be in the presence of Sin. Habakkuk 1:12 states this truth about God, *"Your eyes* are too pure to look on evil; you cannot tolerate wrongdoing." The Father turned His back on the sin that the Son had assumed on Himself thus the Godhead, Who has never been separate for all of eternity, experienced a separation! The beloved Son cried out in agony from the torture of the Crucifixion, *"My God, my God, why have your forsaken me?"* (Matthew 27:46)

Max Lucado wrote concerning the poignancy of the moment. "'Here is the cup, my Son. Drink it alone.' God must have wept as he performed his task. Every lie, every lure, every act done in shadows was in that cup. Slowly, hideously they were absorbed into the body of the Son. The final act of incarnation. The Spotless Lamb was blemished. Flames began to lick his feet...The undiluted wrath of a sin-hating Father falls upon his sin-filled Son. The fire envelops him. The Son looks for his Father, but the Father cannot be seen. 'My God, my God...why?'"[12] During the separation from His Father and through the transaction in which He assumed upon Himself all mankind's sin, Jesus paid the price of eternity in Hell for all men.

How could this separation have happened? It is important to realize that "[T]he unity of the Father and the Son is not identity. Jesus said indeed that 'the Father and I are one' ([John] 10:30), but this is explained in the words: 'that the Father is in me and I am in the Father' (10:38). The Father and Son are one, but not the same."[13] They are separate Persons in the Trinity and in the plan of Salvation, they had to separate. Not only did Jesus have to take sin upon Himself, but He also had to do the unthinkable: God had to taste death! As His lifeblood ebbed away, Jesus entrusted Himself to His Father. With His last rasping, dying breath, Jesus quoted Psalm 31:5 as He said in a loud voice, *"Father, into your hands I commit my spirit."* (Luke 23:46)

Dead. Jesus' body hung lifeless on the Cross until it was brutalized by a Roman spear and then brought down for burial. Joseph of Arimethea petitioned Pontius Pilate for the right to bury Jesus. After receiving permission, he and his fellow Sanhedrin member, Nicodemus, prepared the body with spices and wrapped it in linen. A separate cloth was wrapped around Jesus' head. Jesus' rapidly cooling body was then laid in Joseph's new tomb, the stone was set, seals were affixed to it, and a guard was posted (see, for example, Matthew 27:62-66). Silence kept vigil in Jesus' tomb that Friday evening.

That next Sunday morning, the world changed. In the early hours of that day, something that had never happened before occurred. Jesus' grave clothes imploded upon themselves as the body that was there disappeared! Jesus never had described His death as being final. His teaching about the coming events always stressed that *"he must be killed and after three days rise again."* (Mark 8:31) His mission was not going to end on the sour discordant note of death but instead with the triumphant trumpet blast of victory! The Resurrection was always the true destination of His walk on Earth's surface. *"He was chosen before the creation of the world, but was revealed in these last times for your sake. Through him you believe in God, who raised him from the dead and glorified him, and so your faith and hope are in God."* (1 Peter 1:20,21)

The Resurrection kindles our faith because that one event visibly places the stamp of God's approval on all that Jesus did. Peter preached on the Day of Pentecost that *"God raised him from the dead, freeing him from the agony of death, because it was impossible for death to keep its hold on him."* (Acts 2:24) We don't preach a dead ideologue. We serve a living Messiah!

In the chapter addressing the Word of God, we concentrated on the passage from 1 Corinthians 15:12-18 in which the Apostle Paul emphasized the importance of the Resurrection event. The point is well taken that what we do with the raising of Christ from the dead either establishes us a Christians or reduces us to non-believers. It is impossible, maybe even slightly insane, to claim to believe in the Gospel but to negate the power of the Resurrection! If Jesus was not raised from the dead then all the gospel accounts only form a fine and wonderful story. The disciples and early Christians placed their lives on the line for what they knew to be true. Within literal days of Pentecost, James the brother of John and Stephen were both martyred while remaining true to their witness. The Christians who formed the early Church were persecuted, beaten, stoned, imprisoned, their lives turned upside down, all because they were certain of the authenticity of Jesus' message confirmed by the Resurrection. Throughout the ages since then and until today, the eyewitness accounts still move men and women to put everything on the line in order to follow the risen Lord Jesus Christ!

There are many who ascribe to Jesus the role of a prophet or that of a teacher. As C. S. Lewis stated in the earlier-quoted passage, this is not what He introduced Himself to be. His birth announcement, proclaimed to a band of shivering shepherds by the angelic host, stated that *"[T]oday in the town of David a Savior has been born to you; he is the Messiah, the Lord."* (Luke 2:11) Jesus plainly said concerning His ministry that *"the Son of Man came to seek and to save the lost."* (19:10) His opponents, ridiculing Him on Golgotha's cross even recognized this aspect of His ministry. They said, *"He saved others but he can't save himself!"* (Matthew 27:42a) In addressing Nicodemus, the member of the Sanhedrin who visited Him by night, Jesus proclaimed that:

For God so loved the world that he gave his one and only Son, that whoever believes in him shall not perish but have eternal life. For God did not send his Son into the world to condemn the world, but to save the world through him. Whoever believes in him is not condemned, but whoever does not believe stands condemned already because they have not believed in the name of God's one and only Son. (John 3:16-18)

It is clear that Jesus always has been and always will be the Savior. His mission was always clear, to save all mankind by paying the price of sin on the Cross and by drawing all people to Himself (e.g. John 12:32) for His saving grace. He did not come to become some wise teacher or a religious philosopher or a world leader. He came to save. *"Salvation is found in no one else, for there is no other name under heaven given to mankind by which we must be save."* (Acts 4:12) The Gospel narrative makes no sense without Jesus' *soteriological*[14] role. He came to call all who had need of salvation. He said to the Pharisees who were criticizing His being surrounded by what they called "sinners and tax collectors" that *"It is not the healthy who need a doctor, but the sick. I have not come to call the righteous, but sinners."* (Mark 2:17) All mankind is sick. All of us are filled with the poison of sin. Thus, Jesus came to call all of us to repentance and to salvation!

God desires fellowship with us. He created man specifically to engage in meaningful fellowship. Nothing is more evident than this aspect of Jesus' ministry. Rarely, very rarely, in the gospel account can you see Jesus not in fellowship with others. In Revelation 3:20, Jesus extends the invitation to fellowship in a very personal way: *"Here I am! I stand at the door and knock. If anyone hears my voice and opens the door, I will come in and eat with him, and he with me."* It is through Jesus as Savior that our relationship with God can be restored, the sin question dealt with, and fellowship with God can finally be established as it was intended to be.

No discussion about Jesus would be complete without touching upon His future role in world history. After the Ascension, the Book of Hebrews states that *"[A]fter he had provided purification for sins, he sat down at the right hand of the Majesty in heaven."* (Hebrews 1:3b) He is currently back in the heavenly realm alongside His Father. He is waiting for the Father's timetable to come to fruition, for the moment when God the Father will declare the time to bring all Creation to its close. God is bearing with the increase of sin, allowing time for the Gospel to bring people to salvation.

His motivation for this forbearance is outlined in 2 Peter 3:9, *"The Lord is not slow in keeping his promise, as some understand slowness. Instead he is patient with you, not wanting anyone to perish, but everyone to come to repentance."* The very next verse reminds us though that there is a time when His patience will expire: *"But the day of the Lord will come like a thief. The heavens will disappear with a roar; the elements will be destroyed by fire, and the earth and everything done in it will be laid bare."* (2 Peter 3:10) That moment in history is known only to the Father. Jesus taught plainly that *"about that day or hour no one knows, not even the angels in heaven, nor the Son, but only the Father."* (Matthew 24:36) Thus Jesus waits patiently, His will submitted to the timetable of the Father, until the precise time that is prescribed for the reconciliation of the books and the destruction of evil.

On that day, a day like no other (Jeremiah 30:7), Jesus will come back, not as the Suffering Servant as He did before, but as the Conquering King. He will redeem His Church (John 14:3) and will lead the hosts of Heaven to victory against Satan and his forces (Revelation 19:11-21). We will touch on the subject of the End Times (the *eschaton*[15]) and Jesus' role in bringing about the close of history when we discuss the Eternal Realm. Jesus will redeem those in the "book of life," those who have accepted Him as Lord and Savior and will save them from an eternity in Hell. It will be at this time that His job of Savior will be complete and He will reconcile everything and lay it at His Father's feet (1 Corinthians 15:26-28).

[1] John 11:35
[2] Immanuel means "God with us."
[3] Colson, Charles <u>The Faith</u>. Zondervan, Grand Rapids, 2008. p 84
[4] Guthrie, Shirley C. <u>Christian Doctrine</u>. Atlanta, John Knox Press, 1968. pp. 229,230
[5] Guthrie, Shirley C. <u>Christian Doctrine</u>, p. 237
[6] Stott, John <u>Basic Christianity</u>.Downers Grove: Intervarsity Press, 2008, Kindle e-book, location 346 of 2515
[7] Lewis, C. S. <u>Mere Christianity</u>, New York, Harper-Collins, 2001, p 68
[8] Lewis, C. S. <u>Mere Christianity</u>, p 67
[9] Stott, John <u>Basic Christianity</u>, location 563 of 2515
[10] Colson, Charles <u>The Faith</u>, p 92
[11] Wesley, Charles "O for a Thousand Tongues to Sing." First published in 1740 as part of a poem entitled "For the anniversary day of one's conversion."
[12] Lucado, Max <u>Six Hours One Friday</u>. Sisters, Multnomah Publishers, Inc., 1989. p 101
[13] Moody, Dale <u>The Word of Truth</u>. Grand Rapids, Wm B. Eerdmans, 1981. p. 406
[14] Soteriological is a theological term that refers to salvation. It is derived from the Greek word *soteros*, which mean savior.
[15] Eschaton is derived the Greek word for "end" and is the theological term for the End Times

14 The Doctrine of the Atonement

Where we left off on our discussion of the Doctrine of Man, we had an intense sense of doom. Man has been created an eternal being and yet, because of the reality of Sin, his eternity is bleak. He has no direct access to Holy God, no direct access to the Tree of Life, and he has been condemned to death because of his rejection of God. Scripture states:

"...for all have sinned and fall short of the glory of God..." (Romans 3:23)

"For the wages of sin is death..." (Romans 6:23a)

Additionally, because man is forced to toil by the sweat of his brow, to be concerned for every moment of his life, and to fight for existence itself, his vision of his eternity is clouded or obscured. Satan's biggest lie that he successfully whispers in every ear is that "this lifetime is all there is." Believing this lie leads to man's being lost and not even realizing that his existence is longer than the puny years of this lifetime! The big Satanic lie has been swallowed by each generation — hook, line, and sinker.

If this news appears to be bleak, it is. Let us never pull any punches when it comes to the state of unrepentant sin. It leads to eternal death. However, there is wonderful news to all mankind in Ezekiel 18:21-23,30-32 and 33:11:

"But if a wicked man turns away from all the sins he has committed and keeps all my decrees and does what is just and right, he will surely live; he will not die. None of the offenses he has committed will be remembered against him. Because of the righteous things he has done, he will live. Do I take any pleasure in the death of the wicked?" declares the Sovereign LORD. "Rather, am I not pleased when they turn from their ways and live?" (Ezekiel 18:21-23)

God categorically has gone on record and stated that He does not take pleasure in the death of the wicked! This is the foundation of any study concerning atonement and salvation. God is not a cackling maniac who rubs his hands in glee when people die in sin for Him to dispatch them to hell. Sadly, I believe that this is an image that some people have of our loving Father. He takes no pleasure *whatsoever* in the death of the wicked. In fact, He so detests that the wicked die unrepentant that he stated it, not once, not twice, but three times within a few verses.

From the moment that the first sin was committed in the Garden of Eden and until the end of this age, God demonstrates a tremendous characteristic called "grace." It is grace that makes atonement possible and it is grace that led God to prepare the plan of salvation. The moment that Adam and Eve committed sin He could have immediately wiped them off of the face of the Earth and started over. Yet, He had designed mankind to have freedom of choice and decided to extend that freedom to choose to love Him more than anything else for the course of their lives. In the Garden we see several instances of grace:

1. Adam and Eve were concerned with their nakedness and attempted to cover themselves with fig leaves sewn together. Man saw a problem within him and attempted to remedy it by himself. God knew that man's solution was not durable and He also understood that there was a better one available. He stepped outside of man's reach and provided a more perfect solution for man's problem, one that required the shedding of innocent blood.
2. In the curses pronounced upon the serpent, God outlined His ultimate plan of salvation. It would involve the offspring of the woman who ultimately would crush the head of the serpent. This section of the study is partly a discussion of the achievement of this One special Person.
3. Removing the possibility of man getting to the Tree of Life by himself while in being in an unrepentant state demonstrates God's love towards man. Imagine the anguish of evil existing eternally. God's grace ensures that this life bound in the space-time continuum is limited and thus evil and sin also are finite.

A very crucial point that we must note is that "*the life of a creature is in the blood, and I have given it to you to make atonement for yourselves on the altar; it is the blood that makes atonement for one's life.*" (Leviticus

17:11) When one sins the first time (see the discussion about Original Sin earlier), one essentially deserves eternal death pursuant to God's statement to Adam in Genesis 2:16,17. One life can only be ransomed by another life, one untainted by sin. Hence the lifeblood of a *savior* is needed for the atonement of every human being who desires eternal life. It is **vital** that we grasp this basic concept.

This principle is very important and has a special name in theology: the Doctrine of Substitution. Every substitution requires two specific criteria to be met in order to be effective:

1. The substituting individual must have **credentials**. He or she must meet or exceed the credentials of the substituted individual. Who here would appreciate being wheeled into surgery and being told by the surgeon, "Sorry, I can't operate on your clogged arteries. I hurt my arm playing squash yesterday. But, don't worry...meet Joe. Joe is our best janitor. I have seen him scrub the messiest floors and make them sparkle like new. I am going to let Joe substitute for me in this operation. I am confident that he can make those arteries as good as new!" The guy may be good at what he does, but he has no credentials for this type of procedure.
2. The substitution must be **legal**, conforming to the rules to prevent repercussions. One cannot bring in a major league baseball player to substitute for a pee-wee league kid who broke his arm and somehow expect the game to remain unchallenged. In the scenario above, the hospital's malpractice insurance certainly would not accept any claim for damages done by Joe. Regardless of Joe's well-meaning and good intentions, he is not a legal substitute for an appropriately credentialed surgeon.

Having broached the concepts of the requirement of blood and described the principle of substitution, let us now turn our attention to another concept, that of sacrifice. To many people, the Old Testament seems brutal and harsh. Much of this perception stems from its emphasis on animal sacrifices. Many wonder if Christ died to save all mankind, then why did all those innocent sheep, goats, and bulls have to die! Additionally, some are concerned if we are not supposed to continue sacrificing even today because God had ordained those sacrifices.

The books of Genesis through Deuteronomy contain references to sacrifices while Exodus through Deuteronomy specifically outline God's Law concerning sacrifice at the Tabernacle. We will not delve in deeply to the sacrifices themselves but let us pick up some critical points concerning sin sacrifices. Read Leviticus 4:1-35. Note especially that the sinner must lay his hand upon the head of the animal (v 4,15,24,29,32) before it is slaughtered before the Lord. Through this simple act, the sinner asserted oneness with the sacrifice for it to become a substitute. Note also the importance of the blood of the sacrifice in the ritual. It was to be sprinkled before the Most Holy Place (v 6,17), spread upon the horns of various altars (v 7,18,25,30,34), and poured out at the base of the altar of burnt offering (v 7,18,25,30,34).

Such is the nature of almost all burned sacrifices with one interesting exception. Turn to Leviticus 16:1-34. This is a special offering, the offering for the Day of Atonement. On this one day, the High Priest was to offer a bull for his sins, take some of its blood behind the curtain into the Most Holy Place and sprinkle it before the Atonement cover of the Ark of the Covenant, before God's own presence. He was then to offer the goat chosen by lot for the sins of the nation and reenter the Most Holy Place to sprinkle its blood before God. The goat represents the nation but is not associated to any specific person through the laying on of hands.

Now, here is the key question concerning the Old Testament sacrificial system that we need to answer and then properly understand that answer. Did the sacrifices of the actual animals in the Old Testament atone for the lives of the people that they were associated with? If they did not, then what purpose did the sacrifices serve?

As we strive to answer this crucial question, let us delve into God's Word and gather the information that we need. Let us start with Hebrews 9:1-10.

Now the first covenant had regulations for worship and also an earthly sanctuary. A tabernacle was set up. In its first room were the lampstand, the table and the consecrated bread; this was called the Holy Place.

Behind the second curtain was a room called the Most Holy Place, which had the golden altar of incense and the gold-covered ark of the covenant. This ark contained the gold jar of manna, Aaron's staff that had budded, and the stone tablets of the covenant. Above the ark were the cherubim of the Glory, overshadowing the atonement cover. But we cannot discuss these things in detail now.

When everything had been arranged like this, the priests entered regularly into the outer room to carry on their ministry. But only the high priest entered the inner room, and that only once a year, and never without blood, which he offered for himself and for the sins the people had committed in ignorance. The Holy Spirit was showing by this that the way into the Most Holy Place had not yet been disclosed as long as the first tabernacle was still standing. This is an illustration for the present time, indicating that the gifts and sacrifices being offered were not able to clear the conscience of the worshiper. They are only a matter of food and drink and various ceremonial washings—external regulations applying until the time of the new order.

Let the words sink in. The time described, that of the Tabernacle and Temple, was the time of the sacrifices. Notice carefully the statement at the end of verse 10: "[E]xternal regulations applying until the time of the new order." Now read Hebrews 10:1-4. Did you happen to catch these key words in verse 4? "[I]t is impossible for the blood of bulls and goats to take away sins."

So, what have we learned so far? We have learned that the sacrifices in the earthly sanctuary (Tabernacle and Temple) cannot take away sins but yet they were prescribed by God. It was He who ordained the Tabernacle. It was He who created the priesthood. It was He who mandated the sacrifices in Leviticus. Yet, if the blood of an animal is not able to take away the sins of a man, what gives? God is not insane and is not senile. He did indeed ordain such things and He did so as "*an illustration for the present time*" (Hebrews 9:9). Clearly, we don't have all of the evidence that we need in our hands yet!

Now let's continue our study by reading Hebrews 9:11-28, some of which is here:

When Christ came as high priest of the good things that are already here, he went through the greater and more perfect tabernacle that is not man-made, that is to say, not a part of this creation. He did not enter by means of the blood of goats and calves; but he entered the Most Holy Place once for all by his own blood, having obtained eternal redemption. The blood of goats and bulls and the ashes of a heifer sprinkled on those who are ceremonially unclean sanctify them so that they are outwardly clean. How much more, then, will the blood of Christ, who through the eternal Spirit offered himself unblemished to God, cleanse our consciences from acts that lead to death, so that we may serve the living God!

For this reason Christ is the mediator of a new covenant, that those who are called may receive the promised eternal inheritance—now that he has died as a ransom to set them free from the sins committed under the first covenant. (Hebrews 9:11-15)

Ah! An illustration is an example or a diagram. In this case, the earthly Tabernacle was a representation of a more perfect Tabernacle, the throne room of God Himself. The act of the priest entering the Most Holy Place was an example of the Perfect Priest Himself, Who would enter, not the Most Holy Place in the earthly sanctuary, but the actual throne room of God. He would not bring in the blood of animals but instead the only blood that can truly substitute for the life of a man, His own. His life would *substitute* for the life of a sinner, in fact, for the lives of many sinners. Not only did He enter the Father's presence in heaven, but He remains there permanently (v 24). His blood atones permanently for all lives (v 28). Even more interesting is the statement in verse 15 where we get a hint that the power of Jesus' blood is retroactive.

To bring this to a finely-honed point, let us read Romans 3:21-26:

But now a righteousness from God, apart from law, has been made known, to which the Law and the Prophets testify. This righteousness from God comes through faith in Jesus Christ to all who believe. There is no difference, for all have sinned and fall short of the glory of God, and are justified freely by his grace through the redemption that came by Christ Jesus. God presented him as a sacrifice of atonement, through faith in his blood. He did this to demonstrate his justice, because in his forbearance he had left the sins committed beforehand unpunished—he did it to demonstrate his justice at the present time, so as to be just and the one who justifies those who have faith in Jesus.

Notice that God left the previously committed sins unpunished (v.25) until the time of Christ. This was in preparation for Jesus' death of substitution for our sins. *"God made him who had no sin to be sin for us, so that in him we might become the righteousness of God."* (2 Corinthians 5:21)

Even before the foundation of the Earth, Jesus stepped up to the plate to accomplish our salvation. Man was not created to fail but God knew that the tremendous lure of choice presented the potential of man choosing against Him and being plunged into a state of sin. Look at 2 Timothy 1:8-10, 1 Peter 1:18-21, and Ephesians 1:4-10. Even before the creation of the world, Jesus (the Second Person of the Trinity) was ready to step into history to pay the price of atonement.

This glimpse into the heavenly realm before the Creation helps us understand why God phrased the curse upon the serpent in the Garden of Eden. He knew that at just the right time, Jesus would set aside the prerogatives of deity and would enter into history as a man, the Lamb of God Who takes away the sin of the world. Unlike all other mankind, His life would be sinless and yet He would unfairly suffer death. His unfair death would carry the power to overcome the chains of sin imprisoning all of mankind (see Romans 3:21-26; 1 John 1:7; Hebrews 9:24-28). Jesus is the ultimate sin offering as stated in Romans 8:3,4:

For what the law was powerless to do in that it was weakened by the sinful nature, God did by sending his own Son in the likeness of sinful man to be a sin offering. And so he condemned sin in sinful man, in order that the righteous requirements of the law might be fully met in us, who do not live according to the sinful nature but according to the Spirit.

Jesus' resurrection from the dead and His subsequent ascension into heaven permits sinful mankind to have an advocate who resides permanently before the Father where He defends us and covers our failures and stumbles (Romans 8:34; Hebrews 7:23-25).

There is one way, and one way only, to salvation. While others may harp on their being multiple paths to God, such represents a utopian human perspective. There are absolutes in life and this is one regardless of our desire to accept it or not. Mankind always attempts to compromise and to wheel and deal but this approach is not conducive to salvation. God's conditions are plainly stated in John 14:5-7:

The disciple Thomas said to him, "Lord, we don't know where you are going, so how can we know the way?" Jesus answered, "I am the way and the truth and the life. No one comes to the Father except through me. If you really knew me, you would know my Father as well. From now on, you do know him and have seen him."

Also read Ephesians 2:11-18 and 1 Peter 2:9,10. Jesus is the one way for both Jew and for Gentile alike. Jesus is the Savior of the entire world! In fact, the truth that Peter spoke to the Sanhedrin is the kernel of the discussion of salvation: *"Salvation is found in no one else, for there is no other name under heaven given to men by which we must be saved."* (Acts 4:12)

If Jesus represents the sacrifice for our atonement, then how do we lay our hands on salvation? It is important that we understand that salvation exists at the crossroads of choice, commitment, and divine grace. God has taken care of the problem between man and Him, that is, the problem of sin. He made the move to remove the problem but He depends upon us to accept it. He has provided Jesus as our substitute. Read Joel 2:32; Acts 2:21; and Romans 10:13. God requires us to call upon Him and to accept Jesus by faith. Look at John 6:29, Galatians 2:7, and 1 John 4:10.

Another key point that we need to grasp is that salvation is a personal experience and is not transferable. Each and every person must come to appropriate the blood sacrifice of Jesus and submit to His Lordship. There is not some concept of corporate salvation in a wholesale manner within God's plan. This fact holds true from the largest established Church to the smallest country chapel. Yet, in some cases, the line becomes so blurred until it becomes a concept that one is somehow saved by *belonging* to the Church and there is reduced emphasis on the individual's repentance and submission at Christ's feet. We need to come to the understanding of "whoever will" for salvation. John 3:36 states this as:

Whoever believes in the Son has eternal life, but whoever rejects the Son will not see life, for God's wrath remains on them.

Jesus Himself stated that:

"I am the resurrection and the life. The one who believes in me will live, even though they die; and whoever lives by believing in me will never die. Do you believe this?" (John 11:25b,26)

On Pentecost Day, the Apostle Peter answered the question of the convicted crowd concerning how they should be saved by saying:

*"Repent and be baptized, **every one of you**, in the name of Jesus Christ for the forgiveness of your sins. And you will receive the gift of the Holy Spirit. The promise is for you and your children and for all who are far off—for all whom the Lord our God will call." (Acts 2:38b,39, bold emphasis is mine)*

As someone has said, and wisely so, "God has no grandchildren." The Word states "*I will be a Father to you, and you will be my sons and daughters, says the Lord Almighty*" in 2 Corinthians 6:18. This is the level of our relationship with Him. To drive the point home, Hebrews 2:10,11 says:

In bringing many sons and daughters to glory, it was fitting that God, for whom and through whom everything exists, should make the pioneer of their salvation perfect through what he suffered. Both the one who makes people holy and those who are made holy are of the same family. So Jesus is not ashamed to call them brothers and sisters.

Thus, we must strive to emphasize the need for salvation at the personal level. Those of us who are in strongly liturgical churches must ensure first that we have made this crucial step ourselves and then we must help those around us, our family and our friends, to make the step of faith also.

If you declare with your mouth, "Jesus is Lord," and believe in your heart that God raised him from the dead, you will be saved. For it is with your heart that you believe and are justified, and it is with your mouth that you profess your faith and are saved. As Scripture says, "Anyone who believes in him will never be put to shame." For there is no difference between Jew and Gentile—the same Lord is Lord of all and richly blesses all who call on him, for, "Everyone who calls on the name of the Lord will be saved." (Romans 10:9-13)

In closing, read this wonderful summary of salvation by Max Lucado. "What is it then, that God wants us to do? What is the work he seeks?

Just believe. Believe in the One he sent.... Someone is reading this and shaking his or her head and asking, 'Are you saying it is possible to go to heaven with no good work?' The answer is no. Good works are a requirement. Someone else is reading and asking, 'Are you saying it is possible to go to heaven without good character?' My answer again is no. Good character is also a requirement. In order to enter heaven one must have good works and good character. But alas, there is the problem. You have neither.... Accept the goodness of Jesus Christ. Abandon your own works and accept his. Abandon your own decency and accept his. Stand before God in his name, not yours." [1]

Salvation is God's supreme gift presented through His love (Romans 5:8). He graciously provided the sacrifice for our sins just as He provided a substitute sacrifice for Isaac[2] in Genesis 22:1-19. From the moment of the first sin in the Garden in the mists of time and until the day He brings history to a close, He will indeed be the God of all Salvation, Yahweh Yireh which means "the Lord Will Provide."

---

[1] Lucado, Max <u>A Gentle Thunder</u>. Nashville, W. Publishing Group. pp. 136-137

[2] If you are interested, you might want to read a theological musing on my general blog called "The Depth of Abraham's Faith." This article can be found at *http://claforet.wordpress.com/2011/04/03/the-depth-of-abrahams-faith/*

15 THE HOLY SPIRIT

From the very opening chapter of the Bible, the Holy Spirit's presence is manifested. "In the beginning God created the heavens and the earth. Now the earth was formless and empty, darkness was over the surface of the deep, and the Spirit of God was hovering over the waters." (Genesis 1:1,2) The Holy Spirit, known also as the Paraclete, the Counselor, the Comforter, the Spirit of God, the Spirit of Jesus, and as merely the Spirit, is a very unique part of the Holy Trinity.

The first thing we must get straight (if we have not already done so) is that the Spirit is a *He,* not an *It.* He is one of the three Persons of the Trinity, not merely some neuter force proceeding from the Godhead. Charles Stanley described his experience of discovering this truth while he was studying at the seminary:

I was sitting at a table with several buddies, and during our conversation, I said something about the Holy Spirit and called Him an "it." I didn't think anything about it. Having been raised in a Pentecostal Holiness church, I had always heard the Holy Spirit, or Holy Ghost, referred to as "it."

When our conversation came to a close, one of the fellows asked me if I would join him in his room. It just so happened that he was a doctoral student, so I felt honored by his invitation....After a few minutes of casual conversation, he reached over to his desk and pulled out this Greek New Testament and handed it to me.

"I noticed that tonight when we were talking about the Holy Spirit, you called Him an 'it.'"

"Yeah," I said. "Why?"

"The Holy Spirit is not an 'it,' he said.

From there he proceeded to take me on a tour of the New Testament. We explored all the key verses where the Holy Spirit is mentioned. To my surprise, I discovered that the New Testament was consistent in its presentation of the Holy Spirit as a "He" rather than an "it."

One verse that particularly caught my attention was John 16:13:

But when he, the Spirit of truth, comes, He will guide you into all the truth.

I knew just enough about the Greek language to know that the term translated "He" could not be translated any other way. John men "He," not "it." Further study revealed that John went out of his way to use the masculine form of the pronoun.[1]

Let's now consider some of the personality traits of the Spirit as revealed in the Bible. First of all, the Spirit has a will of His own. In 1 Corinthians 12:11, the Apostle Paul indicated that *"[A]ll these are the work of one and the same Spirit, and he distributes them to each one, just as he determines."* Jesus also stated that, *"The wind blows wherever it pleases. You hear its sound, but you cannot tell where it comes from or where it is going. So it is with everyone born of the Spirit."* (John 3:8) The Spirit comes and goes according to His will and moves people accordingly.

Second, the Holy Spirit possesses emotion. In Ephesians 4:30, Paul admonishes believers to *"not grieve the Holy Spirit of God, with whom you were sealed for the day of redemption."* Likewise in Isaiah 63:10, the Israelites *"rebelled and grieved His Holy Spirit."* Also consider Hebrews 10:29, *"How much more severely do you think someone deserves to be punished who has trampled the Son of God underfoot, who has treated as an unholy thing the blood of the covenant that sanctified them, and who has insulted the Spirit of grace?"*

Third, the Spirit speaks and communicates. He bears witness (John 15:26) and speaks within the Church. In Revelation 2:7, the Bible states, *"Whoever has ears, let them hear what the Spirit says to the churches."* For other examples of the Spirit speaking directly, see Acts 8:29 and 13:2.

Fourth, the Spirit has a mind and knowledge. The Apostle Paul stated in Romans 8:27 that *"he who searches our hears knows the mind of the Spirit, because the Spirit intercedes for God's people in accordance with the will of God."* The Holy Spirit also *"searches all things, even the deep things of God. For who knows a person's thoughts except their own spirit* within them? In the same way no one knows the thoughts of God except the Spirit of God." (1 Corinthians 2:10b,11) Jesus Himself described the Spirit's knowledge:

"But when he, the Spirit of truth, comes, he will guide you into all the truth. He will not speak on his own; he will speak only what he hears, and he will tell you what is yet to come. He will glorify me because it is from me that he will receive what he will make known to you. All that belongs to the Father is mine. That is why I said the Spirit will receive from me what he will make known to you." (John 16:13-15)

The Holy Spirit carries on important work, mostly in the form of ministry. As a general rule, the Father wills, the Son obeys, and the Spirit moves. As we saw in the Creation narrative, the Holy Spirit hovered over the waters and more than likely was the motivating force for the accomplishments of the Creation. The Father willed, the Son spoke, and the Spirit moved to make it happen.

The Holy Spirit works in ministry by revealing God to us. Earlier we looked at 1 Corinthians 2:10,11 and we must also look at Ephesians 3:2-5:

Surely you have heard about the administration of God's grace that was given to me for you, that is, the mystery made known to me by revelation, as I have already written briefly. In reading this, then, you will be able to understand my insight into the mystery of Christ, which was not made known to people in other generations as it has now been revealed by the Spirit to God's holy apostles and prophets.

In Ephesians 1:17, the Apostle Paul prays *"asking that the God of our Lord Jesus Christ, the glorious Father, may give you the Spirit of wisdom and revelation, so that you may know him better."* As part and parcel of this revelation, He also convicts the sinner and allows them to accept the Truth of the Gospel. Jesus described the work of the Comforter by stating, *"When he comes, he will prove the world to be in the wrong about sin and righteousness and judgment: about sin, because people do not believe in me; about righteousness, because I am going to the Father, where you can see me no longer; and about judgment, because the prince of this world now stands condemned."* (John 16:8-11) Jesus also added that, *"when he, the Spirit of truth comes, he will guide you into all the truth."* (John 16:13a)

The Spirit of God has been poured out on believers and brings the mind of God into our regenerated selves (see Romans 8:1-13). Through this mind we can aspire to discovering God's will and submitting to it (v. 6,7). Paul revealed that *"[T]he person with the Spirit makes judgments about all things, but such a person is not subject to merely human judgments, for 'Who has known the mind of the Lord so as to instruct him?' But we have the mind of Christ."* (1 Corinthians 2:15,16)

Not only this, but the Spirit acts on our behalf in the realm of prayer. *"In the same way, the Spirit helps us in our weakness. We do not know what we ought to pray for, but the Spirit himself intercedes for us through wordless groans. And he who searches our hearts knows the mind of the Spirit, because the Spirit interceded for God's people in accordance with the will of God."* (Romans 8:26,27) This specific role of the Holy Spirit in prayer was also picked up by Jude:

But you, dear friends, by building yourselves up in your most holy faith and praying **in the Holy Spirit**, *keep yourselves in God's love as you wait for the mercy of our Lord Jesus Christ to bring you to eternal life. (Jude 1:20,21)*

The Holy Spirit also is the Christian's Teacher. He specifically will teach *"all things and will remind you of everything I have said to you."* (John 14:26) Not only this, but He will teach us what to say in order to defend the faith when we are called to witness. *"When you are brought before synagogues, rulers and authorities, do not worry about how you will defend yourselves or what you will say, for the Holy Spirit will teach you at that time what you should say."* (Luke 12:11,12)

One of the key tasks of the Paraclete is that of marking or sealing the People of God. Paul, the apostle of grace, reminded the Ephesians that *"you also were included in Christ when you heard the message of truth, the gospel of your salvation. When you believed, you were marked in him with a seal, the promised Holy Spirit, who is a deposit guaranteeing our inheritance until the redemption of those who are God's possession—to the praise of his glory."* (1:13,14) The same concept was seen earlier in Ephesians 4:30 and also in 2 Corinthians 1:21,22: *"Now it is God who makes both us and you stand firm in Christ. He anointed us, set his seal of ownership on us, and put his Spirit in our hearts as a deposit, guaranteeing what is to come."* The Spirit's seal upon us confirms us as God's children (see Romans 8:14-16 and Galatians 4:4-7).

One special case of the Spirit's marking is worth mention here. In the Synoptic gospels (Matthew, Mark, and Luke), there is a parallel passage concerning Jesus' baptism. The Spirit played a very important part in the baptism in marking Jesus as the long-awaited Son of God and Messiah. One of the passages states:

At that time Jesus came from Nazareth in Galilee and was baptized by John in the Jordan. Just as Jesus was coming up out of the water, he saw heaven being torn open and the Spirit descending on him like a dove. And a voice came from heaven: "You are my Son, whom I love; with you I am well pleased." (Mark 1:9-11, parallel in Matt 3:16 and Luke 3:22)

We saw this passage earlier in context of the Doctrine of the Trinity and mentioned the fact that here we can easily see all three Persons of the Trinity acting independently at the same time within the same space. In the gospel according to John, John the Baptist *"gave this testimony: 'I saw the Spirit come down from heaven as a dove and remain on him. And I myself did not know him, but the one who sent me to baptize with water told me, 'The man on whom you see the Spirit come down and remain is the one who will baptize with the Holy Spirit.' I have seen and I testify that this is God's Chosen One.'"* (John 1:32-34)

The Spirit's descent and the Father's voice were witnessed not only by John and Jesus, but by all those standing around. The crowd included the priests and Pharisees before whom John the Baptist witnessed about the coming Messiah (see Matthew 3:7-12). Some of them must have witnessed the events of that day and merely ignored them, thus denying Jesus had the authority of God upon Him. This denial by Israel's spiritual leaders came to a head in Matthew 21:23-27 (parallel in Mark 11:27-33 and Luke 20:1-8) when they challenged Jesus' authority following His cleansing of the Temple.

Jesus entered the temple courts, and, while he was teaching, the chief priests and the elders of the people came to him. "By what authority are you doing these things?" they asked. "And who gave you this authority?"

Jesus replied, "I will also ask you one question. If you answer me, I will tell you by what authority I am doing these things. John's baptism—where did it come from? Was it from heaven, or of human origin?"

They discussed it among themselves and said, "If we say, 'From heaven,' he will ask, 'Then why didn't you believe him?' But if we say, 'Of human origin'—we are afraid of the people, for they all hold that John was a prophet."

So they answered Jesus, "We don't know."

Then he said, "Neither will I tell you by what authority I am doing these things."

In other words, the Jewish leaders had totally ignored the Holy Spirit's special mark of approval on Jesus' ministry. They were spiritually blind to the movement of God's Spirit in their midst, preferring to exercise their political power than to submit to God's prompting!

One of the most tantalizing aspects of the Holy Spirit's ministry is found in Galatians 5:22-25. Through His indwelling us, He is able to bring forth Godly fruit from our lives.

But the fruit of the Spirit is love, joy, peace, patience, kindness, goodness, faithfulness, gentleness and self-control. Against such things there is no law. Those who belong to Christ Jesus have crucified the sinful nature with its passions and desires. Since we live by the Spirit, let us keep in step with the Spirit.

Notice that this fruit is *"of the Spirit"* and not of us. We cannot hope to pop out such fruit under our own power, at least, for any long period of time. This fruit of a Godly character is borne only when we live within His strength and in step with Him. The purpose of the fruit is to bring us closer into conformance with the image of Christ in us and to make us visible to those around us, marking us as children of God.

The Spirit Himself in addition to giving gifts is, in turn, God's Gift to Christians. Jesus, in Luke 11:13 stated, *"If you then, though you are evil, know how to give good gifts to your children, how much more will your Father in heaven give the Holy Spirit to those who ask him!"* He also told

His disciples that He *"will ask the Father, and he will give you another advocate to help you and be with you forever—the Spirit of truth."* (John 14:16,17a) His final words to the assembled disciples, just before His Ascension, were a promise.

"But you will receive power when the Holy Spirit comes on you; and you will be my witnesses in Jerusalem, and in all Judea and Samaria, and to the ends of the earth." (Acts 1:8)

As just mentioned, the Spirit gives gifts to believers. In some cases, He enhances abilities that God had created in each of these people and in others, He places special abilities that cannot be explained in terms of genetic predisposition. The Apostle Paul described these special gifts as:

There are different kinds of gifts, but the same Spirit distributes them. There are different kinds of service, but the same Lord. There are different kinds of working, but in all of them and in everyone it is the same God at work.

Now to each one the manifestation of the Spirit is given for the common good. To one there is given through the Spirit a message of wisdom, to another a message of knowledge by means of the same Spirit, to another faith by the same Spirit, to another gifts of healing by that one Spirit, to another miraculous powers, to another prophecy, to another distinguishing between spirits, to another speaking in different kinds of tongues, and to still another the interpretation of tongues. All these are the work of one and the same Spirit, and he distributes them to each one, just as he determines. (1 Corinthians 12:4-11)

The gifts of prophesy and of tongues are among some of the most hotly disputed topics in Christianity. There is one thing that we must acknowledge. They are both listed in the Bible among the gifts of the Holy Spirit and thus cannot be dismissed. To not believe in these will be violating God's Word. However, various denominations deal with the prophetic and *glossolaeia* (tongues) differently and thus our approaches to these manifestations of the Spirit may make some of us uncomfortable in some settings.

In Acts 21:10,11, there is a clear passage concerning the prophetic word being proclaimed through the Spirit:

After we had been there a number of days, a prophet named Agabus came down from Judea. Coming over to us, he took Paul's belt, tied his own hands and feet with it and said, "The Holy Spirit says, 'In this way the Jewish leaders in Jerusalem will bind the owner of this belt and will hand him over to the Gentiles.'"

This prophetic word was absolutely correct and not news to Paul, who had days before, told the Ephesian elders that *"now, compelled by the Spirit, I am going to Jerusalem, not knowing what will happen to me there. I only know that in every city the Holy Spirit warns me that prison and hardships are facing me."* (Acts 20:22,23) It is clear from these passages that the Holy Spirit does move among certain of God's people to permit them to utter truths concerning the coming future.

There are those who claim that the gift of tongues was merely a practical gift that was needed by the early Church in order to spread the gospel. They point to the Great Commission, to Acts 1:8, and to the immediate response to the Holy Spirit being poured out on the disciples at Pentecost:

Now there were staying in Jerusalem God-fearing Jews from every nation under heaven. When they heard this sound, a crowd came together in bewilderment, because each one heard their own language being spoken. Utterly amazed, they asked: "Aren't all these who are speaking Galileans? Then how is it that each of us hears them in our native language? Parthians, Medes and Elamites; residents of Mesopotamia, Judea and Cappadocia, Pontus and Asia, Phrygia and Pamphylia, Egypt and the parts of Libya near Cyrene; visitors from Rome (both Jews and converts to Judaism); Cretans and Arabs—we hear them declaring the wonders of God in our own tongues!" (Acts 2:5-11)

Most can certainly agree that this is definitely one of the meanings of Spirit-given tongues but there is clearly a different "type" of tongue also implied. Paul referred to the fact of speaking *"in the tongues of men or of angels"* in 1 Corinthians 13:1. He also indicated that tongues (of whatever form) are *"a sign, not for believers but for unbelievers"* (1 Corinthians 14:22a) and urged the Church, *"do not forbid speaking in tongues. But everything should be done in a fitting an orderly way."* (14:39b,40) There are two keys to understand here. First, that tongues are indeed the Spirit's manifestation but must be used properly in public (14:27,28) and, second, they are subordinate to prophesy (14:22-25;39a).

The Holy Spirit is very important within the lives of believers and within the Church itself. His gifts build up the Church (1 Corinthians 14:12) and bind Christians into being one body (1 Corinthians 12:13). His work among us is important. Without His Presence, we could not hope to understand the gospel and be convicted unto salvation in the first place. He seals us and guards us until we enter into Heaven's gates and prays on our behalf. As God, He possesses all of the character and nature of the Godhead and seeks to impart this to us through His indwelling.

In closing, consider the words of the evangelist Billy Graham who wrote: "Pentecost was the day of power of the Holy Spirit. It was the day the Christian Church was born. We do not expect that Pentecost will be repeated any more than that Jesus will die on the cross again. But we do expect Pentecostal blessings when the conditions for God's moving are met, and especially as we approach 'the latter days.' We as Christians are to prepare the way. We are to be ready for the Spirit to fill us and use us."[2]

---

[1] Stanley, Charles <u>The Wonderful Spirit Filled Life</u>, Nashville, Thomas Nelson, 1995. pp. 17,18

[2] Graham, Billy <u>The Holy Spirit</u>, Nashville, Word Publishing, 1988. p. 295

16 THE DOCTRINE OF THE CHURCH

The Church is known by many names in the New Testament. Of course, one obvious name is the Church (in Greek, *ekklesia*, from which we get the word "ecclesiastical" which refers to church-related items), but also as the Body of Christ, the Flock, the Brethren, the Temple (or Building), the Kingdom of righteousness and peace, and the Bride of Christ. Regardless of whatever name is used, the Church is a universal organization without parallel in the Bible.

Let us never be confused into thinking that the Church equates to any specific brick-and-mortar building. Whenever the Church is mentioned in Scripture, it is the institution created directly by Jesus Himself even at the outset of His ministry on Earth. In John 15:16, He revealed to His disciples that *"[Y]ou did not choose me, but I chose you and appointed you so that you might go and bear fruit—fruit that will last—and so that whatever you ask in my name the Father will give you."* There is a direct lineage of faith that connects a believer today with Jesus Himself through the family of the Church.

There are those who attempt to equate the Church with the Temple *cultus*[1] of the Old Testament, but the Church defies this comparison. The Temple existed to constantly expiate the sin of the people of God but Christ Himself has accomplished this once and for all (see Hebrews 8 and 9). Others have pointed to the Synagogue as the model for the Church but even this analogy falls apart. Even though the Synagogue does serve to preserve the community of faith, as does the Church, its mandate is still subjected to the existence of a functioning Priesthood. It exists to unite Jews under their common culture and to keep their faith intact during the times of *Diaspora* (separation from their beloved land). The membership of the Church, in contrast, is completely free from the need to expiate sin through the sacrificial structure of the Temple and its mandate is radically distinct from that of the Synagogue.

Christian commentators vary on their precise definition of the Church but there is considerable overlap. Chuck Colson, for example, defines four marks that identify the Church. These are the Word, its Sacraments or

Ordinances, the maintenance of Discipline, and the establishment of Community.[2] The Southern Baptist theologian, Dale Moody, defined it in terms of three missions: that of *witness* (per Peter), that of *service* (according to Paul), and that of *fellowship* (as described by John).[3]

So what is the Church's mandate? It is to "*go.*" The Church accomplishes its mission on shoe-leather. Jesus' direct commandment to His original disciples is still His commandment to us. He told His disciples gathered in the upper room, *"Peace be with you! As the Father has sent me, I am sending you."* (John 20:21) and then among the last words to them was the Great Commission: *"Therefore go and make disciples of all nations, baptizing them in the name of the Father and of the Son and of the Holy Spirit, and teaching them to obey everything I have commanded you. And surely I am with you always, to the very end of the age."* (Matthew 28:19,20) Jesus proclaimed this under His authority which is "*all authority in heaven and on earth.*" (v 18) The Church is built on the mandate of a mission. Until all the requirements that Jesus has placed upon it have been met, the Church cannot stop going and its members must not sit down and be still. In fact, if there is anything that history has taught us, it is that an idle Church is a weak, ineffective, and even in some cases, a sin-embracing, Church.

Yet, even though the Church has a missionary mandate, the reason for its existence goes beyond that. The Church's Scriptural appellation of the "body of Christ" implies fellowship. Jesus Himself, in the High Priestly prayer over His disciples in John 17, prayed *"They are not of the world, even as I am not of it. Sanctify them by the truth; your word is truth. As you sent me into the world, I have sent them into the world....My prayer is not for them alone. I pray also for those who will believe in me through their message, that all of them may be one, Father, just as you are in me and I am in you. May they also be in us so that the world may believe that you have sent me. I have given them the glory that you gave me, that they may be one as we are one—I in them and you in me—so that they may be brought to complete unity. Then the world will know that you sent me and have loved them even as you have loved me."* (verses 16,17,20-23) Unity is the hallmark of the Trinity and must be also the hallmark of the Church and such unity is expressed by selfless love (see 1 Corinthians 13) resulting in *koinonia* (fellowship).

The Apostle Paul stated in his first letter to the Corinthian church that, "*Just as a body, though one, has many parts, but all its many parts form one body, so it is with Christ. For we were all baptized by one Spirit so as to form one body—whether Jews or Gentiles, slave or free—and we were all given the one Spirit to drink. Even so the body is not made up of one part but of many.*" (1 Corinthians 12:12-14)   David Prior, in his commentary on this letter, wrote, "Paul is clearly referring here to the way Christ today manifests himself by the Spirit to the world through his church. Bittlenger comments: 'In order to accomplish his work on earth, Jesus had a body made of flesh and blood. In order to accomplish his work today, Jesus has a body that consists of living human beings.' Paul is affirming both the rich variety and the deep unity in Christ himself. In this all Christians share as members of this one body through this one Spirit...Its context makes it clear that there can be no legitimate exegesis which divides Christians into two (or more) groups, let alone into first-class and second-class Christians."[4]

In the New Testament, the Church is also identified as the "bride of Christ," a name which summons the love that Jesus has for her and the care that He extends to her. Jesus taught His disciples that He was going to send the Paraclete, the Holy Spirit, to indwell them and to unite them with Him in a supernatural way. He said, "*If you love me, keep my commands. And I will ask the Father, and he will give you another advocate to help you and be with you forever—the Spirit of truth. The world cannot accept him, because it neither sees him nor knows him. But you know him, for he lives with you and will be in you. I will not leave you as orphans; I will come to you. Before long, the world will not see me anymore, but you will see me. Because I live, you also will live.*" (John 14:15-20) The Church is branded with a unity, not only the lateral one of *koinonia*, but a vertical unity with God Himself through the indwelling of the Holy Spirit. Paul described this relationship eloquently in the letter to the Ephesians as he described the relationship of a Christian husband in terms of the love of Jesus for His Church:

Husbands, love your wives, just as Christ loved the church and gave himself up for her to make her holy, cleansing her by the washing with water through the word, and to present her to himself as a radiant church, without stain or wrinkle or any other blemish, but holy and blameless. In this same way, husbands ought to love their wives as their own bodies. He who loves his wife loves himself. After all, no one ever hated their own body, but they feed and care for their body, just as Christ does the church—for we are members of his body. (Ephesians 5:25-30)

The Church, as the united body of believers, exists also to focus on worship. Chuck Colson stated, "We worship God because God is worthy of our worship. The Church glorifies God on earth, and this is a primary means by which we participate in God's life....We worship God in our churches so we can follow Him in the world."[5] Worship is the natural outpouring of honor and praise to the Lord from the hearts of His people. We worship God because He is worthy of our praise. Many times within the Psalms we are reminded of this fact.

"For great is the Lord and most worthy of praise; he is to be feared above all gods. For all the gods of the nations are idols, but the Lord made the heavens. Splendor and majesty are before him; strength and glory are in his sanctuary." (Psalm 96:4-6)

The worship of believers in the context of the Church is a foreshadowing of the continual worship in the throne-room of Heaven itself as described in Revelation 5. The believers within the Church, all of whom have been redeemed by the blood of Jesus, can surely exclaim *"Worthy is the Lamb, who was slain, to receive power and wealth and wisdom and strength and honor and glory and praise!"* (Revelation 5:12)

As obvious as it may seem at times, we sometimes forget that the Church was founded by Jesus Himself and that He holds the title to it. It is because of this that it requires our understanding of the whys and hows of its existence. It makes sense in this study to begin with Matthew 16:13-20 where Jesus was privately teaching His disciples. The dialog that ensued between Teacher and students was as follows:

When Jesus came to the region of Caesarea Philippi, he asked his disciples, "Who do people say the Son of Man is?" They replied, "Some say John the Baptist; others say Elijah; and still others, Jeremiah or one of the prophets."

"But what about you?" he asked. "Who do you say I am?" Simon Peter answered, "You are the Messiah, the Son of the living God."

Jesus replied, "Blessed are you, Simon son of Jonah, for this was not revealed to you by flesh and blood, but by my Father in heaven. And I tell you that you are Peter, and on this rock I will build my church, and the gates of Hades will not overcome it. I will give you the keys of the kingdom of heaven; whatever you bind on earth will be bound in heaven, and whatever you loose on earth will be loosed in heaven." Then he ordered his disciples not to tell anyone that he was the Messiah.

In this passage, Jesus played off of Peter's dual Hebrew and Greek names, Simon (*Shimon*, Hebrew, meaning "he has heard" or "he listened") and Peter (*Petros*, Greek, meaning "the rock"). After asking His disciples who they believed Him to be, Simon Peter provided a definitive description of Jesus' Personhood. He used definite articles ("the") for each of the assertions. Jesus is *The* Messiah (or the word "Christ" in the Greek), *The* Son of *The* living God.

Jesus' response indicated that Peter had pegged the answer perfectly, and the key we must understand is that Peter did not know this because of experience or because of deductive reason. He knew this to be truth because he "heard" the Spiritual revelation. Jesus' words, "you are *Petros*, and on this rock (*petros*) I will build my church, and the gates of Hades (or Hell) will not overcome it" has been misinterpreted in Church history to refer to the *person* of Peter. The established Church at Rome, and later in Byzantium/Constantinople, took this passage to establish their Doctrine of the Primacy of Peter. In this doctrine, it is believed that Jesus was addressing Peter and indicating that it was *he* who was that rock. It is not my intent or desire to insult our Orthodox and Roman Catholic brethren but we must truly understand the context of the message to grasp its meaning to the entire Body of the Church.

Jesus was using wordplay to combine Peter (the person) with the truth of the revelation. The literal meaning should be taken as, "You are Petros (the disciple), and on this petros (rock, the statement of truth you just uttered) will I build my church." The Church is founded upon Jesus Christ, the Second Person of the Trinity, and not upon the flesh and blood of Peter. In the light of this, the following sentence makes perfect sense because the Church is anointed with the Authority of Jesus Himself. Through this foundation built upon His authority:

- The Church cannot be undermined by Satan and its other spiritual foes;
- The Church holds out the gospel of salvation and brings souls bound to an eternity in Hell under God's saving grace, thus changing their destiny to an eternity in Heaven; and
- The Church will exercise God's will and shall have His authority on all Spiritual matters.

The sure foundation of the Church is the immovable Person of Jesus Christ. Peter, the disciple who answered the question above, wrote that as all believers come to Jesus, *"the living Stone—rejected by humans but chosen by God and precious to him—you also, like living stones, are being built into a spiritual house to be a holy priesthood, offering spiritual sacrifices acceptable to God through Jesus Christ."* (1 Peter 2:4,5) Paul wrote concerning those who work within the Church, *"For no one can lay any foundation other than the one already laid, which is Jesus Christ. If anyone builds on this foundation using gold, silver, costly stones, wood, hay or straw, their work will be shown for what it is..."* (1 Corinthians 3:11-13a) We each choose what kind of building material we will use, either the truth of the gospel, or the falsehood of worldly entanglements.

In writing about the Church, Chuck Colson said, "In our creeds we confess our belief in one holy, catholic, apostolic Church. What does that mean? The Church is *one* because all true Christians, while we participate in different confessing congregations, are part of one body. That body is *holy* because its essential nature is found in Christ. The Church is *catholic* because it is universal, which is what *catholic* means – the Church is open to everyone. Finally, the Church is *apostolic*, which means that its teachings are those of the apostles. We have not invented a religion. We are part of the faith God revealed."[6]

The Church is a God's newest creation. It is where both Jew and Gentile can come together to be one body, the Body of Jesus the Messiah. This is clearly outlined by the Apostle Paul in the letter to the Ephesians:

*Therefore, remember that formerly you who are Gentiles by birth and called "uncircumcised" by those who call themselves "the circumcision" (which is done in the body by human hands)—remember that at that time you were separate from Christ, **excluded from citizenship in Israel** and foreigners to the covenants of the promise, without hope and without God* *in the world. But now in Christ Jesus you who once were far away have* **been brought near by the blood of Christ.**

For he himself is our peace, who has made the two groups one and has destroyed the barrier, the dividing wall of hostility, by setting aside in his flesh the law with its commands and regulations. **His purpose was to create in himself one new humanity out of the two, thus making peace, and in one body to reconcile both of them to God through the cross, by which he put to death their hostility.** *He came and preached peace to you who were far away and peace to those who were near. For through him we both have access to the Father by one Spirit.*

Consequently, you are no longer foreigners and strangers, but **fellow citizens with God's people** *and also members of his household, built on the foundation of the apostles and prophets, with Christ Jesus himself as the chief cornerstone.* **In him the whole building is joined together and rises to become a holy temple in the Lord. And in him you too are being built together to become a dwelling in which God lives by his Spirit.** *(Ephesians 2:11-22, bold emphasis is mine)*

The Holy Spirit's presence in the Church cannot be unstated or understated. In fact, the Church is empowered completely though His indwelling Presence. In the Great Commission, the Church's marching orders were stated by Jesus: *"Therefore go and make disciples of all nations, baptizing them in the name of the Father and of the Son and the Holy Spirit... "* as was quoted earlier. The Holy Spirit, as outlined in this baptismal formula, is *the* fundamental agent in each believer's conversion and in maintaining Jesus' Presence in the world.

This fact was further clarified just before Jesus ascended into Heaven and left His disciples the task of forming the Church. In Acts 1:8, He told them, *"But you will receive power when the Holy Spirit comes on you; and you will be my witnesses in Jerusalem, and in all Judea and Samaria, and to the ends of the earth."* His mandate was to "go and make disciples" but this mandate was never meant to be achieved by mere human effort. No, the power to accomplish the mission is in the Presence of the Holy Spirit. Mere days after the Ascension, on the Day of Pentecost (Acts 2), the One known as the Spirit of Jesus (the Holy Spirit) came upon the rag-tag group of early believers and ignited the growth of the Church which continues unabated even today, over two thousand years later! Every generation of believers receives the Holy Spirit and through His special power becomes another part in the growing Body of Christ, just as Paul indicated in Ephesians 2:21.

Jesus is with us always through His Spirit, as was previously mentioned. This is the central hub of His teachings found in John 14-17. Everything that the Church needs is delivered through the Spirit's unique ministry. He teaches and exhorts (14:23-26). He cements us in peace (14:27) which is one of His gifts (Galatians 5:15). He testifies about Jesus and puts the gospel on our lips (15:26,27) even while convicting sinners (16:7-11). He serves to extend God's protection (17:11,12) to believers, protection from evil. The Apostle Paul also declared that the Spirit seals us and keeps us for the "day of redemption" (Ephesians 4:30) in keeping with Jesus' prayer in 17:12. Paul also emphasized that the Holy Spirit prays for us, translating our weak fleshly prayer into effective petitions before the throne of God (Romans 8:26-28).

Even in Jesus' analogy of the vine in John 15:1-17, the Holy Spirit's presence is essential for the Church's growth. Charles Stanley, in his book entitled The Wonderful Spirit Filled Life, made this wonderful assertion: "Jesus makes a clear delineation between the vine and the branch. The two are not the same. *He* is the vine; *we* are the branches. The two are joined but not one. The common denominator is the sap. The sap is the life of the vine and its branches. Cut off the flow of sap to the branch, and it slowly withers and dies. As the branch draws its life from the vine, so we draw life from Christ. *To abide in Christ is to draw upon His life.* His life is made available through the presence of the Holy Spirit in our lives. The abiding presence of the Holy Spirit is the life of Christ in us."[7]

Another topic that is worth discussion concerning Church life is our responsibility towards our home congregation. Listen carefully to how Chuck Colson stated his belief that "Church community demands commitment. When people ask where I go to church, I correct them. I don't go; I'm a member….We cannot treat the local church like a restaurant, picking and choosing from the menu, visiting another when we feel like it. Church membership involves making a covenant with fellow believers."[8] This concept seems to be completely foreign in today's Christian environment. There are many who choose to not participate in Church at all, preferring the convenience of watching one or two tele-evangelists instead of belonging to a local congregation. Others participate in a local congregation but do not commit to becoming members and putting themselves under the shepherding of the pastor. If we are to be the Body of Christ, we must be engrafted into the body of the Church itself. We must commit to enter into a covenant with a local body which will serve to teach us, engage us, encourage us, and even discipline us.

While on the subject of participation in a local Church body, let us briefly touch on the subject of tithing. Many object to it or just don't practice it. Some have even considered it to be "old school" and not relevant any longer. Regardless of your position on the matter, consider the fact that tithing is a spiritual discipline. God has never gone on record and revoked tithing as a practice. In Malachi, the last word of prophesy in the Old Testament, God states:

"Will a mere mortal rob God? Yet you rob me. But you ask, 'How are we robbing you?'

In tithes and offerings. You are under a curse—your whole nation— because you are robbing me. Bring the whole tithe into the storehouse, that there may be food in my house. Test me in this," says the Lord Almighty, "and see if I will not throw open the floodgates of heaven and pour out so much blessing that there will not be room enough to store it." (Malachi 3:8-10)

Jesus commented upon the faithfulness of an unnamed widow in giving her offering:

Jesus sat down opposite the place where the offerings were put and watched the crowd putting their money into the temple treasury. Many rich people threw in large amounts. But a poor widow came and put in two very small copper coins, worth only a few cents.

Calling his disciples to him, Jesus said, "Truly I tell you, this poor widow has put more into the treasury than all the others. They all gave out of their wealth; but she, out of her poverty, put in everything—all she had to live on." (Mark 12:41-44)

Tithes and offerings are an important part of being **in** the Church. *"Give to Caesar what is Caesar's"* (Matthew 22:21), said Jesus. We pay taxes and do not fail out of fear of the government and the repercussions of not paying them properly. He continued by saying, *"[Give] to God what is God's."* Do we not fear Him? How can we can obey and respect our respective governments but not accord the same honor to our God?

So what is the tithe? A tithe is 10% of one's gross earnings or one's increase such as gifts. It covered a tenth of the herds and flocks (Leviticus 27:32), a tenth of the produce of the fields (Deuteronomy 14:22), and even a tenth of the blessings that the Priesthood received (Numbers 18:26). So, it is clear, a tithe is 10% of gross which is given specifically to your home congregation for its functioning. Of course, if you feel led or have been especially blessed, other offerings (to your home church or other organizations) can be given on top of this. Consider carefully what James says under the conviction of the Holy Spirit:

You desire but do not have, so you kill. You covet but you cannot get what you want, so you quarrel and fight. You do not have because you do not ask God. When you ask, you do not receive, because you ask with wrong motives, that you may spend what you get on your pleasures. (James 4:2,3)

There are many who choose to argue against all this but all I can tell you is that it is just an obedience thing. If you will indulge me, let me get personal for a moment. I praise the day that God first moved in me to obey Him and tithe. It has proven to be a source of great spiritual enjoyment. It made a real difference in me and I have heard many a testimony from fellow believers who make the same claim. I also have the privilege of being in a Church body that doesn't need to preach about tithing…it is just done. We don't pass plates that might tend to make people feel guilty. We know what God expects of us and we quietly put our tithes in one of the coffers on the way in or out of the service. I have heard Pastor Howard Thompson mention tithing *in passing* in sermons maybe a handful of times in the decade of being under his care. Trust God in this. It is truly liberating!

Earlier, it was mentioned that Chuck Colson believes that discipline is one of the marks that defines the Church. Specifically he said, "Sadly, discipline is not adequately practiced in most churches. Sometimes pastors and governing boards are unwilling to exercise discipline for fear of hurting church recruitment or—perish the thought—for fear of appearing intolerant in this golden age of tolerance. But not to enforce church discipline, not to hold people accountable for holy and righteous living, is to make a mockery of the Church."[9]

Throughout the New Testament, Church discipline is outlined as being practiced. The Apostle Paul called on the church at Corinth to expel a member committing incest (1 Corinthians 5) while Peter dealt with Ananias' and Sapphira's lying to the Holy Spirit in Acts 5. In Galatians 6:1, Paul admonishes, *"Brothers and sisters, if someone is caught in a sin, you who live by the Spirit should restore that person gently. But watch yourselves, or you also may be tempted."* Jesus Himself spoke about this issue in Luke 17:3 and in Matthew 18:15-17, *"If your brother or sister sins, go and point out their fault, just between the two of you. If they listen to you, you have won them over. But if they will not listen, take one or two others along, so that 'every matter may be established by the testimony of two or three witnesses.' If they still refuse to listen, tell it to the church; and if they refuse to listen even to the church, treat them as you would a pagan or a tax collector."* The risen Lord, in the letters to the seven churches transcribed by John the Divine, said to the lukewarm Church of Laodicea, *"Those whom I love I rebuke and discipline. So be earnest and repent."* (Revelation 3:19)

Churches are also required to apply prescriptive formulas in evaluating, selecting, and keeping both pastors and deacons in 1 Timothy 3:1-12 and Titus 1:5-9. The decisions involved in choosing leaders should be prayerfully and carefully lifted before the Lord. Consider how the early believers allowed the Holy Spirit to move them in Acts 1:13-26. Such leaders must understand the tremendous importance of their work and Who has actually called them. Paul reminded the Ephesian elders to *"[K]eep watch over yourselves and all the flock of which the Holy Spirit has made you overseers. Be shepherds of the church of God, which he bought with his own blood."* (Acts 20:28) Christian accountability is even of more importance within the leadership of the Church and one must be extremely suspect of a leader who decries such accountability and even more so if they justify their inviolability by misusing 1 Samuel 26:11 concerning "the Lord's anointed."

Finally, in bringing this chapter to a close, it would be an error to not address the subject of the true ownership of the Church. Nothing irks me more than when someone describes a church, other than describing it as the one they attend, as "my church." No, it is Jesus' Church! Gustav Aulén stated that "[T]he church and Christ belong together. They constitute an inseparable unity. The church exists in and through Christ. But neither does Christ exist apart from his church. Just as the church cannot be conceived of without Christ, so neither can we think of *Christus-Kyrios* [Christ the Lord] without his dominion, without connection with that fellowship which belongs to him. Where Christ is, there is the church."[10]   The two are inseparable for where one finds Christ today, there is His Church. Where you can find the Spirit-indwelled members of His Body, there He is also. The Church has no reason to exist apart from the Lord Jesus.

Unfortunately, we are seeing more and more instances of "churches" that are formed without Christ at their center. Many of these are successful, thriving, "mega-church" movements but, sadly, they are built on anything but Jesus and His righteousness (be aware that I am not saying that every mega-church conforms to this model). We live in the age when there is a preponderance of feel-good, do-what-pleases-me, unaccountable, take-down-that-offensive-cross, tickle-my-ears, blood-free Christianity and the message of such preaching has certainly found fertile ground.

The question that does not seem to occur to many members of these congregations is *whose* church are they part of. If the church belongs to Christ, then He and His blood-stained Cross must be at its center. Chuck Colson wrote, "We are the bride for whom Christ, the Bridegroom, gave Himself (Ephesians 5:25). Think about that scriptural analogy – Christ shed His blood for the Church; shame on us when we trivialize her."[11]   The Cross must be an offense (Galatians 5:10) and Christ-crucified must be a stumbling block to all (1 Corinthians 1:23)! We are only set free from our sins by bowing at the foot of that Cross and being "smeared" with the saving blood of Jesus. Political and social correctness aside, ours has to be a "bloody religion" for only it is "the blood that makes atonement for one's life" (Leviticus 17:11b) and that blood is Christ's (Romans 3:24).

We who are in the Jesus' Church need to wake up and rededicate ourselves. May we take careful heed to the words of Jesus in the letter to the Church of Ephesus in Revelation. *"Yet I hold this against you: You have forsaken the love you had at first. Consider how far you have fallen! Repent and do the things you did at first. If you do not repent, I will come to you and remove your lampstand from its place."* (Revelation 2:4,5)

Lord, may we hear you and obey. May we humble ourselves and repent of our pride and arrogance. May we, O Lord, who are the Church called by your Name, seek to serve you as your faithful Bride. Amen.

---

[1] *Cultus* is a term that means the practices of religious worship.
[2] Colson, Charles The Faith, Grand Rapids, Zondervan, 2008. pp 149-156
[3] Moody, Dale The Word of Truth, Grand Rapids, William B. Eerdmans, 1983. pp. 429-433
[4] Prior, David The Message of 1 Corinthians, Downers Grove, Inter-Varsity Press, 1985. p 210
[5] Colson, Charles The Faith, p. 149
[6] Colson, Charles The Faith, pp. 155,6
[7] Stanley, Charles The Wonderful Spirit Filled Life, Nashville, Thomas Nelson, 1995. p. 64
[8] Colson, Charles The Faith, p. 155
[9] Colson, Charles The Faith, p. 153
[10] Aulén, Gustaf The Faith of the Christian Church, Philadelphia, Fortress Press, 1960. p. 294
[11] Colson, Charles The Faith, p. 149

17 THE ETERNAL REALM

Eternity is God's realm. Unbounded by time or space, God simply is. He, and He alone, is uncreated and without beginning. While this concept may be foreign to our finitely-bound minds, we must accept the fact that this is how God has introduced Himself and has described Himself in His special revelation to mankind. He is boundless. He created everything else, some to be eternal in nature and others not. For example, we know that He created the angels (see Nehemiah 9:6; Psalm 148:5) at some point before the creation of the Earth (see Job 38:4-7). We know that it was Jesus, the Second Person of the Trinity, Who was the Agent of Creation (see Colossians 1:16,17) and thus He must have also created the angelic hosts. Angels were created to be eternal beings as were humans (see Psalm 8:5; Genesis 1:26,27), finite only in terms of their beginning but with no end.

God rules over all. All Eternity and everything within it is subject to His rule. The time-space continuum of the Creation and everything contained within its borders is likewise subject to His rule. "God reigns over the nations; God is seated on his holy throne," states Psalm 47:8. Heaven is God's realm from whence He rules. The throne-room of God is described in Revelation 4:

After this I looked, and there before me was a door standing open in heaven. And the voice I had first heard speaking to me like a trumpet said, "Come up here, and I will show you what must take place after this." At once I was in the Spirit, and there before me was a throne in heaven with someone sitting on it. And the one who sat there had the appearance of jasper and ruby. A rainbow that shone like an emerald encircled the throne. Surrounding the throne were twenty-four other thrones, and seated on them were twenty-four elders. They were dressed in white and had crowns of gold on their heads. 5 From the throne came flashes of lightning, rumblings and peals of thunder. In front of the throne, seven lamps were blazing. These are the seven spirits of God. Also in front of the throne there was what looked like a sea of glass, clear as crystal.

In the center, around the throne, were four living creatures, and they were covered with eyes, in front and in back. The first living creature was like a lion, the second was like an ox, the third had a face like a man, the fourth was like a flying eagle. Each of the four living creatures had six wings and was covered with eyes all around, even under its wings. Day and night they never stop saying:

"'Holy, holy, holy
is the Lord God Almighty,'
who was, and is, and is to come." (Revelation 4:1-8)

Heaven is the aspiration for all who seek God. Jesus taught that *"[Y]ou believe in God; believe also in me. My Father's house has many rooms; if that were not so, would I have told you that I am going there to prepare a place for you? And if I go and prepare a place for you, I will come back and take you to be with me so that you also may be where I am."* (John 14:1b-3) Paul, the Apostle, stated that *"...our citizenship is in heaven. And we eagerly await a Savior from there, the Lord Jesus Christ, who, by the power that enables him to bring everything under his control, will transform our lowly bodies so that they will be like his glorious body."* (Philippians 3:20,21)

Heaven is a literal place that all the faithful worshippers of God await. In the middle of the "roll call of faith" chapter of Hebrews, one can read that *"[A]ll these people were still living by faith when they died. They did not receive the things promised; they only saw them and welcomed them from a distance, admitting that they were foreigners and strangers on earth. People who say such things show that they are looking for a country of their own. If they had been thinking of the country they had left, they would have had opportunity to return. Instead, they were longing for a better country—a heavenly one. Therefore God is not ashamed to be called their God, for he has prepared a city for them."* (Hebrews 11:13-16)

However, It is impossible to consider the realm of Eternity without dealing with the question of Evil. Of course, we opened this can of proverbial worms when we addressed the Doctrine of Sin. Those of us who are "in Christ" must be very aware of the existence and the destructive power of evil otherwise our conversion was in vain. Surely, we each must have reached a point in our lives when we agreed with God that our lives were captured by sin and we were bound for an eternity in Hell. We repented of our sin while turning the title of our lives over to Jesus our Savior. Evil is not a laughing matter; the consequences are eternally serious!

Satan is often caricatured as a comic, bumbling character with a poor fashion sense. We must seek to put out of our heads this human figure wearing a red velveteen suit with matching red shoes, one who is festooned with a pair of comical red horns and an equally comical long pointed tail. This merely desensitizes us to the *enemy* who, according to Peter the Disciple, is one who *"prowls around like a roaring lion looking for someone to devour."* (1 Peter 5:8) He and his minions are lethal! It is not for a trivial reason that Paul admonishes believers to *"put on the full armor of God, so that you can take your stand against the devil's schemes. For our struggle is not against flesh and blood, but against the rulers, against the authorities, against the powers of this dark world and against the spiritual forces of evil in the heavenly realms. Therefore put on the full armor of God, so that when the day of evil comes, you may be able to stand your ground, and after you have done everything, to stand."* (Ephesians 6:11-13)

As we discussed in an earlier chapter, Satan desired to be "like God" and led a rebellion in Heaven that conscripted a third of the angelic host to his side (Revelation 12:2,3). The rebellion was quashed and Satan and his followers were cast out of heaven into the newly created universe (Ezekiel 28:16b-17). Thus, Satan entered the pristine goodness of the new Creation and corrupted it with his pure evil. Since the time he first spoke to Eve and until the day this universe is drawn to a close, he infects man with the same desire that he has always had. *"For God knows that when you eat from it [the Tree of the Knowledge of Good and Evil] your eyes will be opened, and you will be like God, knowing good and evil."* (Genesis 3:5)

Generation after generation come and go, each repeating the Fall by replacing God with themselves as their supreme being. The lie of Satan is twofold: First, that this life is all that there is and so it makes sense to grasp at everything one can (Genesis 3:4); and second, that God and His commands are inconsequential and can merely be trivialized and dismissed (Genesis 3:1,5).

How many fruit trees do you imagine were in the Garden of Eden? Tens of thousands? Hundreds of thousands? Millions? In this vast microcosm of countless fruit-bearing trees, what made *this* one so important? Until this moment of time, both Adam and Eve completely avoided this tree, never giving it a second's thought. Had a thought passed through their mind, they readily remembered God's admonition and went right along to one of the other umpteen trees that provided of their rich bounty for their sustenance. Yet, in one moment, a few words deceptively spoken made that tree more important than life itself. The serpentine incarnation of Satan hissed the tantalizing words that the fruit of that tree could make them "like God!" In moments, the thousands or millions of other suitable trees faded from memory. Their trusting knowledge of God being totally true and honest evaporated. Mankind's understanding of having been created as an eternal being also came to an abrupt end.

Thus, since the Fall, millions upon millions have been deceived and have chosen to fashion their lives against God. They have all died in their sins to spend their eternity in Hell. All of this needless sadness is in spite of God's plans and the opportunities for salvation that He has provided. God has stated, *"Do I take any pleasure in the death of the wicked? Rather am I not pleased when they turn from their ways and live?"* (see Ezekiel 18:23,32; 33:11) God's offer of redemption is the central message of the oft-quoted John 3:16. The Apostle Paul stated that *"[T]hey perish because they refused to love the truth and so be saved."* (2 Thessalonians salonians 2:10b) Jesus said, using some examples of recent disasters, *"But unless you repent, you too will all perish."* (see Luke 13:3;5) As we discussed in the Doctrine of Sin, God's call to repentance is clear and embedded even in the natural man's conscience.

We live in a society that scoffs at the existence of Hell. In many cases, Hell is either considered "politically incorrect" or is viewed to be a useless myth. Unfortunately, these mindsets have made their way into the Church and have led some to absurd concepts such as "universal salvation" and "conditional immortality." Without a healthy understanding of Hell and its impact on sinful man, how in the world can anyone explain why God would send His own Son into the world to bear the burden of mankind's accumulated sin? If the consequences of sin are not dire and disastrous, why would Jesus have paid such a tremendous price to save us (see 1 Peter 1:18-21)? In fact, it is fair to state that without a literal Hell a lot of the Biblical narrative makes absolutely no sense.

Hell exists. It is real and literal. It is the eternal place that is characterized by extreme absence...the absence of God and of His love. Jesus described it as a place of torment (Luke 16:23) and fire (Mark 9:43,49). It is better to be maimed in this life, according to Him, than to use your limbs in a way that causes you to stumble and end up thrown into Hell (Mark 9:43-49). He quoted Isaiah 66:24 in which the Lord stated:

"And they will go out and look on the dead bodies of those who rebelled against me; the worms that eat them will not die, the fire that burns them will not be quenched, and they will be loathsome to all mankind."

In Revelation 20, the Bible pulls no punches about the existence or the seriousness of Hell. *"Then death and Hades were thrown into the lake of fire. The lake of fire is the second death. Anyone whose name was not found written in the book of life was thrown into the lake of fire."* (20:14,15) Antecedent to this passage, it said that *"the devil...was thrown into the lake of burning sulfur, where the beast and the false prophet had been thrown. They will be tormented day and night for ever and ever."* (20:10) That lake was described in Revelation 19:20 as *"the fiery lake of burning sulfur"* which unites the lake of fire with the lake of burning sulfur into one concept, a place of eternal suffering. The everlastingness of this place also is stated by the prophet Daniel who said, *"Multitudes who sleep in the dust of the earth will awake: some to everlasting life, others to shame and everlasting contempt."* (Daniel 12:2)

In answer to those who reduce Hell by holding universal salvation[1] or annihilatist[2] positions, the Baptist theologian Dale Moody stated: "The belief in the mercy of God and the desire for a final harmony of all things in God make one hope for such an outcome, but destruction and the second death confront us under the symbol of the 'lake of fire' where all the notoriously wicked 'will be tormented day and night for ever and ever (Revelation 20:10). *Gehenna* was 'prepared for the devil and his angels' (Matthew 25:41), but men may end there by spurning the love of God (Revelation 20:14)."[3] Chuck Colson wrote the following to those who might think that God is either incapable or unwilling to dispatch souls to Hell: "He [God] doesn't want 'anyone to perish, but everyone to come to repentance' (2 Peter 3:9). He promises that every individual who comes to Him in genuine faith and repents of his sins will be saved and spend eternity with God. But God gives each person a free will. Reluctantly, He respects the choice the person makes to remain alienated from Him while alive. He doesn't send the unrepentant person to hell; the unrepentant person chooses it."[4]

So here we have them, Heaven and Hell, both contained within the Realm of Eternity. Since man is born with an eternal soul he will spend eternity in one or the other. We have seen that access to Heaven depends partly upon the choice a person makes and partly upon the redemptive work of Jesus when He is chosen as Lord and Savior. This is such an important decision that it should neither be delayed nor rejected! The gospel message is not to be taken lightly.

An argument that arises constantly from the mouths of both believers and unbelievers is that if Jesus is indeed **the** only way to God (as He claimed), then what would happen to those who have not had an opportunity to hear the Gospel preached? To them, it is totally unfair, and they try to use this approach to open the heretical door of there being many ways to God. Man's finite mind and corrupted character cannot begin to understand how God's righteousness will deal with this issue.

There are some interesting hints in Scripture that should help us understand that He does have everything completely in control. Consider, for example, the tantalizing statement in 1 Peter 3:18-20a, *"For Christ also suffered once for sins, the righteous for the unrighteous, to bring you to God. He was put to death in the body but made alive in the Spirit. After being made alive, he went and made proclamation to the imprisoned spirits—to those who were disobedient long ago when God waited patiently in the days of Noah while the ark was being built."* There are many views to the interpretation of this passage of who the "imprisoned spirits" may be but what is interesting to us is that God implements plans to ensure that "people are without excuse." In Hebrews 11:39,40 Scripture states, *"These [who lived by faith in the time before Jesus became flesh] were all commended for their faith, yet none of them received what had been promised, since God had planned something better for us so that only together with us would they be made perfect."* Likewise, Jesus stated to the Jewish leaders, *"Your father Abraham rejoiced at the thought of seeing my day; he saw it and was glad."* (John 8:56)

Colson's take on this issue is "...while Scripture isn't entirely clear about how truth becomes known to people who have not heard the Gospel, and how God's perfect justice and mercy will apply to them, believers trust in the goodness and mercy of God and, obedient to His command, are calling all people everywhere to repent and believe the Good News of

Jesus Christ (Acts 17:30). As the book of Job says, 'It is unthinkable that God would do wrong, that the Almighty will pervert justice' (34:12)"[5] The point of this is that we must let God be God and trust Him to be perfectly just in administering His righteous judgment. It is not for us to know all of the variations of His plans other than He does not lie and has specifically pronounced His judgment on those who reject His rule.

The prescription is clear. Those who are in Christ must be faithful to the Great Commission and preach the Gospel to a lost and dying world, while those who are not under His saving grace and who have read or heard the Gospel are under His indictment right now. There is no fallback position, no loophole through which salvation is offered to those who are deliberately rejecting God. Heed the words of Hebrews 4:7, *"God again set a certain day, calling it 'Today.' This he did when a long time later he spoke through David, as in the passage already quoted: 'Today, if you hear his voice, do not harden your hearts'"* for the consequences are dire and eternal. Today needs to be your day of salvation if you missed it yesterday!

It is impossible to talk about Eternity without touching upon the End Times. The Creation is finite and its days are numbered. It will be brought to a close one day. Ironically, this subject is popular among both Christians and non believers alike. There are those who, while they might not lend credence to Jesus or do not believe in God, are extremely eager to dig into the Book of Revelation.

God is clear about the time when He will reconcile the books and bring an end to rebellion and sin. In Ezekiel 39, He stated:

"I will make known my holy name among my people Israel. I will no longer let my holy name be profaned, and the nations will know that I the Lord am the Holy One in Israel. It is coming! It will surely take place, declares the Sovereign Lord. This is the day I have spoken of." (Eze 39:7,8)

The Psalmist wrote, *"The Lord is at your [Messiah's] right hand, he will crush kings on the day of this wrath. He will judge the nations, heaping up the dead and crushing the rulers of the whole earth."* (Psalm 110:5,6) Isaiah prophesied, *"See the day of the LORD is coming—a cruel day, with wrath and fierce anger—to make the land desolate and destroy the sinners within it. The stars of heaven and their constellations will not show their light. The rising sun will be darkened and the moon will not give its light. I will punish the world for its evil, the wicked for their sins."* (Isaiah 13:9-11a) Zephaniah, considering that day, said, *"The great day of the LORD is near—near and coming quickly....That day will be a day of wrath—a day of distress and anguish, a day of trouble and ruin, a day of darkness and gloom, a day of clouds and blackness—a day of trumpet and battle cry against the fortified cities and against the corner towers."* (Zephaniah 1:14-16) Joel referred to this coming time as the *"great and dreadful day of the LORD"* (Joel 2:31) as also did Malachi (4:5).

The prophetic words concerning the End Times are not merely found in Revelation. It is not Scripturally sound to concentrate only upon this one book in attempting to understand the *"great and dreadful day of the Lord"* as some are in the habit of doing. It is also fair to say that non-believers cannot truly understand the Word of God since the Holy Spirit needs to come alongside and help readers to interpret it. It stands to reason that any interpretation a non-Christian may do of these passages (or any Biblical text at all) must be considered highly suspect!

The following represents a list of End Times passages that must all be read and considered together. Scripture dovetails passages with each other so only by prayerful consideration of all that the Bible has to say about this topic can one actually gain some level of understanding of this critical subject.

- Isaiah, many passages, especially chapters 2-4, 24-26
- Jeremiah, especially chapter 31
- Ezekiel, many passages, especially chapter 38
- Daniel chapters 7-12
- Joel
- Zechariah
- Zephaniah
- Micah, especially chapter 4
- Malachi chapter 4
- Matthew chapter 24 and 25
- Mark chapter 13
- Luke chapter 21
- 1 Thessalonians
- 2 Thessalonians

- 2 Peter
- Jude 1:17-22
- Revelation

The point we must grasp throughout all of these passages is that God has assigned a day when He will bring the world to an end. *"See, the LORD is going to lay waste the earth and devastate it...the earth will be completely laid waste and totally plundered,"* said Isaiah in 24:1,3. At that time, we understand that Satan would have propped up a false "Christ" who is called the anti-Christ. This person will deceive the world into worshipping him and in aligning themselves against God and His Elect. The end will come at a battle in which all the forces of men and demons will align themselves against God's army. This rebellion will be short-lived because Jesus will reappear at the head of the heavenly hosts as a conquering King.

I saw heaven standing open and there before me was a white horse, whose rider is called Faithful and True. With justice he judges and wages war. His eyes are like blazing fire, and on his head are many crowns. He has a name written on him that no one knows but he himself. He is dressed in a robe dipped in blood, and his name is the Word of God. The armies of heaven were following him, riding on white horses and dressed in fine linen, white and clean. Coming out of his mouth is a sharp sword with which to strike down the nations. "He will rule them with an iron scepter." He treads the winepress of the fury of the wrath of God Almighty. On his robe and on his thigh he has this name written:

KING OF KINGS AND LORD OF LORDS.

And I saw an angel standing in the sun, who cried in a loud voice to all the birds flying in midair, "Come, gather together for the great supper of God, so that you may eat the flesh of kings, generals, and the mighty, of horses and their riders, and the flesh of all people, free and slave, great and small."

Then I saw the beast and the kings of the earth and their armies gathered together to wage war against the rider on the horse and his army. But the beast was captured, and with it the false prophet who had performed the signs on its behalf. With these signs he had deluded those who had received the mark of the beast and worshiped its image. The two of them were thrown alive into the fiery lake of burning sulfur. The rest were killed with the sword coming out of the mouth of the rider on the horse, and all the birds gorged themselves on their flesh. (Revelation 19:11-21)

Following this, ultimately, Satan and his minions will be judged and then all mankind will also be judged (Revelation 20:7-15). Some of the saddest words in all of the Bible are found in Revelation 20:15: *"Anyone whose name was not found written in the book of life was thrown into the lake of fire."* These are twice sad, first because God does not take pleasure in the death of the wicked (Ezekiel 18:23;32;33:11), and second that there are men and women so foolish that they would not reach out their hand and pluck the free gift of God's grace of salvation through Christ Jesus (Ephesians 2:8,9; Revelation 22:14).

The final point that needs to be made concerning the End Times is in reference to the Resurrection of the Dead. Jesus was raised from the dead by the love of the Father as *"the firstfruits of those who have fallen asleep."* (1 Corinthians 15:20) This is the crux of the Christian hope that beats within each of our chests. The promise, as enunciated by the Apostle Paul, is that *"[B]y his power God raised the Lord from the dead, and he will raise us also."* (1 Corinthians 6:14) We, like the Thessalonian church, *"wait for his Son from heaven, whom he raised from the dead— Jesus, who rescues us from the coming wrath."* (1 Thessalonians salonians 1:10)

If we choose to not believe in the Resurrection, then our faith is certainly in vain. Why would we choose to follow the way of Christ if this is not true. Paul pulled no punches when he told the Corinthians that:

But if it is preached that Christ has been raised from the dead, how can some of you say that there is no resurrection of the dead? If there is no resurrection of the dead, then not even Christ has been raised. And if Christ has not been raised, our preaching is useless and so is your faith. More than that, we are then found to be false witnesses about God, for we have testified about God that he raised Christ from the dead. But he did not raise him if in fact the dead are not raised. For if the dead are not raised, then Christ has not been raised either. And if Christ has not been raised, your faith is futile; you are still in your sins. Then those also who have fallen asleep in Christ are lost. If only for this life we have hope in Christ, we are of all people most to be pitied. (1 Corinthians 15:12-18)

Without the Resurrection, there is absolutely no hope! However, we join with Paul and proclaim that *"Christ has indeed been raised from the dead!"* (1 Corinthians 15:20a) He will come back to Earth and gather His children. *"We will not all sleep, but we will all be changed—in a flash, in the twinkling of an eye, at the last trumpet. For the trumpet will sound, the dead will be raised imperishable, and we will be changed. For the perishable must clothe itself with the imperishable, and the mortal with immortality. When the perishable has been clothed with the imperishable, and the mortal with immortality, then the saying that is written will come true: 'Death has been swallowed up in victory.'"* (1 Corinthians 15:51-54) To the church in Thessalonica, Paul described the event as:

According to the Lord's word, we tell you that we who are still alive, who are left until the coming of the Lord, will certainly not precede those who have fallen asleep. For the Lord himself will come down from heaven, with a loud command, with the voice of the archangel and with the trumpet call of God, and the dead in Christ will rise first. After that, we who are still alive and are left will be caught up together with them in the clouds to meet the Lord in the air. And so we will be with the Lord forever. (1 Thessalonians 4:15-17)

There are four different views concerning the timing of the *parousia* (the Second Coming), one of which is completely heretical since it is against Scripture.

1. Pre-Tribulation view: Jesus will come and rapture His Church before the anti-Christ gains power, seven years before the Day of Judgment.
2. Mid-Tribulation view: Jesus will come and rapture His Church before the anti-Christ turns evil, three and a half years before the Day of Judgment.
3. Post-Tribulation view: Jesus will come and rapture His Church out of the world before the final battle described in Revelation 19.
4. Non-Tribulation view: Jesus will not rapture the Church at all. This argument cannot hold water in the light of the passages quoted above and thus is false.

In most cases, the exact timing of the Rapture could be considered a "disputable matter" (per Romans 14:1). Many Christians hold one position or the other and hotly debate it but Scripture does not specifically lay out a timetable. There are Scriptural passages which can be pressed into defense of any of the valid positions. If I were to take an exclusively Pre-Tribulation view, then why did Jesus make specific comments about fleeing when one sees the abomination that causes desolation in the holy place (Matthew 24:15-24)? Similar arguments can be lodged against the Mid-Tribulation and Post-Tribulation standpoints.

My stance is that God is God and will do what He deems necessary *when* He deems it necessary. We know that He will take us out of this world, we just don't have the exact itinerary in our hands. Let us simply trust Him to be faithful to His Word.

---

[1] Basically, the position of Universal Salvation states that since God is all love, He will not go through with His plan to send the unrepentant into an eternity in Hell. This is a false view which sacrifices God's attributes of righteousness and justice on the altar of convenience. This stands against God's revealed truth in Scripture.

[2] Annihilism is another false view in which proponents diminish or remove the understanding of eternity from Hell. To them, God will either immediately totally destroy (annihilate) the souls of the unrepentant or will bring Hell to a finite end. This position stands against Scripture. Consider, for example, Jesus' words in Mark 9:43-45 in which He stated, "It is better for you to enter life lame, rather than having two feet, to be cast into hell, into the fire that shall **never** be quenched."

[3] Moody, Dale The Word of Truth. Grand Rapids, Wm B. Eerdmans, 1981. p. 515

[4] Colson, Charles The Faith, Grand Rapids, Zondervan, 2008. p. 194

[5] Colson, Charles The Faith, p. 196

18 THE CHRISTIAN WALK

In my personal observance of Christianity today, I can see two dangerous currents which somewhat overlap. The first of these is the dilution of the concept of absolute Truth by the post-modernistic worldview that pervades even our pews. This attack serves to reduce the Word of God to a set of "good sayings" which may be "true" for one person but not for another and which a person can choose to believe or reject as they see fit. The second current is the advent of a "feel-good" approach to Christianity in which emotions dominate the believer's experience of God. Together, these two falsehoods serve to totally destroy the Christian's footing.

We already dealt with the concept of Truth in an earlier chapter. Now, as we concentrate on what it means to be a true follower of Jesus Christ, we will touch on the second of these — emotion.

Consider that when God created man and breathed the breath of life into him, He created man in his own image (Genesis 1:26-28) and assigned him a godly role of subduing the Earth and ruling over this area of Creation (what Chuck Colson called the "Cultural Commission"[1]). In doing this, he imbued man with instinct (like the animals), emotions, and intellect. In creating man with intellect He provided the basis of choice, the ability to make a decision consciously and deliberately. Instinct and emotion might produce a right decision for any situation but only intellect can weigh the decision and make a choice and even reflect upon the wisdom or folly of that choice in hindsight in order to better choose in a future situation.

You may be asking, "what does this have to do with Truth and emotion?" First, it is our intellect that God uses to know Him. In Romans 1:18-22, the Apostle Paul wrote:

"The wrath of God is being revealed from heaven against all the godlessness and wickedness of men who suppress the truth by their wickedness, since what may be known about God is plain to them, because God has made it plain to them. For since the creation of the world God's invisible qualities—his eternal power and divine nature—have been clearly seen, being understood from what has been made, so that men are

without excuse. For although they knew God, they neither glorified him as God nor gave thanks to him, but their thinking became futile and their foolish hearts were darkened. Although they claimed to be wise, they became fools and exchanged the glory of the immortal God for images made to look like mortal man and birds and animals and reptiles."

God provides clues to His existence throughout the Creation that demand both man's observation and his reason. Yet, man's natural response to them tends to be one rooted in emotion and instinct. He chooses to worship the created things (wind, stars, bulls, fish, Gaia, etc.) rather than to reason that all of creation points to one Creator.

The understanding of the existence of universal truth is a logical assertion that it derives from our proper understanding of the Creator. If there is One who made everything then that One has established His rules for the created space. If that One, Who is God, has revealed these rules to man through both the innate understanding He mapped into us when He made us and through His directly speaking to us (Scripture), then these rules form the framework of Truth. This understanding then provides us a true and logical approach for knowing God's will and understanding His character and His nature.

However, we must also realize that God also created emotion in mankind. Does this mean that we must lean on emotion to know and serve Him? How does emotion work with intellect? Should we rely on our emotion to drive us in our worship of God? Is faith merely a facet of emotion? Some believers think so. Church, to some people, is a roller-coaster of joyful highs and sobbing lows that seeks to make one *feel* significant as God's child.

However, I believe that God expects us to apply our intellect to our relationship with Him. As pointed out above, God expects us to discover His existence by looking at the created order and reasoning that there is a Creator. He then expects us to search diligently for Him through His Truth, first of all our innate understanding of Truth, then through His revealed Truth which resonates with that understanding. Hebrews 11:6 demonstrates this twofold approach to God by stating that *"without faith it is impossible to please God, because anyone who comes to him must believe that he exists and that he rewards those who earnestly seek him."*

We cannot approach Church by checking our intellect at the door. The Psalmist did *not* say, "Be still and **feel good** that I am God." No, the inspired writing of David calls us to *"Come and see the works of the Lord"* (Psalm 46:8a) and, *"Be still, and know that I am God."* (Psalm 46:10a). The admonition to *know* requires each person to engage his or her intellect.

As our supreme example, note how Jesus dealt with temptation. He did not say (for example), "I **don't feel** that God wants me to turn these rocks into bread" but by instead He declared definitively that, *"It is written, 'Man does not live on bread alone (but on every word that comes from the mouth of God)'"* (Luke 4:4 in which Jesus referenced Deuteronomy 8:3). His firm stance was based upon knowledge of the Word of God and a reasoning that it would be sin for Him to have made bread out of the rocks to feed Himself when the Father's command (through the leading of the Spirit) was for Him to fast and faithfully face temptation in the desert for forty days (Luke 4:1,2).

On the other hand, we cannot simply negate emotion as some monastic orders have attempted to do over time. God also created emotion and it can also serve along with our other attributes to completely worship and serve Him. We must use our intellect fed by the Word of God with the understanding that intellect devoid of emotion is mere legalism. On the other hand, emotion devoid of intellect and understanding is brute instinct. Only when emotion is coupled with the knowledge of God's power, grace, and love (derived from intellect) can it work to make a man complete.

For example, Jesus expressed emotion in John 11:33-35 where, confronted by the grief of Mary and Martha at the untimely death of their brother Lazarus, He was *"deeply moved in spirit and troubled"* and wept. However, His weeping was also in subjection to His intellect — it was not a senseless crying over loss. His was a reaction to the plight of Fallen man, expressed through the pain of the wailing bystanders, all of whom were victims of sin's sting of death. He was completely aware of Lazarus' place in eternity and what He was about to do.

Likewise, Jesus expressed emotion in the execution of His ministry. See, for example, the emotional language of Matthew 9:36 which declared that He preached and healed the crowds because He *"had compassion on them, because they were harassed and helpless, like sheep without a shepherd."* Once again, it was not just senseless emotion expressing itself. He knew that He came to be the Good Shepherd (John 10:11-18) and to redeem them of their state of sin and fear.

The Barna Group published a study in 2009 in which they sampled the views of U.S. adults on issues of morality.[2] The results indicated that 60% of all adults in the U.S. consider co-habitation to be morally acceptable. Yet, breaking the results down by Christian groupings showed that 12% of Evangelicals and a whopping 49% of "born again Christians" who are not self-described as evangelical, agreed with this view. In the same study, the 33% of this same non-evangelical "born again" group did not consider having an abortion as being morally wrong. Likewise, while 36% of the entire adult population did not consider use of profanity as morally reprehensible, 7% of those within the Evangelical silo and 29% within the same "born again" silo agreed with this assertion. In terms of extra-marital sex (pre-martial and adulterous sexual activity), 7% of the Evangelical group and 35% of the "born again" group consider it as being morally ok. Pornography was also acceptable to 5% of Evangelicals and 28% of non-evangelical "born again" Christians.

Dallas Willard examined the disconnect between those who self-identify as "born-again Christians" in terms of their definition of the word "gospel" only in terms of *justification* (being made right with God) and eliminating the fact that it also defines *regeneration* (a complete repentance and change in direction). What this leads to are the horrifying statistics that we saw above and also in the chapter entitled "What is Truth?" in which believers do not know the fundamentals of the Christian life and do not live according to God's control. He stated, "Widespread acceptance of this interpretation of salvation within the evangelical and conservative churches of North America is what has produced the situation sketched earlier, in which those who profess Christian commitment consistently show little or no behavioral and psychological difference from those who do not."[3]

The problem here is that Christians are prone to let other ideas mix with the Word of God and thus *syncretize*[4] the Christian call with worldly concepts. As the Christian walks behind his or her Savior, it is important to not accept other "gospels." Paul discussed this in his letter to the Galatians (1:6-12) and he stated, *"I am astonished that you are so quickly deserting the one who called you to live in the grace of Christ and are* turning to a different gospel—which is really no gospel at all." This certainly could be the message to today's Church!

So, how can the people ransomed by the grace of Christ stay true to the will of God? God calls His born-again children to begin expressing their new "Spiritual DNA" (for want of a descriptive term) that He bestowed upon them. When we are regenerated through the saving grace of Jesus Christ, we become "new creatures" (2 Corinthians 5:17). In John 1:12,13, the Disciple wrote that,

[Yet] to all who did receive him, to those who believed in his name, he gave the right to become children of God— children born not of natural descent, nor of human decision or a husband's will, but born of God.

The Apostle Paul, writing to the Romans stated:

What shall we say, then? Shall we go on sinning so that grace may increase? By no means! We are those who have died to sin; how can we live in it any longer? Or don't you know that all of us who were baptized into Christ Jesus were baptized into his death? We were therefore buried with him through baptism into death in order that, just as Christ was raised from the dead through the glory of the Father, we too may live a new life. (Romans 6:1-4)

Our "carnal DNA" has been supplanted by a spiritual one. It is just as compelling as the carnal in the sense that we cannot control its expression, only cover it, maybe. We cannot will to change the genetic disposition that defines our height, our hair color, our gender, our race, or our bald spot! Regeneration through the conversion experience should lead each believer to show our new Spiritual traits. This new "Spiritual DNA" is that of our heavenly Father who has defined the life of faith simply as *"I am the LORD your God; consecrate yourselves and be holy, because I am holy."* (Leviticus 11:44a) Jesus demands us to *"[B]e perfect, therefore, as your heavenly Father is perfect."* (Matthew 5:48) The Apostle Paul told Timothy, *"He has saved us and called us to a holy life."* (2 Timothy 1:9a) It is abundantly clear that the Christian walk must begin demonstrating the desires and behaviors of holiness!

With this having been said, why is it that so many Christians live defeated, carnal lives? Why are they wrapped up in sin and, in many cases, are indistinguishable from the members of a lost world? Why do we see such devastating worldviews in self-proclaimed, born-again believers (as we demonstrated in the chapter entitled "What is Truth?"). Why do believers trivialize the name of their Lord and even deny it during the week? How can the reborn "children of God" live disconnected from the Godhead instead of spending significant time in prayer and worship? How can many consider themselves "in Christ" and yet rarely even visit a Church? It is clear that the holy life demands much more than this. It requires quality time spent in the presence of Holy God and within the life of an active congregation (as described in the chapter about the Church). The holy life compels the Christian to be distinguishable from the rest of the population because Holiness is totally different from the profane.

Do not be yoked together with unbelievers. For what do righteousness and wickedness have in common? Or what fellowship can light have with darkness? What harmony is there between Christ and Belial **[or the Devil or false gods or evil]***? Or what does a believer have in common with an unbeliever? What agreement is there between the temple of God and idols? For we are the temple of the living God. As God has said: "I will live with them and walk among them, and I will be their God, and they will be my people." Therefore, "Come out from them and be separate, says the Lord. Touch no unclean thing, and I will receive you." And, "I will be a Father to you, and you will be my sons and daughters, says the Lord Almighty." (2 Corinthians 6:14-18, bold clarifying comment is mine)*

The Apostle Paul summarized the Christian Walk as our constant ongoing voluntary submission to Christ and setting our minds upon the things of God:

Since, then, you have been raised with Christ, **set your hearts on things above***, where Christ is, seated at the right hand of God.* **Set your minds on things above***, not on earthly things. For you died, and your life is now hidden with Christ in God. When Christ, who is your life, appears, then you also will appear with him in glory.*

Put to death, therefore, whatever belongs to your earthly nature: *sexual immorality, impurity, lust, evil desires and greed, which is idolatry. Because of these, the wrath of God is coming. You used to walk in these ways, in the life you once lived. But now you must also* **rid yourselves of all such things as these**: *anger, rage, malice, slander, and filthy language from your lips. Do not lie to each other, since you have taken off your old* *self with its practices and have put on the new self, which is being renewed in knowledge in the image of its Creator. Here there is no Gentile or Jew, circumcised or uncircumcised, barbarian, Scythian, slave or free, but Christ is all, and is in all.*

Therefore, as God's chosen people, holy and dearly loved, **clothe yourselves with compassion, kindness, humility, gentleness and patience.** *Bear with each other and forgive one another if any of you has a grievance against someone.* **Forgive** *as the Lord forgave you. And over all these virtues put on love, which binds them all together in perfect unity.*

Let the peace of Christ rule in your hearts, *since as members of one body you were called to peace. And be thankful.* **Let the message of Christ dwell among you richly** *as you teach and admonish one another with all wisdom through psalms, hymns, and songs from the Spirit, singing to God with gratitude in your hearts. And whatever you do, whether in word or deed,* **do it all in the name of the Lord Jesus**, *giving thanks to God the Father through him. (Colossians 3:1-17, bold emphasis is mine)*

Christ's redemptive work does not give us a "cheap grace" license for us to continue our lives of sin. We were called out from such a life, redeemed through Jesus' selfless and unbelievable sacrificial love, and rendered "not-guilty" by the covering of our sins by His blood. Peter calls us to live in "reverent fear" in 1 Peter 1:17-19 because of the tremendous enormity of the sacrifice it took to cleanse us.

Since you call on a Father who judges each person's work impartially, live out your time as foreigners here in reverent fear. For you know that it was not with perishable things such as silver or gold that you were redeemed from the empty way of life handed down to you from your ancestors, **but with the precious blood of Christ**, *a lamb without blemish or defect. (Bold emphasis is mine)*

Every Christian is called to live a life that is in accordance with the holiness of God Himself. Under no condition can a person separate their state of being redeemed called into a new life of salvation from their day-to-day actions. We must all reflect the character and nature of God in every way; through our speech, our actions, our aspirations, and our testimony we must consistently show that we are our Father's children. This cannot be done, of course, by only our strength and will-power. In fact, a key to the

Christian's walk is to relinquish control to God's control. Every believer should constantly and earnestly pray as David did, *"Direct my footsteps according to your word; let no sin rule over me."* (Psalm 119:133)

The other side of the discussion approaches the Christian walk from the God's perspective. Jesus plainly stated that *"My sheep listen to my voice; I know them, and they follow me. I give them eternal life, and they shall never perish; no one will snatch them out of my hand. My Father, who has given them to me, is greater than all; no one can snatch them out of my Father's hand."* in John 10:27-29. This passage which defines a believer's eternal security[5] is, in a way, a double-edged sword. The positive side is that when we have entrusted our lives to Jesus, He has us firmly and eternally in His grasp and thus no external force can remove us. The "unpleasant" side (to us) is the need for our discipline. In any truly loving parent-child relationship, there must be a consistent application of discipline to prune and focus the child's wild tendencies and thus produce a well-mannered and moral adult. Likewise, as part of being placed in Jesus' hand for safekeeping, God will use discipline to mold and develop His children.

Deuteronomy 8:5,6 states, *"Know then in your heart that as a man disciplines his son, so the Lord your God disciplines you. Observe the commands of the Lord your God, walking in obedience to him and revering him."* This same line of thought is picked up and developed in Hebrews where the inspired author of the book wrote:

In your struggle against sin, you have not yet resisted to the point of shedding your blood. And have you completely forgotten this word of encouragement that addresses you as a father addresses his son? It says, "My son, do not make light of the Lord's discipline, and do not lose heart when he rebukes you, because the Lord disciplines the one he loves, and he chastens everyone he accepts as his son."

Endure hardship as discipline; God is treating you as his children. For what children are not disciplined by their father? If you are not disciplined—and everyone undergoes discipline—then you are not legitimate, not true sons and daughters at all. Moreover, we have all had human fathers who disciplined us and we respected them for it. How much more should we submit to the Father of spirits and live! They disciplined us for a little while as they thought best; but God disciplines us for our good, in order that we may share in his holiness. No discipline seems pleasant at the time, but painful. Later on, however, it produces a harvest of righteousness and peace for those who have been trained by it. (Hebrews 12:4-11)

Our loving heavenly Father applies discipline to us so that we may grow to be spiritually strong. Ultimately, even though it is "not pleasant," it serves to forge our characters towards holiness. Sometimes, if we are attentive in seeking God's will in our lives, His discipline is "soft" and molds us through positive encouragement. However, at other times, if we choose to be rebellious and ignore Him, God uses stronger methods of discipline to get our attention. Do note, however, that the above qualifications of "soft" and "stronger" do not refer to what we would consider minor or major.

Sometimes God will allow some of His most receptive children to go through deep valleys in order to refine and deepen their faith. As we know from the Book of Job, there is no direct, measurable correlation between a person's walk and an affliction such as cancer or the death of a child. Jesus stated in the Sermon on the Mount that God *"causes his sun to rise on the evil and the good, and sends rain on the righteous and the unrighteous."* (Matthew 5:45b) Blessings and hardships and the ratio between them are never meant to be used as a measuring stick of one's closeness to God.

In keeping with this understanding of discipline and our need to walk in the paths of God's holiness, we must understand that we are God's witnesses before the world. Since we are identified with God, our every action will reflect upon Him in the eyes of bystanders, our family, friends, coworkers, and everyone else with whom we interact! With this in mind, let's read God's indictment on the Israelites in Judah found in Ezekiel 22:26:

Her priests do violence to my law and profane my holy things; they do not distinguish between the holy and the common; they teach that there is no difference between the unclean and the clean; and they shut their eyes to the keeping of my Sabbaths, so that I am profaned among them.

Under no condition can the people of God allow themselves to trivialize God's Person, His character, His Law, or His holy institutions. In fact, God specifically demanded that the Priesthood of the Old Testament learn to distinguish between what is holy and what is profane (Leviticus 10:10). Bearing in mind, consider that in the New Testament, through the saving power of the Lord Jesus Christ, born-again Christians are forged into a new Priesthood. Revelation 1:5,6 states, *"To him [Jesus] who loves us and has freed us from our sins by his blood, and has made us to be a kingdom and priests to serve his God and Father."* The same concept emerges from the inspired pen of the Apostle Peter:

But you are a chosen people, a royal priesthood, a holy nation, God's special possession, that you may declare the praises of him who called you out of darkness into his wonderful light. (1 Peter 2:9)

The believers in the Church thus form a God-established "kingdom of priests." Therefore, Christians who form the new priesthood must also distinguish between holiness and that which is profane just as the Levite priests of the Tabernacle were warned in Leviticus. A key skill of the Christian walk is to recognize what is holy and to keep it holy and never to trivialize such crucial elements as God's character and His worship. Likewise, the converse is true: Believers must distinguish what is profane and eliminate it from their lives.

In closing, let us who are called by the name of our Lord consider the following warning very carefully:

Woe to those who call evil good and good evil,
who put darkness for light and light for darkness,
who put bitter for sweet and sweet for bitter. (Isaiah 5:20)

---

[1] See, for example, Colson, Charles The Faith. Grand Rapids, Zondervan, 2008. p 107

[2] http://www.barna.org/barna-update/article/5-barna-update/129-morality-continues-to-decay

[3] Willard, Dallas The Divine Conspiracy. HarperCollins Publishers, New York, 1997. p 43

[4] Syncretism is the practice of taking more than one system of beliefs (normally religious beliefs) and blending them together into something new which doesn't represent either of the original ones. A perfect example of syncretism is found in

how the Old Testament Israelites blended the worship of Baal (fertility idolatry) with the commandments of God (Who, incidentally, in the first commandment mandated that only He should be worshipped (Exodus 20:2-4)) into a miserable, blended, pagan practice.

[5] Eternal Security is best defined as "once saved, always saved." This is one of the passages in which we are assured of God's faithfulness in keeping those who have entrusted their eternal souls to Him. This is a somewhat controversial subject across the spectrum of Christian churches but suffice it to say, the agreement is based upon the definition of "truly entrusting." It is clear that some of this process is human (our wills must be made subject to God) and some is the work of the Holy Spirit (Who convicts us, illuminates the Word to us, Who makes us ready to accept Jesus as Lord and Savior, and ultimately seals us for the day of redemption). Another area that we must consider is the concept of self-removal from salvation, a one-off operation referred to in some passages such as Hebrews 6. This depends upon your reading of "no one" in John 10:29 – does this refer to one's own will also? A complete discussion of this is well beyond the scope of this chapter or even this book but the fact that Scripture provides warnings about such things should give the Christian great pause. We should be careful to not trivialize the grace that holds us and never turn our wills away from God! If there is a reason to be continually faithful to seek Him every moment of every day, *to "demolish arguments and every pretension that sets itself up against the knowledge of God, and we take captive every thought to make it obedient to Christ"* (2 Corinthians 10:5), this is it.

EPILOGUE: CALLED TO PURITY

Throughout this book, I have stressed that we need to **know** what we believe. The thrust of this is specifically to give us a strong foundation for our faith and thus to better be able to defend it whenever it might be attacked. However, the more that we know, the more that we must be accountable to that knowledge. Jesus Himself taught in the parable of the wise manager, *"The servant who knows the master's will and does not get ready or does not do what the master wants will be beaten with many blows. But the one who does not know and does things deserving punishment will be beaten with few blows.* **From everyone who has been given much, much will be demanded; and from the one who has been entrusted with much, much more will be asked."** (Luke 12:47,48, bold emphasis is mine) We can't offer an excuse of ignorance of God's demands upon our lives.

Let us take A. W. Tozer's words to heart in which he wrote, "The doctrine of justification by faith—a biblical truth, and a blessed relief from sterile legalism and unavailing self-effort—has in our time fallen into evil company and been interpreted by man in such a manner as to actually bar men from the knowledge of God. The whole transaction of religious conversion has been made mechanical and spiritless. Faith may now be exercised without a jar to the moral life and without embarrassment to the Adamic ego. Christ may be 'received' without creating any special love for Him in the soul of the receiver. The man is 'saved,' but he is not hungry nor thirsty after God. In fact, he is specifically taught to be satisfied and is encouraged to be content with little."[1] The key concept here is that even in 1948, when Tozer penned these words, there was a rampant exercise of what Dietrich Bonhoeffer called "cheap grace." Grace cannot be taken to be a simple "get-out-of-hell-free card." The conversion experience is rooted in knowledge of sin and salvation, in knowing God and His love, and in a 180 degree turn around in one's views and way of life!

Thus, while the standards of purity are not overtly touched upon in most creedal confessions, they are actually extremely important in the life of the believer. It may be that the early confessors understood the relationship of purity to Christianity and thus did not need to explicitly define such standards. However, **the** standard of all purity of all time was outlined by God in His call to His people in Leviticus 19:2 to obey His commandments. There is no wiggle-room. His requirement is crystal-clear as he said:

"Speak to the entire assembly of Israel and say to them: 'Be holy because I, the Lord your God, am holy.'"

This divine requirement was picked up and brought into the Christian life by the Apostle Paul who said to Timothy:

*"But join with me in suffering for the gospel, by the power of God, **who has saved us and called us to a holy life**—not because of anything we have done but because of his own purpose and grace. This grace was given us in Christ Jesus before the beginning of time, but it has now been revealed through the appearing of our Savior, Christ Jesus, who has destroyed death and has brought life and immortality to light through the gospel." (2 Timothy 1:8b-10, bold emphasis is mine)*

John Stott, in his book Basic Christianity, drew the following conclusion: "So is basic Christianity the belief that Jesus is the Son of God who came to be the Saviour of the world? No, it is not even that. To accept that he is divine, to acknowledge our need of salvation, and to believe in the effectiveness of what he did for us are still not enough. Christianity is not just about what we *believe*; it's also about how we *behave*. Our intellectual belief may be beyond criticism; but we have to put our beliefs into practice."[2] Accepting Jesus as Lord and Savior must change us fundamentally which is why this moment is referred to as a "conversion." Through our actions, our lives have to reflect this incredible change in allegiance that our respective conversions brought.

The key to understanding where this chapter fits into the overall discussion is that even our innate standards of purity (arising from what we call our conscience) are *not* merely man-made "best practices" that came about after careful consideration of morals and mores. Instead, they are rooted in God's perfect character. They are not merely ethics. They actually result from God's very image in us. Our holiness must reflect the Holiness of the Almighty Himself!

It can be argued that being able to defend one's faith and living the Christian life of purity are really two sides of the same coin. Consider the Apostle Paul's words to his "son in the faith," Timothy:

But you, man of God, flee from all this, and pursue righteousness, godliness, faith, love, endurance and gentleness. Fight the good fight of the faith. Take hold of the eternal life to which you were called when you made your good confession in the presence of many witnesses. In the sight of God, who gives life to everything, and of Christ Jesus, who while testifying before Pontius Pilate made the good confession, I charge you to keep this command without spot or blame until the appearing of our Lord Jesus Christ, which God will bring about in his own time—God, the blessed and only Ruler, the King of kings and Lord of lords, who alone is immortal and who lives in unapproachable light, whom no one has seen or can see. To him be honor and might forever. Amen. (2 Timothy 6:11-16)

To Paul, the fight of faith, a life driven by the Spirit, and standing strong in one's testimony are all part and parcel of the Christian's calling. In fact, a few sentences later, Paul specifically admonishes Timothy to *"...guard what has been entrusted to your care. Turn away from godless chatter and the opposing ideas of what is falsely called knowledge, which some have professed and in so doing have departed from the faith."* (2 Timothy 6:20,21) There can be no doubt here that the Apostle of Grace believed strongly in defending the Truth of the Gospel against erosive controversies. In fact, his words to Timothy must become our marching orders also:

Do your best to present yourself to God as one approved, a worker who does not need to be ashamed and who correctly handles the word of truth. (2 Timothy 2:15)

The Christian mandate is to stand firm upon God's Word and to use it correctly and appropriately. In order to "correctly handle the word of truth" it is imperative to know the Word inside and out, backwards and forwards. Only by so doing can we properly defend the faith against misuse of Scripture and heretical statements. We **must** dedicate ourselves to knowing God's Word and knowing Him through it. The sure way to recognize counterfeit is to intimately know the real thing. It is well known that the people who have to guard against counterfeit currency (e.g. bank tellers, US Secret Service and Treasury agents) spend much of their training time handling and smelling the real bills over and over before fake bills are slipped in. This works because the trainees become so familiar with real currency that they almost develop an instinctive recognition of false bills. So should our understanding of the real Word of God and our relationship with God Himself be so that anyone trying to introduce something fake will be immediately obvious!

This must also be true for our Christian walk. Once we have come to know God intimately and to understand His aversion to sin, how can we willingly decide to engage in sinful acts? How can we dare to play a justification game with what we know is wrong (e.g. "Since God is love, why would He be against my girlfriend and me living together and expressing 'love?'")? How can we cheapen God's grace and Jesus' suffering on Calvary by playing a legalistic cause-and-effect game and in deliberately making up our minds ahead of time to serve our carnal desires with a predetermined expectation of full forgiveness afterwards? The Apostle Paul stated clearly, *"Do not lie to each other, since you have taken off your old self with its practices."* (Colossians 3:9) Our practices must correspond to our new, redeemed, and regenerated selves! Peter said, under the Holy Spirit's guidance:

Dear friends, I urge you, as foreigners and exiles, to **abstain from sinful desires**, *which wage war against your soul. Live such* **good lives** *among the pagans that, though they accuse you of doing wrong, they may see your good deeds and glorify God on the day he visits us. (1 Peter 2:11,12. bold emphasis is mine)*

Of course, we must *purpose* in our hearts to follow God and to live properly for Him but our strength to overcome comes from Him through the Holy Spirit's indwelling. Our carnal desires will continue to tug upon our hearts until we leave this world and are given our glorified bodies at the Resurrection. This implies that our lives must be tied closely to God and that we must constantly seek both His will and His Presence through prayer. Galatians 5:24,25 outlines this by stating, *"Those who belong to Christ Jesus have crucified the flesh with its passions and desires. Since we live by the Spirit, let us keep in step with the Spirit."* Jesus admonished Peter and His disciples on the night He was betrayed :

"Watch and pray so that you will not fall into temptation. The spirit is willing, but the flesh is weak." (Matthew 26:41)

In the letter to the Church at Colossae, Paul outlined the principles of Christian living:

Since, then, you have been raised with Christ, set your hearts on things above, where Christ is, seated at the right hand of God. Set your minds on things above, not on earthly things. For you died, and your life is now hidden with Christ in God. When Christ, who is your life, appears, then you also will appear with him in glory.

Put to death, therefore, whatever belongs to your earthly nature: sexual immorality, impurity, lust, evil desires and greed, which is idolatry. Because of these, the wrath of God is coming. You used to walk in these ways, in the life you once lived. But now you must also rid yourselves of all such things as these: anger, rage, malice, slander, and filthy language from your lips. Do not lie to each other, since you have taken off your old self with its practices and have put on the new self, which is being renewed in knowledge in the image of its Creator. (Colossians 3:1-10)

As Christians, emblazoned with the Name of the One who died for our sins, let us covenant one with the other to live lives that bring glory to God. Let us not be misled by Satan, false teachers, or our fleshly desires into living defeated lives. In closing, may these words of Paul spur us on to rededicate ourselves to purity: *"Therefore, since we have these promises, dear friends, let us purify ourselves from everything that contaminates body and spirit, perfecting holiness out of reverence for God."* (2 Corinthians 7:1) Amen, and Amen!

---

[1] Tozer, A. W. The Pursuit of God. Harrisburg, Christian Publications, Inc., 1948, Kindle e-book, location 82 of 1179.

[2] Stott, John <u>Basic Christianity</u>. Downers Grove: Intervarsity Press, 2008, Kindle e-book, location 145 of 2515.

Study Group Questions and Discussion Points

1. Introducing this Book
    a. Why are mainstream churches suffering today? Why is this bad for the Church?
    b. How can we guard against being misled by false teachings?
    c. Does your home church have a statement of beliefs? If so, what does it say?
    d. What made creeds effective?
    e. In your words, why should each Christian spend time developing a strong Theological position?
    f. Are creeds a substitute for Scripture?

2. Early Confessions, Hymns and Creeds in Scripture
    a. What, in your words, are confessions?
    b. Are Christian confessions true at all times, under all conditions, and in all places?
    c. What is the earliest and most basic Christian affirmation according to Shirley Guthrie?
    d. What does "Christological" mean?
    e. Is the Trinity merely a man-made construct or is it defined in the Bible?
    f. What does "Doxology" mean?
    g. What does "Eschatological" mean?

3. The Development of Creeds
    a. What are Binatarianism and Trinitarianism?
    b. In your words, describe what a creed is?
    c. Why was the "Apostle's Creed" developed?

d. Why is it dangerous theologically to not believe or understand that Jesus was born as a 100% man?
   e. Why was the "Niceno-Constantinople" creed developed?
   f. Describe the heresy that Gnosticism introduced to the early Church?
   g. What was the heresy of Arianism?
   h. Memorize one of the creeds in this chapter.

4. Understanding Theological Tension
   a. What is "Theological Tension?"
   b. Why is it important to recognize Theological topics that must be held in tension?
   c. How important is it to understand Jesus' nature in terms of tension?
   d. Where do you fall in the ratio of Jesus' divine and human natures? Have you changed your mind from how you thought before?
   e. Can you see the need to maintain tension in the following concepts?
      i. The Holy Trinity?
      ii. Man's and God's actions in the process of Salvation?

5. Authority
   a. What happens when there is no ultimate source of authority?
   b. Where should our quest for Authority begin in Theology?
   c. What is the physical tool that God has provided us so that we can understand Him?
   d. Do you believe that the Bible is completely Authoritative on all that it says about God? Why or why not?
   e. Has Jesus delegated authority to His Church? Can you defend this position from the Bible?
   f. What are the dangers of second-guessing the validity or Authority of any part of Scripture?

g. Should a prophet stand in your midst and prophesy something that overrides the Word of God along with doing several miracles be considered legitimate and believable? Why or why not?

6. The Doctrine of God and His Revelation
    a. Do you agree with the statement that "sin is only sin because it is sin against God?"
    b. We started with the declaration that God exists because we are Christians and must have already made this discovery. Is there Scripture that requires that we have to make this step of faith anyway if we are seeking God?
    c. What are the two distinct types of God's revelation?
    d. Which type of revelation is more specific and direct?
    e. Do you understand and agree with the point that God's revelation is always Person-to-person? Do you want to give your testimony about your first meeting God "face-to-face?"
    f. How did God supremely reveal Himself to us?
    g. Can you describe the concept of general revelation?
    h. Imagine the experience of Moses, Joshua, or Isaiah. Would this be an awe-inspiring experience?
    i. How does the issue of Sin get dealt with when we come face-to-face with God? Can we fix it?
    j. Do you agree with the assertion that "since Jesus has been revealed to the world, all encounters with God are mediated through Him?" Why or why not?

7. "What is Truth?"
    a. Do you agree that the understanding of absolute truth is under attack today?
    b. What is cultural relativism?
    c. How is it that a wishy-washy understanding of Truth can affect the Church?

d. Do you have a Biblical worldview or are you influenced by cultural relativism?
   e. How is Jesus the Truth personified?
   f. How many different ways are there to God? Can you defend your position?
   g. Where does a Christian's worldview derive from?
   h. In your own words, describe why a Christian cannot live two different lives: a Christian one and a secular one.
   i. Does God call His children out of their former lives and into a new one that reflects His light?
   j. How does a solid understanding of absolute Truth and the development of a strong Christian worldview help us to make sense out of life?

8. The Bible: The Written Word of God
   a. Should the Bible be accepted at face value?
   b. Are there dangers in picking and choosing what to believe and what not to believe?
   c. What is the main purpose of the Bible?
   d. What does "canonization" mean?
   e. What is believed to have been the first of the gospel accounts to be written?
   f. What are the three languages that the Bible was written in?
   g. What is your favorite Bible version and why?

9. God's Character and Nature
   a. What are some of God's attributes?
   b. What are some characteristics of holiness?
   c. Describe God's wrath and what is it tied to.
   d. How can we determine that the Son is the One who was the agent of Creation?
   e. Can God tolerate evil? Why or why not?
   f. Discuss God's love and why is it the fountain of God's grace.

g. Since God is eternal, He created everything. Did He create the Holy Spirit? Did He create Jesus? Why or why not?
h. What holds the universe together?

10. The Doctrine of the Trinity
    a. Is the Doctrine of the Trinity difficult for you to understand?
    b. Describe what happens if you overstress the Godhead's threeness over its oneness.
    c. Describe what happens if you overstress the Godheads oneness over its threeness.
    d. Can you show the Trinity co-existing and co-operating in the Bible?
    e. What is Binatarianism? Is this a stage in the early Church towards understanding the Trinity?
    f. Discuss the Trinatarianism in the Great Commission.
    g. What is the key concept that we must all understand about Scripture that will prevent us from being misled by heresy and heretical groups?
    h. Why do you think that every Christian should dedicate a fair amount of their time into reading all of the Bible?
    i. Are there any books in the Bible that you have not read? Why or why not?

11. The Doctrine of Man
    a. How would you answer the Psalmist's question, "What is man that God thinks of him?"
    b. How is man's creation different from the creation of everything else?
    c. Does man still have God's image in him? What do you think?
    d. What was the commandment that God gave the newly-created man and woman?

    e. How is man different from the other animals including apes?
    f. Is man's fleshly body evil? Why or why not?
    g. Why was woman created? What model of government does God use to hold man and woman accountable to Him?
    h. How does God view the unborn, as just a mass of tissue or as a person?

12. The Doctrine of Sin
    a. What is the root cause of evil in the creation?
    b. What is the opposite of God?
    c. God's holiness separates Him from sin and evil. True or false?
    d. What were the consequences of the first sin in the Garden of Eden?
    e. Is there sin without God in the mix?
    f. What is the price required to pay for sin, any sin?
    g. Since Christians have been saved by Jesus' blood, is it OK to sin whenever they feel it is justified since they are under salvation? Why or why not?
    h. Does Satan's power overcome God's? How is Satan different from God?

13. The Person of Jesus
    a. In your own words, how does Jesus make the Invisible God visible?
    b. Why did Jesus "become flesh?"
    c. Was the Holy Spirit Jesus' father in the Incarnation? In your words, what happened then?
    d. Why is it important that Jesus lived sinlessly, growing up "in favor with God and man?"
    e. Did Mary lose sight of Jesus' mission? Why or why not?
    f. When did the road to the Cross begin in earnest?

g. What were the three major temptations for Jesus to duck the Cross?
h. The claims of Jesus either are the claims of God or those of a madman. What factors allow you to see Him to be the Son of God, as He claims?
i. What happened at the Cross? How would you describe the concept of Jesus becoming a *substitutionary* sacrifice?
j. Why is the Resurrection important and why can we not consider it a "myth" as some theologians do?
k. What is Jesus' ultimate role? Was He merely to be a wise teacher or philosopher?
l. Can you think of concrete examples in the Bible in which Jesus had fellowship with people like you and me?
m. Jesus came to be both the Suffering Servant and the Conquering King. Briefly describe the when and how of both aspects of His ministry.

14. The Doctrine of the Atonement
    a. What is the lie that Satan whispers into every human ear? If you believe that lie, how does it affect your choices in this life?
    b. Describe some ways that God gave grace to Adam and Eve after the Fall.
    c. What are the criteria for the Doctrine of Substitution?
    d. Why do some people think that the Old Testament is brutal?
    e. Did the Old Testament sacrifices clean people or is there another factor that we must take into account?
    f. How did Jesus serve as the ultimate and final sacrifice?
    g. How does Jesus fulfill the curse pronounced on Satan in Genesis 3:15?
    h. The saying goes that "God does not have grandchildren." What does this mean in terms of Salvation?

i. How would you describe "believing in Jesus?" Is it a simple mental exercise or do you think there is something else involved?

15. The Holy Spirit
    a. Is the Holy Spirit a neuter force?
    b. What are some of the personality traits of the Holy Spirit?
    c. Is the Holy Spirit God? Why or why not?
    d. How does the Holy Spirit work in the realm of prayer?
    e. Discuss the Holy Spirit's marking of believers.
    f. Why was the baptism of Jesus a mark of God's authority on His mission?
    g. What are the fruit of the Spirit? What can we do to improve the yield of the fruit?
    h. Does the Spirit give gifts to believers?
    i. What do you think about the "sign gifts" like tongues and prophesy?

16. The Doctrine of the Church
    a. What are some of the New Testament names for the Church? Does one of these names speak to you specially?
    b. Is the Church the New Testament equivalent of the Old Testament Temple?
    c. What is the mandate of the Church?
    d. What are some characteristics of the Church?
    e. What is the Primacy of Peter? Do you agree or disagree with it?
    f. What does the word "catholic" mean in the Niceno-Constantinople creed?
    g. Who enables the Church to function?
    h. Do you agree or disagree with Church discipline? Is it Biblical? Can it be misapplied or misused?
    i. Who owns the Church?
    j. Is tithing an "out of date" practice? Why or why not?

17. The Eternal Realm
    a. Who owns all the Eternal Realm?
    b. How do you visualize Heaven? Is your view in accordance with Scripture?
    c. Where did the Evil in the world come from?
    d. Is Satan just a comic character or a figment of man's overactive imagination? Why or why not?
    e. What are the big lies that were foisted upon the human race in the Fall?
    f. Is there a literal Hell? How would you describe this place? Is your view in accordance with Scripture?
    g. Does God rub His hands with glee as He dispatches fallen souls to the depths of Hell?
    h. Is this world eternal? If not, what is going to happen to it?
    i. Why is belief in a literal bodily resurrection of Jesus important to our faith?
    j. What are the three major Biblically-sound views of the Rapture? Which one do you believe in today and why?

18. The Christian Walk
    a. Describe the two Commissions that God has given to man?
    b. How does intellect and emotion work together to understand God's Word and to worship Him?
    c. Can we leave our intellect at the door as we enter Church? In other words, is faith something emotional?
    d. Is there any evidence that Jesus used emotion and intellect in balance one with the other?
    e. Do you think that being "born-again" places a responsibility of change in our behavior on us? Why or why not?
    f. What is "Syncretism?" Can you give an example of syncretism in today's Christian practices?

g. How is it that Christians live defeated and carnal lives? Should the life that God calls His Church to live be different?
h. Why does God discipline His children? Have you ever faced His discipline and come out from it more refined and holy?
i. Prayerfully consider areas in your life in which you may be trivializing God. Will you hand these over into the hands of your loving Father to deal with?

Appendix: Choosing and Using a Bible

Since the Bible is your "sword of the Spirit" (Ephesians 6:16), it makes sense to have one that you read consistently and are very familiar with. A Bible must be read daily and you should use strategies that enable you to have full coverage of all the books over some finite period of time. I personally use several different strategies during different years to mix things up and see Scripture in different contexts. One option is to read it from cover to cover, several chapters per day over the course of a year. Another one is to use a dual-Testament reading plan in which you read chapters from both the Old and New Testaments every day throughout a year. Another is to use a chronological Bible and read it through (e.g. the Daily Bible or the Narrated Bible) which brings a new perspective to the Word as you see events unfold in order. I also will use mixed approaches such as reading the Gospels, the Torah, Acts, Joshua through Chronicles, the letters of Paul, the Prophets, the general letters of the New Testament, Psalms through Ecclesiastes, Revelation, then pick up the other books of the Old Testament.

The Bible that you choose for your daily use should be a solid committee-translated Bible. I urge you to read the translators' preface and/or notes because most of the time this will help you understand how each committee approached logical problems of translation that come about from merely moving from one language to another. It is naive to think that translation is simply a matter of converting one word in the source language to a word in the destination language. Words and phrases contain shades of meaning that cannot be easily translated mechanically, sometimes because they have deeper cultural significance.

The King James Version (KJV) is a solid translation that certainly is very technical in nature. The language used is a little old to our modern day ears, but if you know the meanings of the words and the pattern of the sentences, it is a fine version.

Since 1611, there have been several others that have attempted to bring the languages and idiomatic expressions underlying the Bible (Hebrew, Aramaic, and Greek) to life in modern languages as well as to keep abreast of the exciting textual finds uncovered by archeology (such as the Dead Sea Scrolls and the discovery of many earlier New Testament manuscripts). In the English realm, there have been the Revised Standard Version (RSV), American Standard Version (ASV), the New American Standard Version (NASB), the New International Version (NIV), and the New King James Version (NKJV) to name some. Each of these has approached translation in as transparent a way as possible but each have their own biases since translating languages cannot be done on a one-to-one word-to-word basis.

There are other specialty Bibles such as paraphrases (e.g. The Living Bible (TLB)), simple English Bibles for the young and those who are not proficient in reading (e.g. Today's English Version (TEV)), and what I call study-aid Bibles (e.g. the Amplified Version) which attempt to give an English reader a better sense of the richness of the words underlying the translated text. These are handy for specialized purposes and even for helping grasp a concept but I don't recommend them for your daily use.

A good way to familiarize yourself with different styles of phrasing in Bibles as you attempt to make a decision of which one you prefer is to use BibleGateway (www.BibleGateway.com). They have, online, umpteen different versions of Bibles including Bibles in other languages such as Spanish, Chinese, and Russian. It actually is one of my favorite sites for quick lookups of Scripture by passage reference or by searching keywords. One truly wonderful feature that they added is the ability to add parallel Bibles so that you can see, side by side, the same text in different versions. This can be very helpful in understanding difficult passages as well as in evaluating which version resonates better with your language skills.

With the advent of the notepad/tablet computing devices such as Android[1], iPad[2], and now Windows 8[3], it is now possible to carry powerful copies of the Bible with you in an electronic form. My caveat is that this does not replace your printed Bible completely. You should have a printed Bible which you devote yourself to reading, highlighting, and affixing notes when appropriate. I also strongly believe in using the printed Bible at Church and am on the fence about using them from the pulpit. However, the electronic Bible is handy for permitting one to easily read while commuting by bus or airplane and for other lightweight uses. One powerful argument for the notepad versions is that the backlighting and font sizes can be changed at will and thus accommodate changing light conditions especially for those of us whose vision is marginal. I personally use an Android™ tablet and have found that Ernzo.com's LiveBible is a wonderfully maturing product that allows me to switch versions or languages easily. This is, of course, one of many but one of its draws for me is the fact that it allows full download of any of its supported Bibles for use while away from the Internet. Finally, a word of caution is in order. If you plan to use your tablet for a talk or from the pulpit, make sure that it is fully charged. You don't want your "sword of the Spirit" to die midway through your speaking! That is one thing to say about a printed Bible: it won't run out of battery power or "crash" ever.

As you pick a printed Bible, I urge you to look at one of the good study Bibles. These contain several good Bible study aids (such as cross references and alternate readings). Of lesser importance, but useful anyway, are the study notes at the bottom of the page referring to the text. It is important to realize that these *are of less value that the Scriptural text itself and the prompting of the Holy Spirit*. Bear in mind that these notes are derived by mere mortals and are not the definitive Word of God. It is easy to fall into the trap of using these as "gospel" when they are not! While they can be extremely helpful and may be right on point in most cases, there are times when a particular bias in the note's author can mislead someone completely! Let discernment and your growing understanding of the whole of Scripture guide you.

Let me close this discussion about study Bibles by showing you some examples and point out a few of their features. First, here is a sample of Scripture taken from <u>The NIV Study Bible</u> (Zondervan Bible Publishers, Grand Rapids, Michigan. 1985)

[14] But as for you, continue in what you have learned and have become convicted of, because you know those from whom you learned it,^{i} [15] and how from infancy^j you have known the holy Scriptures,^{k} which are able to make you wise^l for salvation through faith in Christ Jesus.	**3:14** *i* 2Ti 1:13 **3:15** *j* 2Ti 1:5 *k* Jn 5:39 *l* Dt 4:6; Ps 119:98,99 **3:16** *m* 2Pe 1:20,21 *n* Ro 4:23,24 *o* Dt 29:29	[16] All Scripture is God-breathed^m and is useful for teaching,^{n} rebuking, correcting and training in righteousness^o, [17] so that the man of God^p may be thoroughly equipped for every good work.^{q}

3:17 p 1Ti 6:11 q 2Ti 2:21	

3:15 *from infancy you have known the holy Scriptures.* A Jewish boy formally began to study the OT when he was five years old. Timothy was taught at home by his mother and grandmother even before he reached this age.

3:16 *All Scripture.* The primary reference is to the OT, since some of the NT books had not even been written at this time. (See 1Ti 5:18; 2Pe 3:15-16 for indications that some NT books – or material ultimately included in the NT – were already considered equal in authority to the OT Scriptures.) *God-breathed.* Paul affirms God's active involvement in the writing of Scripture, an involvement so powerful and pervasive that what is written is the infallible and authoritative word of God (see 2Pe 1:20-21 and notes).

Now let us look at an example from a different study Bible using a different translation version. This is excerpted from the MacArthur Study Bible (NKJV) published by Word Bibles, Nashville, Tennessee, 1997.

¹⁴ But you must ˢcontinue in the things which you have learned and been assured of, knowing from whom you have learned *them*, ¹⁵ and that from childhood you have known ᵗthe Holy Scriptures, which are able to make you wise for salvation through faith which is in Christ Jesus.	**14** ˢ 2 Tim 1:13;Titus 1:9 **15** ᵗ Ps 119:97-104;John 5:39 **16** ᵘ [2 Pet 1:20] ᵛ Rom 4:23;15:4 ³*training, discipline* **17** ʷ 1 Tim 6:11 ˣ 2 Tim 2:21;Heb 13:21	¹⁶ "All Scripture *is* given by inspiration of God, ᵛand *is* profitable for doctrine, for reproof, for correction, for ³instruction in righteousness, ¹⁷ ʷthat the man of God may be complete, ˣthoroughly equipped for every good work.

3:14 from whom you have learned. See note on 1:13. To further encourage Timothy to stand firm, Paul reminds him of his godly heritage. The plural form of the pronoun "whom" suggests Timothy was indebted not just to Paul, but to others as well (1:5).

3:15 from childhood. Lit. "from infancy." Two people whom Timothy was especially indebted to were his mother and his grandmother (see note on 1:5) who faithfully taught him the truths of OT Scripture from his earliest childhood, so that he was ready to receive the gospel when Paul preached it. **you have known the Holy Scriptures.** Lit. "the sacred writings." A common designation of the OT by Greek-speaking Jews. wise for salvation. The OT Scriptures pointed to Christ (John 5:37-39) and revealed the need for faith in God's promises (Genesis 15:6;cf. Rom 4:1-3). This, they were able to lead people to acknowledge their sin and need for justification in Christ (Galatians 3:24). Salvation is brought by the Holy Spirit using the Word. *See notes on Rom 10:14-17;Eph 5:26; 1 Pet 1:23-25.* **faith which is in Christ Jesus.** Though not understanding all the details involved (cf. 1 Pet 1:10-12), OT believers including Abraham (John 8:56) and Moses (Hebrews 11:26) looked forward to the coming of the Messiah (Isaiah 7:14;9:6) and His atonement for sin (Isaiah 53:5,6). So did Timothy, who responded when he heard the gospel.

3:16 All Scripture. Grammatically similar Gr. constructions (Romans 7:12;2 Cor 10:10; 1 Tim 1:15;2:3;4:4) argue persuasively that the translation of "all Scripture is given by inspiration..." is accurate. Both OT and NT Scripture are included (*see notes on 2 Pet 3:15,16,* which identify NT writings as Scripture). **given by inspiration of God.** Lit. "breathed out by God." Or "God-breathed." Sometimes God told the Bible writers the exact words to say (e.g. Jer 1:9), but more often He used their minds, vocabularies, and experienced to produce His own perfect infallible, inerrant Word (*see notes on 1 Thess 2:13;Heb 1:1;2 Pet 1:20,21*). It is important to note that inspiration applies only to the original autographs of Scripture, not the Bible writers; there are no inspired Scripture writers, only inspired Scripture. So identified is God with His Word that when Scripture speaks, God speaks (cf. Rom 9:17;Gal 3:8). Scripture is called "the oracles of God" (Romans 3:2;1 Pet 4:11), and cannot be altered (John 10:35;Matt 5:17,18;Luke 16:17;Rev 22:18,19). **doctrine.** The divine instruction or doctrinal content of both the OT and the NT (cf. 2:15;Acts 20:18,20,21,27;1 Cor 2:14-16;Col 3:16;1 John 2:20,24,27). The Scripture provides the comprehensive and complete body of divine truth necessary for life and godliness. Cf. Ps 119:97-105. **reproof.** Rebuke for wrong behavior or wrong belief. The Scripture exposes sin (Hebrews 4:12,13) that can then be dealt with through confession and repentance. **correction.** The restoration of something to its proper condition. The word appears only here in the NT, but was used in extrabiblical Gr. of righting a fallen object, or helping back to their feet those who had stumbled. Scripture not only rebukes wrong behavior, but also points the way back to godly living. Cf. Ps 119:9-11;John 15:1,2. **instruction in righteousness.** Scripture provides positive training ("instruction: originally referred to training a child) in godly behavior, not merely rebuke and correction of wrong behavior (Acts 20:32; 1 Tim 4:6; 1 Pet 2:1,2).

3:17 man of God. A technical term for an official preacher of divine truth. See note on 1 Tim 6:11. **complete.** Capable of doing everything one is called to do (cf. Col 2:10). **thoroughly equipped.** Enabled to meet all the demands of godly ministry and righteous living. The Word not only accomplishes this in the life of the man of God but in all who follow him (Ephesians 4:11-13).

Both of these examples illustrate some of the best parts of study Bibles. The center-column contains cross-references that may be of interest to better understand a concept or word. Notice that generally the word or conceptual block is marked with a letter or number which reflects in the center-column. Arrayed along the bottom are the study notes. Notice that sometimes, a word or phrase may have an alternate rendition that the translators deemed important enough to include. These are generally marked with a letter or number and are reflected either in the center-column or at the bottom of the page. A good example of this is found in the NKJV text of 2 Tim 3:16 above. The word "instruction" is marked and an indication is included that the underlying Greek word has the flavor of "training" or "discipline."

Another handy tool that is included in many study Bibles is a concordance. This tool permits the user to look up a word and find references where that word is used. Generally, most Bibles do not have an "exhaustive" concordance[4] which lists *every* instance of the word in the specific translation, however what they do provide proves to be very useful in practice. I do counsel every devoted Bible student invest in an exhaustive concordance at some point in his or her life but this is becoming less important with the electronic searches online and in computer Bible software.

As you read your Bible, I urge you to not be afraid to make notes in it. God wants you to understand His Word and will not object to you making notes of things that speak to you about a passage. These notes may reflect someone's excellent interpretation of that passage or the Holy Spirit's prompting you to make some special connection. It is my opinion that you should make such notes neatly using a pencil or special Bible pen along the margins of your Bible.

I also urge you to keep track of crucial dates during your Christian walk in the front of your Bible. Things like baptisms, miraculous events, inspiring moments, and such can be powerful testimonials to you as you struggle with the issues of life. These can be helpful to see the activity of God during your own walk. I once heard a funeral sermon preached in which the pastor used the decedent's Bible and led us through some of her favorite verses, in some cases touching on her margin notes, and he tied them to events in her life. Needless to say, it was one of the most marvelous glimpses of a life spent searching God's Word and a challenge to all of us to be just as diligent.

Finally, do not be afraid to highlight words, phrases, or passages to make them memorable or readily recognizable. There are special Bible highlighters that will not bleed through the delicate paper of a Bible. I personally recommend the crayon or gel highlighters which will never bleed through. Some people color-code their references (e.g. red is grace, yellow is salvation, etc.) . This system works well if you can keep up with your color coding. The system that I use is to use a different color each time I read a passage and recognize something new. In this way, years later, I can see the tracks of the Holy Spirit's prompting me at different times.

---

[1] Android is a trademark of Google, Inc.
[2] iPad is a trademark of Apple, Inc.
[3] Windows is a trademark of Microsoft, Inc.
[4] An exhaustive concordance touches on every word and every place it is used in the Bible under a specific translation. An example of one of these is Strong's Exhaustive Concordance.

INDEX

"

"general" revelation · 27
"special" revelation · 27

A

Abraham · 17, 24, 77, 82, 114
adam · 89, 100
Adam · 23, 63, 89, 90, 94, 95, 97, 100, 110, 111, 112, 113, 114
Adam and Eve · 63, 95, 110
anarchy · 27
Angel Gabriel · 118
Angels · 12
Anglican · *See* Church of England
Apostle Paul · 9, 17, 29, 32, 43, 50, 52, 53, 55, 63, 64, 87, 108, 115, 124, 126, 142, 143, 147, 153, 156, 158, 161, 168, 174, 177, 181, 182, 190, 191, 192
Apostle Peter · 32, 108, 186
Apostle's Creed · 15, 19
Aramaic · 62
arguments · 86, 187
Arian · 19
Arianism · 19, 20, 24
Ark of the Covenant · 134
Armenian · 24
Articles of Religion · 5
Ascension · 128, 147, 157
Assemblies of God · 4
atonement · 6, 7, 17, 18, 72, 89, 105, 113, 114, 118, 131, 132, 135, 136, 137, 138, 162
Atonement · 11, 50, 96, 105, 124, 131, 134, 201, *See* atonement
attribute · 70, 73, 77, 92

attributes · 69, 70, 71, 77, 79, 92, 98, 179
Augsburg Confession · 5
authority · 6, 7, 27, 28, 29, 30, 32, 33, 50, 55, 63, 64, 65, 83, 95, 122, 145, 146, 152, 155, 156, 196, 202

B

baptismal · 15
baptized · 2, 82, 121, 139, 145, 153, 181
Barna Group · 47, 180
beliefs · 5, 7, 15, 16, 23, 55, 86
believers · 2, 3, 6, 7, 18, 28, 32, 52, 59, 76, 85, 93, 178, 180, 182, 186
Bethlehem · 36, 122
Bible · 1, 5, 6, 7, 23, 27, 29, 30, 31, 33, 48, 51, 55, 56, 57, 63, 65, 66, 67, 73, 81, 86, 88, 107
Biblical · 18, 30, 33, 56, 63, 64, 66, 67, 91
Billy Graham · 30, 149
Binatarian · 83
Binitarianism · 15, 84
blessing · 11, 43, 84, 85, 91, 99, 111, 121, 159
blood · 16, 44, 84, 92, 93, 102, 105, 109, 112, 113, 117, 118, 122, 124, 132, 133, 134, 135, 136, 138, 142, 153, 154, 155, 157, 161, 162, 167, 173, 183, 184, 186, 200
boast · 71, 99
book of life · 18, 128, 169, 174
born · 1, 9, 16, 24, 48, 73, 91, 98, 100, 103, 114, 180, 181, 182, 186
born again · 180
brokenness · 105

213

C

C. S. Lewis · 123, 126
Charles Stanley · 141, 158
Christ · 1, 2, 4, 6, 7, 9, 10, 11, 12, 13, 15, 16, 17, 18, 19, 20, 21, 23, 27, 28, 30, 36, 37, 38, 40, 42, 43, 44, 47, 49, 50, 51, 52, 53, 57, 59, 60, 64, 69, 78, 82, 84, 85, 87, 91, 92, 98, 99, 105, 115, 116, 124, 126, 133, 136, 137, 138, 139, 140, 143, 144, 146, 151, 152, 153, 155, 156, 157, 158, 159, 162, 166, 170, 171, 173, 174, 175, 177, 180, 181, 182, 183, 186, 187, 189, 190, 191, 192, 193
Christian · i, 1, 3, 4, 6, 7, 9, 10, 11, 12, 13, 20, 21, 23, 27, 30, 32, 48, 49, 50, 51, 52, 53, 59, 60, 81, 91, 92, 102, 103, 112, 116, 129, 177, 180, 181, 182, 183, 184, 186, 187
Christian walk · 1, 4, 181, 184, 186
Christians · 2, 3, 4, 5, 9, 10, 11, 12, 13, 47, 48, 52, 55, 59, 62, 67, 69, 108, 109, 180, 181, 186
Christological · 11, 12, 13
Chuck Colson · 48, 87, 115, 151, 154, 156, 158, 160, 162, 177
Church · vii, viii, 1, 2, 3, 4, 5, 6, 7, 9, 11, 16, 18, 19, 20, 28, 29, 30, 32, 42, 49, 50, 51, 52, 53, 55, 57, 59, 60, 61, 63, 65, 81, 98, 99, 103, 116, 119, 126, 128, 138, 142, 148, 149, 151, 152, 153, 154, 155, 156, 157, 158, 159, 160, 161, 162, 163, 168, 175, 176, 178, 179, 181, 182, 186, 193, 195, 196, 197, 199, 202, 203, 204
Church of England · 4
churches · See Church
Comforter · See Holy Spirit
commandments · 29, 30, 78, 93, 112
community · 88, 95
conception · 100, 102
confession · 4, 9, 10, 11, 12, 13, 16, 20, 76
confessional · 1, 5, 9
confessions · 5, 6, 7, 9, 11, 15, 20
Confessions · 5, 9
constant of gravitation · 76

conviction · 123, 124, 160
correcting · 29, 51, 56
Counselor · See Holy Spirit
covenant · 58, 77, 79, 93
created · 6, 11, 20, 24, 25, 49, 73, 75, 76, 77, 78, 86, 89, 90, 92, 95, 96, 97, 98, 100, 101, 102, 103, 105, 106, 108, 109, 110, 177, 178, 179
creation · 10, 24, 27, 69, 74, 76, 84, 89, 90, 91, 93, 94, 96, 97, 100, 101, 102, 106, 177, 178
Creation · 7, 27, 35, 37, 38, 44, 49, 50, 51, 53, 63, 74, 75, 76, 85, 90, 91, 96, 99, 106, 107, 109, 118, 128, 137, 143, 165, 167, 171, 177, 198
Creator · 27, 47, 50, 57, 73, 75, 76, 94, 178, 183
credentials · 133
creedal · 4, 6, 7, 15
creeds · 1, 4, 5, 7, 9, 11, 15, 20
cults · 1, 2, 3, 4, 7, 20, 86
curse · 87, 93, 137, 159, 201

D

Dale Moody · 69, 89, 112, 152
Dallas Willard · 65, 180
Daniel · 58, 61
David · 53, 70, 77, 100, 179, 184
death · 9, 10, 16, 17, 18, 24, 25, 82, 92, 111, 112, 113, 115, 116, 179, 181, 182, 185
denominations · 2, 4
disciples · 4, 12, 28, 31, 60, 78, 85, 87, 106
discipleship · 2
discipline · 29, 102, 184, 185
divine · 23, 24, 25, 31, 69, 94, 97, 177
Divine · 25, 67, 186
divinity · 20
Doctrine of Substitution · 133
doctrines · 7, 13
dogma · 55

E

Earth · 6, 18, 76, 77, 89, 90, 96, 107, 108, 177
ecclesiastical · 151
Egypt · 56, 64
empty tomb · 17
End Times · *See* Eschatology
Episcopalians · 4
Eschatology · 7
eschaton · 128
eternal · 3, 12, 18, 20, 23, 24, 27, 50, 51, 57, 73, 83, 85, 87, 92, 95, 102, 108, 113, 177, 184, 187
eternity · 23, 24, 25, 27, 57, 73, 111, 179
Evangelical · 2, 4, 180
Evangelicals · 180
Eve · 97, 110, 111
everlasting · 16, 73, 79
evil · 11, 47, 71, 72, 73, 92, 99, 102, 106, 107, 108, 109, 182, 185, 186
exile · 59, 77
eyewitnesses · 59, 60

F

faith · 4, 5, 7, 9, 10, 11, 12, 17, 20, 21, 30, 31, 48, 50, 51, 63, 64, 65, 79, 85, 108, 112, 178, 181, 185
Faith · i, 4, 34, 48, 54, 65, 88, 103, 116, 186
Father's will · 121, 122
fellowship · 28, 95, 96, 117, 127, 152, 162, 182, 201
flesh · 12, 16, 18, 28, 33, 90, 92, 101, 102, 109
forbearance · 128, 136, 146
friends · 32, 78, 85, 108, 109, 185
fruit of the Spirit · 146

G

Garden of Eden · 113, 114, 117, 132, 167, 200
gender · 3, 96, 98, 100, 181

Genesis · 56, 57, 74, 85, 89, 90, 92, 93, 94, 96, 97, 99, 100, 105, 109, 113
Gentile · 37, 138, 139, 156, 183
gifts · 30, 84, 146, 147, 149, 158
Gnostic · 18
Gnosticism · 16, 18, 24
Gnostics · 16
goat · 134
God · 1, 2, 3, 4, 6, 7, 9, 10, 11, 12, 13, 15, 16, 17, 18, 19, 20, 23, 24, 25, 27, 28, 29, 30, 31, 32, 33, 35, 47, 49, 50, 51, 52, 53, 56, 57, 58, 59, 61, 62, 63, 64, 65, 66, 67, 69, 70, 71, 72, 73, 74, 75, 76, 77, 78, 79, 80, 81, 82, 84, 85, 86, 87, 89, 90, 91, 92, 93, 94, 95, 96, 97, 98, 99, 100, 101, 102, 103, 105, 106, 107, 108, 109, 110, 111, 112, 113, 114, 115, 116, 177, 178, 179, 180, 181, 182, 183, 184, 185, 186, 187
God with us · 28, 117, 118, 129
Godhead · 11, 18, 20, 23, 24, 25, 49, 69, 81, 82, 84, 85, 86, 87, 123, 125, 141, 149, 182, 199
God's love · 78, 79, 117, 118, 132, 144, 198
God's Truth · 2, 53
God's will · 102, 178, 185
God's Word · 6, 27, 30, 31, 57, 58, 66, 97
Golgotha · 79, 122, 127
good · 1, 2, 10, 12, 16, 17, 49, 51, 56, 61, 62, 66, 67, 74, 82, 91, 92, 95, 97, 105, 106, 107, 109, 110, 177, 179, 184, 185, 186
grace · 3, 4, 7, 27, 52, 56, 57, 85, 105, 108, 111, 112, 113, 179, 180, 181, 187
Grace · 11, 43, 132, 144, 189, 191
grave clothes · 124, 126
Great Commission · 85
Gustav Aulén · 112, 162
Gutenberg · 62

H

heaven · 10, 12, 16, 17, 19, 29, 31, 55, 58, 61, 72, 76, 77, 82, 83, 84, 87, 96, 102, 106, 116, 177
heresies · 20
heretical · 1, 2, 5, 9, 19, 20, 23, 25, 86
heterosexuality · 100
high priest · 17, 24, 42, 58, 114, 135, 136
His Body · 28
holiness · 69, 70, 71, 72, 73, 181, 183, 185, 186
Holiness · 70, 182
holy · 16, 19, 30, 51, 52, 53, 69, 70, 71, 73, 84, 85, 99, 107, 108, 181, 182, 183, 185, 186
Holy Ghost · *See* Holy Spirit
Holy Place · 134, 136
Holy Spirit · 28, 32, 44, 66, 118, 135, 139, 141, 142, 143, 144, 145, 146, 147, 148, 149, 152, 153, 157, 158, 160, 161, 172, 192, 199, 200, 202, *See* Spirit
homosexual · *See* Homosexuality
Homosexuality · 100
Humpty Dumpty · 105
Husbands · 99
hymns · 5, 6, 7, 9, 15, 183

I

idolatry · 77, 182
image · 76, 85, 89, 92, 93, 94, 95, 96, 97, 99, 102, 177, 183
Immanuel · 28, 118, 129
immortal · 12, 13, 178
Incarnation · 24, 25, 28, 64, 118, 119, 123, 200
incest · 29
intelligent design · 38
Isaiah · 57, 58, 69, 71, 73, 75, 82, 90, 94, 100, 101, 106, 107, 113, 115, 186

J

Jehovah's Witnesses · 2, 20, 24
Jerusalem · 32, 58, 59, 75, 79, 102
Jesus · iii, viii, ix, 2, 3, 5, 6, 8, 9, 10, 11, 12, 15, 16, 17, 18, 19, 20, 23, 24, 25, 27, 28, 29, 31, 33, 37, 41, 42, 43, 44, 47, 49, 50, 52, 53, 56, 57, 58, 59, 60, 61, 63, 64, 69, 72, 76, 78, 79, 82, 83, 84, 85, 87, 89, 93, 95, 98, 100, 102, 105, 106, 107,飴114, 115, 116, 117, 118, 119, 120, 121, 122, 123, 124, 125, 126, 127, 128, 136, 137, 138, 139, 140, 142, 143, 144, 145, 146, 149, 151, 152, 153, 154, 155, 156, 157, 158, 159, 161, 162, 165, 166, 167, 168, 169, 170, 171, 173, 174, 175, 176, 177, 179, 181, 183, 184, 185, 186, 187, 189, 190, 191, 192, 196, 197, 198, 199, 200, 201, 202, 203
Jew · 37, 98, 138, 139, 156, 183
Job · 74, 75, 92, 101, 106, 107, 109, 185
John · 2, 3, 9, 13, 18, 20, 24, 27, 28, 31, 32, 47, 49, 50, 56, 60, 61, 73, 76, 78, 82, 83, 84, 86, 87, 97, 103, 109, 129, 179, 180, 181, 184, 187
John Stott · 122, 124, 190
John the Baptist · 121, 145, 154
Jonah · 57, 63
Joseph · 118, 119, 120, 125
Joseph of Arimathea · 122
Joshua · 56, 63
Judah · 58, 75, 77, 102, 115, 185
judgment · 17, 18, 28, 72, 84, 102

K

Kethuvim · 55, 57, 59
Kingdom · 6
Koine · 62

L

Lamb · 72, 79

last days · *See* Eschatology
Law · 31, 57, 58, 59, 93, 185
Lazarus · 117, 179
legalistic · 34
life · 1, 2, 3, 4, 9, 12, 13, 16, 17, 18, 19, 20, 23, 27, 30, 31, 49, 50, 51, 52, 53, 57, 59, 64, 65, 66, 69, 70, 77, 78, 79, 82, 83, 85, 89, 90, 92, 93, 95, 96, 99, 100, 101, 110, 111, 112, 113, 115, 177, 180, 181, 182, 183, 184
likeness · 10, 76, 85, 89, 92, 93, 94, 95, 102
LORD · 1, 7, 9, 10, 11, 12, 15, 19, 20, 23, 31, 33, 47, 49, 50, 51, 52, 56, 57, 58, 60, 63, 67, 71, 73, 74, 75, 77, 84, 85, 91, 93, 94, 96, 98, 101, 108, 109, 112, 116, 179, 181, 182, 183, 184, 186, 187
love · 6, 23, 52, 56, 69, 72, 73, 77, 78, 79, 82, 85, 87, 92, 93, 94, 95, 96, 99, 110, 113, 116, 179, 183
Luke · 23, 24, 34, 60, 61, 82, 106, 107, 179

M

Magi · 119
man · 6, 7, 10, 16, 19, 24, 27, 56, 63, 64, 65, 66, 71, 76, 78, 85, 89, 90, 91, 92, 93, 94, 95, 96, 97, 98, 99, 100, 101, 102, 105, 106, 109, 110, 111, 112, 113, 114, 115, 116, 177, 178, 179, 184
Man's · 57, 111, 112
manuscripts · 62
Mark · 34, 60, 61, 82
marriage · 97, 98, 100
Mary · 16, 19, 119, 120, 179, 200
Max Lucado · 125, 139
Megachurch · 2
Megachurches · *See* Megachurch
memory aids · 5, 7, 15
Messiah · 9, 44, 121, 126, 127, 145, 154, 155, 156, 171
Milky Way · 91
miracles · 77, 83
Monarchians · 81

morality · 48, 180, 186
Mormonism · 20, 24
Mormons · 2
Moses · 27, 69, 73, 78
Most Holy Place · 134, 135, 136

N

Nancy Pearcey · 48
Nazareth · 119, 120, 145
Nevi'im · 55, 57, 58, 59
New Testament · 9, 55, 56, 57, 59, 61, 62, 76, 186
Nicea · 19
Nicene · 19
Niceno-Constantinople Creed · 19

O

of extra-marital sex · 180
Old Testament · 32, 55, 57, 59, 61, 62, 77, 100, 185
Oneness · 23, 50, 81, 86, 88
Orthodox · 24

P

Paraclete · *See* Holy Spirit
Pentecost · 148, 149, 157
pentecostal · *See* Pentecost
Peter · 17, 24, 32, 33, 36, 41, 60, 63, 85, 108, 112, 121, 123, 126, 128, 137, 138, 139, 152, 154, 155, 156, 161, 167, 168, 169, 170, 173, 183, 186, 192, 202
Pharisees · 33, 93
philosopher · 127, 201
philosophical · 9, 49, 52
plenary, verbal inspiration · 30, 63
Pontius Pilate · 12, 16, 19, 47
post-modern · 47
prayer · 31, 69, 182
Presbyterians · 4
profane · 69, 70, 71, 182, 185, 186
pronouncements · 32, 33, 55, 56

217

prophesy · 32, 33, 75, 147, 148, 159
prophets · 19, 31, 32, 33, 58, 63, 79, 102
Prophets · 57, 58, 59, 93
prosperity gospel · 3
Protestant · 2, 48, 55, 57, 114, 115

R

race · 27, 49, 96, 116, 181
reality · 24, 47, 64
rebellion · 78, 95, 106
rebuking · 29, 51, 56
relationship · 27, 57, 79, 86, 95, 97, 98, 99, 105, 110, 114, 178, 184
resurrection · 16, 17, 18, 20, 64, 82
Resurrection · 64, 124, 126, 174, 175, 192, 201
revelation · 27, 50, 55, 63, 69, 78
risen · 1, 23
ritual · 70
Roman Catholics · 32
Rome · 60
ruler · 13, 87, 96
Ruler · 12, 27

S

sacred · 55, 59, 69, 102
sacrifice · 6, 17, 25, 52, 79, 102, 112, 117, 124, 133, 134, 136, 138, 140, 183, 201
sacrifices · 133, 134, 135, 156, 201
sacrificial system · 134
sadness · 117, 168
salvation · 6, 7, 19, 28, 37, 38, 57, 72, 78, 85, 107, 113, 118, 127, 128, 129, 131, 132, 137, 138, 139, 144, 149, 156, 168, 169, 171, 174, 180, 183, 187, 189, 190, 200
Salvation · 35, 50, 125, 127, 138, 140, 196, 201
Satan · 2, 7, 47, 49, 106, 107, 108, 109, 110, 111, 114, 119, 121, 122, 128, 131, 156, 167, 168, 173, 174, 193, 200, 201, 203

saved · 4, 8, 12, 15, 52, 57, 92, 114, 116, 181, 187
savior · 87, 118, 129, 133
Savior · 1, 16, 49, 50, 57, 98, 111, 127, 128, 138, 166, 167, 170, 180, 187, 190
scientists · 77
Scribes · 33
Scriptural · 2, 3, 7, 24, 25, 30, 33, 67, 82
Scripture · 2, 6, 7, 9, 16, 20, 23, 24, 25, 27, 29, 31, 32, 33, 34, 50, 51, 55, 56, 57, 58, 59, 61, 63, 67, 69, 78, 81, 82, 84, 85, 86, 92, 98, 101, 103, 106, 108, 109, 116, 178, 187
self-sacrificial · 6, 78
separation · vii, 64, 111, 113, 117, 125, 151
serpent · 109, 110, 111, 132, 137
Sex · 96, 103
sexuality · 96
Shirley Guthrie · 9, 37
signs · 33, 77
sin · 1, 5, 6, 17, 23, 24, 25, 28, 35, 37, 41, 53, 65, 72, 73, 78, 89, 92, 94, 100, 102, 103, 105, 106, 110, 111, 112, 113, 114, 115, 116, 117, 120, 123, 124, 125, 127, 128, 131, 132, 133, 134, 137, 138, 140, 143, 151, 152, 161, 167, 168, 171, 179, 180, 181, 183, 184, 189, 192, 197, 200
Sin · 35, 50, 96, 105, 112, 114, 115, 116, 124, 131, 133, 166, 168, 197, 200
sinful · 6, 57, 72, 78, 137, 168, 192
sinlessly · 121, 200
sinned · 47, 112, 113, 115
snapshot · 117
sob · 117
Son · *See* Jesus
Son of God · 10, 118, 122, 123, 124, 142, 145, 190, 201
Son of Man · 122, 123, 127, 154
Son of the Living God · 118
Soteriological · 129
Southern Baptists · 2, 4
Sovereign · 71
space · 73, 76, 107, 178
speed of light · 76
spirit · 20, 32, 33, 53, 71, 92, 101, 102, 115, 179

218

Spirit · 6, 11, 12, 15, 16, 18, 19, 20, 23, 28, 29, 32, 33, 47, 52, 61, 63, 66, 82, 83, 84, 85, 86, 87, 88, 141, 179, 183, 187, *See* Holy Spirit
Spirit of God · *See* Holy Spirit, *See* Holy Spirit
Spirit of Jesus · *See* Holy Spirit
spiritual · 31, 48, 56, 84, 95, 108, 109, 112
steadfast love · 78, 79
Stewardship · 90
strong force · 76
submission · 17, 121, 122, 138, 182
submissive · 88, 99
submit · 30, 98, 99, 184
substitute · 119, 133, 134, 136, 140, 195
Suffering Servant · 118, 128, 201
Sunday School · 2
Synagogue · 151
Synod of Carthage · 61
Systematic Theology · 5

T

tabernacle · 134, 135, 136
Tabernacle · 70, 134, 135, 136, 186
TANAKH · 55, 57
teacher · 123, 126, 127, 201
tear · 117
Temple · 40, 59, 70, 119, 135, 145, 151, 202
temptation · 4, 23, 24, 25, 52, 121, 179, 192
temptations · *See* temptation
tension · 23, 24, 25, 69, 81, 82, 86
the Almighty · 39, 73, 171, 190
the Fall · 63, 92, 93, 109, 112, 115
the Father · 6, 10, 15, 16, 17, 18, 19, 20, 23, 27, 28, 29, 49, 64, 69, 82, 83, 84, 85, 87, 179, 181, 183, 184
the Flood · 63, 64
the foundation of the Earth · 137
the Great Commission · 148, 152, 157, 171
the Lord Will Provide · *See* Yahweh Yireh
the Son · 11, 16, 19, 20, 28, 29, 76, 82, 83, 84, 85, 87, 116

the unborn · 102
the Word · 31, 36, 38, 56, 67, 118, 191
theological · 1, 5, 8, 10, 11, 15, 23, 25, 27, 55, 81, 86, 92, 114, *See* Theological
theology · 4, 5, 6, 15, 50, 55, 81, 82, 86, 89, 91, 114
Theology · 4, 21, 23
Threeness · 81, 82, 86, 88
Time · 73
timelessness · 73
tongues · 147, 148
Torah · 55, 57, 58, 59
Tree of Life · 95, 109, 110, 111, 113, 131
Tree of the Knowledge of Good and Evil · 109, 110
Trinitarian · 18, 84, 85
Trinitarianism · 15
Trinity · 3, 7, 11, 18, 19, 20, 25, 28, 29, 43, 44, 50, 76, 81, 82, 83, 85, 86, 87, 95, 102, 116, 118, 119, 121, 123, 125, 137, 141, 145, 152, 155, 165, 195, 196, 199
trivialize · 69, 182, 185, 187
truth · 1, 2, 3, 20, 27, 28, 31, 32, 47, 48, 49, 50, 51, 52, 53, 58, 72, 77, 85, 94, 95, 99, 105, 112, 177, 178
Truth · 21, 23, 47, 48, 49, 50, 52, 53, 54, 69, 79, 93, 103, 116, 129, 177, 178, 180, 182

U

universe · *See* Universe
Universe · 6, 47, 76, 89, 90, 91
unrepentant sin · 131

V

virgin · 16, 118
Virgin birth · *See* Vigin Birth
Virgin Birth · 111

W

Westminster Confession of Faith · 5
Wives · 98
woman · 76, 90, 95, 97, 98, 99, 110, 111, 112, 113
Word · iii, viii, 1, 7, 21, 27, 30, 31, 33, 36, 37, 50, 51, 53, 55, 56, 57, 58, 59, 61, 62, 63, 65, 67, 69, 76, 79, 81, 84, 93, 103, 116, 117, 118, 119, 121, 122, 126, 129, 134, 139, 147, 149, 151, 163, 172, 173, 176, 177, 179, 180, 187, 191, 197, 198, 203
Word of God · 7, 21, 30, 31, 55, 56, 57, 58, 59, 61, 62, 65, 84, 177, 179, 180
world leader · 127
worldview · 47, 48, 51, 52, 177
wrath · 52, 69, 71, 72, 77, 79, 84, 102, 177, 182

Y

Yahweh Yireh · 140

About the Author

While a teenager, Chris became a born-again Christian in 1980 in a small Southern Baptist congregation in Caracas, Venezuela. He holds a degree from Campbell University and took some studies at Southeastern Baptist Theological Seminary in Wake Forest, North Carolina. While his career is in software development, he is a dedicated lay teacher and has spent many years teaching adult and youth Bible studies and Sunday School classes. Chris' personal favorite subjects are theology and the Biblical original languages, especially Greek.

Chris has been married for the past 28 years to his wonderful wife, Sherry. They have one daughter, Rebekah, who is the apple of their eye. Over the years, they have had the benefit of sitting under some excellent pastoral teaching and currently are members of Burlington Assembly of God in Burlington, North Carolina. It is Chris' conviction that a Christian's growth demands their all (e.g. Matthew 13:44) and thus is one of the subjects that he writes and speaks about often.

When Chris is not working at his day job crafting software and he is not involved in Church, he is an avid photographer. He shares some of his photographic work online on Flickr and also through a photo-blog on Wordpress. If you like photography that highlights "our Father's world," these can be found at the following addresses:

http://www.flickr.com/photos/claforet
http://iceblueline.wordpress.com

www.ingramcontent.com/pod-product-compliance
Lightning Source LLC
Chambersburg PA
CBHW071525040426
42452CB00008B/889